D0987144

Iris Murdoch's Paradoxical Novels

Critics have compared Iris Murdoch's comic plots to Shakespeare's and have put her name forward for the Nobel Prize in Literature; her novels have been translated into twenty-nine languages; and no less a critic than Harold Bloom has said of her "no other contemporary British novelist seems to me to be of Murdoch's eminence." Collecting the major critics who have described for the last third of a century the phenomena of Iris Murdoch's fiction, this study analyzes the stories her critics tell about her artistic processes. Murdoch passed away in February 1999 after a long struggle with Alzheimer's Disease, and now it seems time to examine her critical reception. There are three major questions at the heart of this reception and at the heart of the present study: to what extent is Murdoch a philosophical novelist, a realistic novelist, a postmodern novelist? The book also deals with the question of Murdoch's reputation in the literary world: an intriguing question in view of the praise of Bloom and other critics and writers. This is the first full-length work to deal with the literary criticism on Murdoch.

Barbara Stevens Heusel is professor of English at Northwest Missouri State University in Maryville, Missouri.

Studies in English and American Literature,
Linguistics, and Culture:
Literary Criticism in Perspective

Literary Criticism in Perspective

James Hardin (*South Carolina*), General Editor

Books in the series *Literary Criticism in Perspective* trace literary scholarship and criticism on major and neglected writers alike, or on a single major work, a group of writers, a literary school or movement. In so doing the authors — authorities on the topic in question who are also well-versed in the principles and history of literary criticism — address a readership consisting of scholars, students of literature at the graduate and undergraduate level, and the general reader. One of the primary purposes of the series is to illuminate the nature of literary criticism itself, to gauge the influence of social and historic currents on aesthetic judgments once thought objective and normative.

Iris Murdoch's Paradoxical Novels

Thirty Years of Critical Reception

Barbara Stevens Heusel

CAMDEN HOUSE

ART INSTITUTE OF ATLANTA
LIBRARY

Copyright © 2001 Barbara Stevens Heusel

All Rights Reserved. Except as permitted under current legislation,
no part of this work may be photocopied, stored in a retrieval system,
published, performed in public, adapted, broadcast, transmitted,
recorded, or reproduced in any form or by any means,
without the prior permission of the copyright owner.

First published 2001
by Camden House

Camden House is an imprint of Boydell & Brewer Inc.
PO Box 41026, Rochester, NY 14604–4126 USA
and of Boydell & Brewer Limited
PO Box 9, Woodbridge, Suffolk IP12 3DF, UK

ISBN: 1–57113–089–6

Library of Congress Cataloging-in-Publication Data

Heusel, Barbara Stevens.
 Iris Murdoch's paradoxical novels: thirty years of critical reception / Barbara
Stevens Heusel.
  p. cm. — (Studies in English and American literature, linguistics, and
culture. Literary criticism in perspective)
Includes bibliographical references and index.
ISBN 1-57113-089-6 (alk. paper)
  1. Murdoch, Iris — Criticism and interpretation — History.   2. Women
and literature — England — History — 20th century.   3. Postmodernism
(Literature) — England.   4. Philosophy in literature.   5. Paradox in literature.
6. Realism in literature. I. Title. II. Studies in English and American literature,
linguistics, and culture (Unnumbered). Literary Criticism in perspective.

PR6063.U7 Z69 2001
823'.914—dc21
                                                                    2001025878

A catalogue record for this title is available from the British Library.

This publication is printed on acid-free paper.
Printed in the United States of America

Dedicated to Dennis Moore

Contents

Preface

THE PRESENT BOOK AIMS TO TRACE, describe, and assess — and give the reader enough information to assess — the critical response to Iris Murdoch's twenty-six novels. Focusing on selected novels, the study organizes a dialogue around the issues that have dominated Murdoch criticism: is she a philosophical novelist? Are her novels examples of realism? Does she use postmodernist strategies? I address the major critics' arguments chronologically, developing the chapters according to the phases into which the critics' questions divide themselves. The reader will notice that frequently I quote Murdoch from within a critic's commentary: what a critic chooses to quote can illustrate much about that critic's values. As a reminder that these critics do not operate in isolation, I also cite their references to each other's positions, thereby showing the interplay among critics and their respective interpretations.

Dramatizing her critical reception in this way is an attempt to be as tolerant and respectful of others' opinions as Iris Murdoch was. I want in this study to grant each critic the freedom to give him- or herself, as one of Murdoch's characters says in *A Fairly Honourable Defeat* (New York: Viking, 1970), "to the situation like a swimmer to the sea" (203). Given her propensity to immerse herself in swimming as much as in writing fiction, such a statement reflects her profound generosity.

In accordance with the practice followed in the Literary Criticism in Perspective series, works cited in each chapter are listed alphabetically by author's last name at the end of the chapter. At the end of the book all works cited are divided into primary and secondary and listed chronologically within each category.

Acknowledgments

F OR PERMISSION TO REPRODUCE copyrighted material, the author and publisher would like to thank *Windsor Review: A Journal of the Arts* and The University of Georgia Press.

My colleagues in the international Iris Murdoch Society have continued to pursue a rigorous exploration of the relationship between Dame Iris's writing and the larger Anglo-American culture.

Professor Cheryl Bove has been especially helpful and thorough. By awarding me a reduced teaching load for one semester, Taylor Barnes, Dean of the School of Arts and Sciences at Northwest Missouri State University, made it possible for me to complete this project.

— Maryville, Missouri, August 2000

Introduction

DURING THE FINAL THIRD of the twentieth century many critical voices described and celebrated Iris Murdoch's fiction. This study analyzes the stories her critics have told about her artistic processes. A stunningly gifted storyteller, Dame Iris published twenty-six novels between 1954 and 1995. One of her stated goals was to use the vehicle of the novel to originate "a house fit for free characters to live in" ("The Sublime and the Beautiful Revisited," 271), the implication being that she wanted to produce characters with minimal authorial control, creating a freedom similar to that which Fyodor Dostoevsky allowed his characters. Her characters reflect her major interest, the morality of humanity in the twentieth century; like real people, they struggle through their worlds, attempting to be good but being sidetracked by temptations. The experience of writing fiction was for Murdoch similar to "a religious activity," for she argued in an interview that "all art is a struggle to be, in a particular sort of way, virtuous" (Haffenden, 193). Discovering ways to free her characters is a major artistic problem that her stories address.

Her readers will never again receive a new Murdoch story — unless, that is, an unpublished manuscript of hers appears. Her husband, John Bayley, announced on February 8, 1999, that Dame Iris had died after having been diagnosed with Alzheimer's disease in 1994. Now is an appropriate time to examine the critical reception of her novels. Her oeuvre includes — in addition to the twenty-six novels — five books of philosophy, five plays, a libretto, two books of poetry, and two collections of essays on philosophy and literature, as well as criticism, verse, short fiction, and two volumes of previously uncollected philosophical and critical essays.

Biography

The kind of life Iris Jean Murdoch was privileged to live — what she called life as an outsider — influenced her philosophy and the directions her novels took. Integral to her multifaceted and often paradoxical perspective on life were her Anglo-Irish background and her careers as an Oxford philosopher and a commercially successful novelist.

Murdoch's father, Wills John Hughes Murdoch, came from a Protestant sheep-farming family in County Down and was a civil servant in Belfast before the First World War. During the war he served as a second lieutenant in King Edward's Horse (Bove, 221).[1] When his unit was not in France, he was stationed at the Curragh, a British military base near Dublin (Haffenden, 200). During his time there he met Irene Alice Richardson; they were married in 1918, when Irene was eighteen, ruining any chance of a musical career for her, although she had a fine voice and studied with a professional teacher in Dublin and later in London (200). Iris was born on July 15, 1919, in Dublin, and appeared to inherit from her Anglo-Irish ancestors an instinctual link to that culture's fascination with the magical. In 1920 Wills Murdoch took Irene and Iris to London to take a civil service post. Her parents, however, continued to nourish Iris's Irish roots on vacations, during which her father taught her to swim in the baths near Kingstown, outside Dublin (Conradi, "Memoir, Festschrift, Biography," 8).

Wills Murdoch started at the bottom of the Whitehall hierarchy and rose to the level of deputy registrar-general (Hauptfuhrer, 18); this bureaucracy became the subject of many of his daughter's fictional worlds. Murdoch attributed not only her interest in such subject matter but also her feeling of exile to her family's move from Ireland to London. She suggested that her experience made her understand why she identified so much with exiles. A family threesome living in "a perfect trinity of love" was the positive effect of their moving to a city where they knew no one else (Haffenden, 200). Her father helped establish her interest in stories, discussing with her the *Alice* books when she was quite young (200). She received her early childhood education at the Froebel Institute in London, living with her parents in the districts of Hammersmith and West Chiswick; in 1933 she received a scholarship to board at Badminton School in Bristol, which continued until she graduated in 1938. The school newspaper published twenty-six of her articles during that time (Fletcher, "The Birth of a Writer: Iris Murdoch before 1950," 3).

Murdoch entered Somerville College, Oxford, in 1938. In Eduard Fraenkel's Greek class she met William Frank Thompson (1920–44), brother of the historian and peace campaigner E. P. Thompson. Eighteen-year-old Frank fell in love with nineteen-year-old Iris during the autumn of that year. While they were at Oxford, he influenced her to join the Communist Party; she remained a member for only a year. She and Frank planned to marry after the Second World War, but in January 1944, as a member of the military's covert operations, he parachuted into Bulgaria, where the Germans captured and executed him

(Hauptfuhrer, 18). In 1947 Frank's brothers published his memoir, which includes his letters to Iris (Fletcher and Bove, 198, 297).[2]

At Oxford, Murdoch began to publish in *The Cherwell* and the *Oxford Forward*, student-managed literary journals, in 1939; in 1942 "she received a first-class degree in Greats (Latin and Greek languages, literature, history, and philosophy)" (Bove, 194). Her experience aiding war refugees, primarily from Eastern Europe, while she worked for the British treasury from 1942 to 1944 and for the United Nations Relief and Rehabilitation Administration in England, Belgium, and Austria as an administrative officer during 1945–46, influenced her later commitment to study moral philosophy. For example, in 1943–44, while employed at the treasury, she wrote three articles concerning morality for *The Adelphi*, another Oxford journal; furthermore, working with displaced persons from Yugoslavia and Poland affected the direction many of her novels took and the themes that pervaded her stories (Haffenden, 201).

In Belgium after the war she became friends, and sometimes more than friends, with several influential existentialist writers. Bayley calls the mathematician and novelist Elias Canetti, who won the Nobel Prize in literature in 1981, "Iris's onetime lover, tyrant, dominator, and master. Teacher, too, and inspiration. The great all-knowing *Dichter"* (*Iris and Her Friends,* 258). To Canetti she dedicated *The Flight from the Enchanter* (1956), the novel that introduces the powerful enchanter figure so important in her later work. She revealed to Harold Hobson that she imitated the style of her friend Raymond Queneau, French novelist and poet, in *Under the Net* (1954), which she dedicated to him (Bove, 222). She met Jean-Paul Sartre in 1945 in Brussels; his influence on her was intellectual — both philosophical and political.

As a result of her brief encounter with the British Communist Party, the United States denied Murdoch a visa in 1946, forcing her to pass up a graduate fellowship to Vassar College. Instead, she obtained a Sarah Smithson studentship in philosophy to Newnham College, Cambridge, during the 1947–48 school year. "Because she came into contact with fervent Wittgensteinian disciples," John Wisdom and Elizabeth Anscombe, during her year at Cambridge, "her interest in moral philosophy — especially existentialism — began to merge with her interest in linguistic philosophy" (Heusel, 26). She met the renowned Ludwig Wittgenstein twice and had the privilege of discussing philosophy with him during an extended private conference. These experiences rounded out her French existentialist and British empiricist influences.

From 1948 to 1963 Murdoch was a fellow of St. Anne's College, Oxford, and university lecturer in philosophy. She published the critical study *Sartre, Romantic Rationalist* in 1953. Perhaps as a result of her practicing her craft by writing five novels that she considered not "fit for publication," her first published novel, *Under the Net* (1954), received outstanding acclaim (Dipple, *Iris Murdoch: Work for the Spirit*, 134).

As Bayley makes clear in his recent memoir of his wife, *Elegy for Iris* (1999), Murdoch, far from being solitary at the time, had an active love life. Courting her from 1954 to 1956, he feared her excursions to London to visit a series of lovers: "the people Iris went to see were . . . intellectuals, writers, artists, civil servants, mostly Jewish, mainly refugees" (58). Before Bayley met her, she had been engaged to the young poet Franz Steiner, a Jewish refugee who died of a heart ailment in 1954 (69). They had become acquainted at Oxford, where he taught anthropology. In 1956 Murdoch married Bayley, a fellow of New College, who in 1973 became Thomas Warton Professor of English Literature at Saint Catherine's College, Oxford; he is an author of more than twenty novels and books of criticism and three books about his life with Murdoch. John Fletcher describes this relationship as "one of the most fruitful literary and critical partnerships of our time, and remarkable in any time" (Fletcher, *Dictionary of Literary Biography*, 550).

In 1963 Murdoch retired from her position at Oxford and became an honorary fellow of St. Anne's; she continued to teach as a part-time lecturer at the Royal College of Art, London, until 1967, when she gave up her teaching career to pursue literary and philosophical writing. Concentrating during that period on two vocations only, she produced exemplary work in each. She stated that she never "felt any . . . tension" between philosophy and art. "The only tension involved there is that both pursuits take up time" (Haffenden, 198). Her novels and her philosophical work are closely intertwined, as the literary critic Harold Bloom demonstrates in his estimate of her first published text, *Sartre, Romantic Rationalist*, which serves as a bridge linking her literary, critical, and philosophical concerns. Bloom finds Murdoch prophetic here for crying out that Sartre's "inability to write a great novel is a tragic symptom of a situation which afflicts us all" (1). Bloom suggests that Murdoch also embodies the style of the age (7), implying that she understood that it is unlikely that novelists will again write great novels. Bloom suggests that her broad perspective, encompassing two fields of expertise, envisioned the twentieth century accurately. Such brilliance has caused interminable problems for critics.

A Critical Estimate of Murdoch's Novels

Generally, critics have found Murdoch's comic vision comprehensive and intellectually rigorous. They have understood that Murdoch chose to revive the eighteenth- and nineteenth-century English novel traditions, in which writers were free to adapt classic theatrical devices and to mix comic, tragic, and satiric modes, as William Shakespeare or Henry Fielding might have. She employed not only older forms such as the picaresque road novel, using digressions and prefaces, as Laurence Sterne did, but also traditions of gothic and detective fiction. Attempting to maintain a traditional, or historical, realism, she rejected many modernist techniques, such as the stream of consciousness. Although some critics group Murdoch's oeuvre into four phases, most choose three, such as early, major or mature, and late. For example, David J. Gordon's 1995 book defines her "Major Phase" as 1968 to 1985; in these novels, Gordon says, Murdoch is "formally more original" and sets new precedents (138). Although critics' estimates vary as to the time when her novels become uniquely "Murdochian," most agree that her early period ends in the 1960s. Many critics are in accord about the first phase of her career — that *Under the Net* is an excellent absurdist novel in the style of Raymond Queneau and Samuel Beckett; that *The Flight from the Enchanter, The Sandcastle* (1957), *An Unofficial Rose* (1962), *The Italian Girl* (1964), *The Red and the Green* (1965), and *The Time of the Angels* (1966) have many weaknesses; and that *The Bell* (1958), *A Severed Head* (1961), and *The Unicorn* (1963) are fine examples of particular modes.

Whereas many critics consider Murdoch's mature phase to begin with *The Nice and the Good* (1968), Richard Todd argues that a temporary artistic breakdown comes after *The Bell* (1958). From *A Severed Head* to *The Time of the Angels* darker themes and intellectualized sexual adventures provoke him to characterize the phase as the doldrums.

In his *Iris Murdoch: The Shakespearian Interest* (1984) Todd argues that in *The Nice and the Good* (1968) Murdoch increases her Shakespearian interest and, quoting Lorna Sage, that she builds up "richness of detail and its disposability" (19). Peter Conradi, on the other hand, sees the darker books from 1961 to 1966 as more confident and wiser than the earlier ones. A scholar of Dostoevsky, Conradi appreciates, especially in *A Severed Head,* her Dostoevskian dark comedy. Furthermore, he says that Murdoch's "mastery" of the Russian's equivocal relations with his protagonists "is extraordinary" (*Iris Murdoch: The Saint and the Artist,* 29). Characterizing Murdoch as "an idealist-without-illusions" (64), he sees no major break between what some critics call the fantasy of *The Time of the Angels* and the reality of *The Nice and the Good;* as he explains the difference, the first is "a 'closed' novel about the dispersion of the spiritual world," and the second is "an 'open' book which points to exactly the missing value (the Good) in its title" (141).

Elizabeth Dipple, focusing on Murdoch's search for her own kind of novel, finds a complex and somewhat chaotic movement. In her *Iris Murdoch: Work for the Spirit* (1982) Dipple sums up the traits of the early novels: "As Murdoch moved back and forth" among styles in her early phase, "three dominant inclinations can be discerned": "the novel of tricks where plotting dominates," "the ruminative novel characterized by deepening of character," and "the increasingly religious novel which is concerned with definitions and enactments of good and evil" (136). Some critics find this classification arbitrary; others find it insightful. As to the later novels, various critics have chosen as candidates for greatness *The Black Prince* (1973), *The Sea, The Sea* (1978), *The Philosopher's Pupil* (1983), and *The Good Apprentice* (1985). Seeing Murdoch's talent as "fecund and exuberant," Bloom was optimistic in 1986 that Murdoch would produce "a great novel": "If *The Good Apprentice* marks the start of her strongest phase, and it may, then a great novel could yet come, rather surprisingly in the incongruous form of the nineteenth-century realistic novel" (1).

Increasing Fame

"Losing Her Mind to Gain the World," a July 26, 1998, *Sunday Times* (London) review, takes stock of Murdoch's reputation. Reflecting an international perspective, it reports that "Her name was often put forward for the Nobel prize for literature." The British government rewarded her in 1987 by making her a Dame Commander of the Order of the British Empire. She received many honorary degrees and literary honors, such as the Royal Society of Literature in 1987 and the Medal of Honor from the National Arts Club in New York in 1990. She was one of only eight women whose writing appeared on the Modern Library's 1998 "100 Best Novels of the Twentieth Century" list: her first novel, *Under the Net,* was Modern Library's ninety-fifth choice. *The Black Prince* won the James Tait Black Memorial Prize in 1973, *The Sacred and Profane Love Machine* won the Whitbread Literary Award in 1974, and *The Sea, The Sea* won the Booker McConnell Prize in 1978. Her novels have been translated into more than twenty-nine languages, including Dutch, Swedish, Danish, Norwegian, Spanish, Catalan, Japanese, Chinese, Korean, Turkish, Latvian, Lithuanian, and Slovak.

Bloom says that "no other contemporary British novelist seems to me of Murdoch's eminence" (7) and that "she resembles no other contemporary novelist, in part because she is essentially a religious fabulist, of an original and unorthodox sort" (2). Although he admits that this "conceptual originality" is confusing to her readers (others go so far as to insist that divination is the only way to find answers to the many mysteries her novels raise), Bloom praises her strengths effusively: "Of all her talents, the gift of plotting is the most formidable, including a near-Shakespearian faculty for intricate double plots" (1). Apparently reacting to Frank Kermode's statement that Murdoch is the heir to E. M. Forster, Conradi writes that "Murdoch is a better writer than Forster or [Virginia] Woolf" (*Iris Murdoch: The Saint and the Artist*, 284). One of Murdoch's bibliographers, Fletcher, says that she is "the most intelligent novelist the English have produced since George Eliot" and "the only Henry James our age deserves or is likely to produce" (*Dictionary of Literary Biography*, 547, 560).

Several bibliographies of the critical reception of Murdoch's oeuvre have appeared; the first, Thomas T. Tominaga and Wilma Schneider-meyer's *Iris Murdoch and Muriel Spark: A Bibliography* (1976), obviously valued the two women as rising literary stars.[3] The second, Kate Begnal's *Iris Murdoch: A Reference Guide* (1987), added annotations of secondary sources from 1953 to 1983. In 1994 Fletcher and Cheryl Bove published *Iris Murdoch: A Descriptive Primary and Annotated Secondary Bibliography*, which provides a plethora of indispensable details for all students of Murdoch and some useful categories for determining her importance as the subject of literary investigation. Scholars were not long in recognizing the value of researching Murdoch's novelistic process: 42 "Books and Journals Devoted Entirely to Iris Murdoch" appeared between 1965 and 1993, 118 "Books Devoted in Part to Iris Murdoch" between 1954 and 1993, 56 "Doctoral Dissertations and Theses Devoted Entirely to Iris Murdoch" between 1965 and 1990, 25 "Doctoral Dissertations Devoted in Part to Iris Murdoch" between 1970 and 1991, 17 "Theses and Diploma Essays Devoted to or Devoted in Part to Iris Murdoch" between 1961 and 1986, and 361 articles between 1956 and 1993. This increasing fame and attention, and Murdoch's verbal responses, led critics in the 1980s and 1990s to search for new explanations for her unusual novelistic views and strategies and to revise old opinions. The *Modern Language Association International Bibliography* cites sixteen articles in books and twenty-seven journal articles published between 1993 and 1999. Although MLA cites only six published books, three of Bayley's cited articles became books by 2000. *Dissertation Abstracts International* lists twenty-eight dissertations that are entirely or in part focused on Murdoch's novels written between 1990 and 1999.

Phases of Critical Interpretation

Murdoch studies tend to arrange not only her novel writing but also the work of the critics into chronological phases. No matter how arbitrary, such systematizing is part of the critics' job. The critical commentary on Murdoch's novels falls primarily into three phases. The present study focuses on the move from the first phase of Murdoch criticism, the orthodox view that took its theme from statements Murdoch apparently made to Byatt and then put in print in the 1970s, to the late 1990s, the view that her theory of the novel allowed her much more freedom than originally seemed possible.

During the years 1965 to 1976 Murdoch's critics were preoccupied with definitions: what a philosophical novelist and a realist are and evidence that she fit neatly into one or the other category. In the 1980s the major critics shifted their attention to finding alternatives to the orthodox position that Murdoch was a philosophical novelist and an unconventional but traditional realist. Todd (1984) led the way for these naysayers, claiming that Murdoch's novelistic vision defied categorization. Following Todd's lead, a range of critics attempted to undermine the orthodox position: Guy Backus (1986) laid bare the critical past, questioning its accuracy and usefulness — especially the work of Byatt (1965), on which many subsequent critics had based their hypotheses. By taking into account Murdoch's own developing spiritual insights of the 1980s, Conradi's interpretation became the basis for the second phase of Murdoch studies; his view of Murdoch as a moral psychologist became the new orthodox position. The third and most recent phase (1987–95) might well have emanated from the increasing number of women writing about Murdoch's novels. Dipple, Deborah Johnson, and Barbara Stevens Heusel moved Murdoch criticism into new territory: postmodernist analysis. The decades of criticism make clear that readers cannot hope to understand the complex intersecting of the three major questions critics ask about Murdoch's novels until they struggle with what Sage calls her "aesthetics of imperfection" (quoted in Johnson, 106).

The controversy about the goals of Murdoch's fiction began with the publication of her first novel, *Under the Net,* in 1954. Her earliest reviewers quibble about whether Murdoch was being funny or intellectual or neither; most did not catch the jokes. In 1984 Todd refers to the critical "uncertainty about the kind of novelist she is" and addresses

Murdoch's contradictions (8). His insight into the general critical debate — over whether she is a philosophical novelist, a realist, or a postmodernist — cautions readers to stop emphasizing her "traditional
realism" and to view her novels instead "as manifestations of curiosity
about the elements and assumptions which made the novel a serious
form of art" (14). He repeats her analysis of an inevitable underlying
theoretical contradiction — or paradox — in her novels: that, even
though she strove to write as a realist in the European nineteenth-
century tradition, "good philosophical and epistemological reasons"
made such writing impossible (13). She always disagreed with theorists
who argued the novel could not survive without radical experimentation; her "historically aware, and genuinely international literary sensibility" foresaw that "fantasy realism" and other kinds of humanistic
realism were valid strategies to use in the contemporary novel (14).

An even more annoying and incomprehensible attitude is Murdoch's audacious defiance of convention in insisting that irony and
paradox are pervasive in human life. Being an "original theorist of fiction" (13) and a Platonist, she sustains an attitude toward the artist,
and herself as an artist, which is unlike that of any other. Her stated
goal — what Gordon in *Iris Murdoch's Fables of Unselfing* (1995) calls
"seeking her *own* 'unselfing'" (4), or using the writing of novels to unself the self — is unique. Such singularity in paradoxically suggesting a
Christ-like stance for the non-Christian artist causes critics to ask questions about Murdoch's fiction that they rarely ask in the same way
about other novelists. Given that her different method of perception
reflects her training as a philosopher, the major issue in Murdoch criticism remains the extent to which she fails to detach herself from her
other role and how much philosophy she brings to her novels. While
there are numerous simplistic answers to the question, this study shows
that the question has no absolute answer. The following chapters demonstrate that the critics' respective answers depend on the definitions
with which they begin, not only the way they define *philosophical novelist* but also their tolerance for contradiction, paradox, and ambiguity
and for a novelist who celebrates imperfection.

Much of the controversy has grown out of Murdoch's propensity
for contradicting herself. As a thinker she never stopped growing and
changing. Except for a finite number of major consistencies, such as her
belief in the Good and the Beautiful, disposable hypotheses are more
abundant in her thinking and writing than absolutes. In her philosophical writings, as well as her novels, Murdoch bridges seemingly opposite
absolutes: she describes herself, for example, as being a "Wittgensteinian neo-Platonist" (Chevalier, 90). Plato's many followers have

often shared a contempt for empirical studies, a longing for a better world, and a spiritual view of life; Ludwig Wittgenstein's ideas, on the other hand, have had a major influence on Logical Positivism (also known as Logical Empiricism). Furthermore, in a January 12, 1983, letter to the author of the present study she wrote: "I see no problem about Plato and 'empiricism'. . . . Plato's Ideas are not distant abstractions but concern the perception of what is real (as contrasted with our usual conditions of casual egoistic illusion)."

Given that paradox is central to Murdoch's thinking and writing, the greatest risk for her readers is to see her novels as simple embodiments of a single idea. One can never assume that she is signifying one view — or even two, for that matter. Such monocular vision would result in misjudgment. Critics who pigeonhole Murdoch's work as traditional are quite baffled by the uniqueness and complexity of her vision. On the other hand, the critics who know her texts best still seem troubled by what they consider her irreverent, inconsistent, cacophonous writing — by her paradoxical questioning of her own stated values. They have trouble grasping why she would undermine, or *dismantle* — to use Charles Arrowby's term in *The Sea, The Sea* (36, 498) — "her [own] fictional worlds" (Baldanza, 98).

Some critics use words such as *makeshift, hesitating, dialectic, mocking,* and *parodic* to refer to what they see as stories that do not reach closure. In "The Pursuit of Imperfection" (1977) Sage goes so far as to argue that Murdoch employs an "aesthetic of imperfection" (quoted in Johnson, 106). Why would an artist such as Murdoch, hoping quite passionately to communicate with her audience, want to leave stories unfinished, to craft stories with loose ends? And why would a philosopher, one of whose best-known essays is "The Idea of Perfection," strive to achieve imperfection in her fiction? By provoking such questions throughout her twenty-six novels, Murdoch demands that her critics carefully explore her literary vision and examine all possible reasons for such a strategy. Her most perceptive critics suggest that she distrusts oversimplification and the illusion that the function of art is to provide completeness.

Murdoch's critics approach her contradictions from various directions. Not surprisingly, however, they are consistent in pointing out contradictory and parodic elements in the novels that critics begin to label postmodernist in the 1980s. Such incisive readers unearth Murdoch's determination to simulate the dynamic reality that, as one of her models — Plato — stated, cannot be perfected. And to show that reality cannot be perfect, she must demonstrate that it is imperfect and disposable; for her "the novel is 'the most imperfect of all the art-forms'"

(Conradi, *Iris Murdoch: The Saint and the Artist*, 75). Conradi cites one of Murdoch's many interviews to link this attitude of disposability to her reading of Plato: "She has always rejected the classic Neoplatonic stance of believing that art is in direct contact with the Forms. 'I cannot accept these "Ideas" even as a metaphor of how the artist works' (Magee 1978)" (75). For Murdoch, art is a craft, a process — not, as the modernists believed, a symbol of perfection. She is a realist, but an unusual one.

Murdoch's "Aesthetic of Imperfection"

From the beginning of her career critics saw evidence of Murdoch's distrust of artistic perfection, but they could find no reasons for it. As Murdoch's fame as a novelist grew, her critics increasingly recognized the importance and the controversial nature of what Sage would later call Murdoch's "aesthetic of imperfection." Between 1965 and 1995 the critical dialogues changed in content and tone as critics learned more about Murdoch and her novels and as Murdoch understood and expressed her theory of the novel more concretely. New studies changed the face of Murdoch criticism by giving critics more perspectives with which to work and by encouraging them to focus on different problems in the novels. In the first critical book, *Degrees of Freedom: The Novels of Iris Murdoch* (1965), Byatt posits that Murdoch's seven novels focus on existential freedom. She finds Murdoch's purpose to be the creation of impenetrable human beings, a feat possible, according to Murdoch, only for a few artists such as Shakespeare, Tolstoy, and Dostoevsky: they grant their characters so much freedom that the reader might mistake them for real people. Todd voices another major position in *Iris Murdoch: The Shakespearian Interest* (1979): that Murdoch builds on Shakespeare's model. Attempting to flesh out Murdoch's broad range of interests, Conradi suggests that it is Dostoevskian; Dipple, that it is moral.

While these critics disagree as to the goals that Murdoch's novels pursue, critics from all chronological phases — from the early orthodox positions to the most recent, least orthodox ones — concur on the paradoxical, ambiguous, ambivalent, and indeterminate nature of the novels. Early critics tend to set aside that particular problem. In 1965 Byatt uses the word *tentativeness* to refer to these qualities. Frank Baldanza's *Iris Murdoch* (1974) describes her strategy of "writing against at least some of her instincts" (21), suggesting that in some novels, beginning in the 1960s, she is not writing the tightly plotted comedy that comes easily to her. He hypothesizes that part of her mind "thirsts for

Dickensian slap-dash composition, but that the deepest resources of her creative genius are inclined toward elegance of finish and neatness of control" (21–22). By calling attention to such a dichotomy, he raises the question whether Murdoch is a divided self or simply an artist orchestrating multiple voices. On the other hand, he shrewdly observes that she keeps her magician figures, or enchanters, at a "teasing distance" so that the reader never has "an 'inner' view of their nature" (19). He finds that as a primary strategy she juggles a variety of voices, whose mystery reflects deliberate irony.

Proposing in 1977 that reading a Murdoch novel is like "the queasy excitement of a ride on a roller coaster" (112), Sage calls Murdoch's plot strategies "plots against plots" (113). Sage's contribution was to make it easier for critics to discuss Murdoch's seemingly incomprehensible novelistic quirks. Conradi praises Sage for isolating this characteristic, referring to her essay "The Pursuit of Imperfection" twelve times in his *Iris Murdoch: The Saint and the Artist* (1986). He describes this Murdochian characteristic as "a device for humiliating those who wish to contain experience or abstract it," as characters do when they think that they are autonomous (79). Conradi notes Murdoch's apparent disregard for building her own vision, claiming that, instead, she dismantles it, moving towards "a use of myth that is consciously disposable and provisional, subordinated to the moral psychology of the characters" (quoted, 75). In addition, he finds that her later texts become increasingly ambivalent over time: "less absolute, more dialectical and playful, patient, comprehensive and open after 1971. The novels do without chapters and increase, one by one, in length" (85). His most significant insight into Murdoch's reason for creating work that appears unfinished is that "like Plato Murdoch always veils with irony the highest truth she wishes to show" (107). His point is well taken: abundant evidence, including a careful reading of Murdoch's *The Fire and the Sun*, points toward her goal of imitating Plato in both his artistic and his dialectical methods. Sage's essay calls attention to the argument the character Brendan poses in *Henry and Cato:* that "all images are obsolescent, provisional, imperfect, and that it's precisely their hypothetical quality which makes consciously — even vulgarly — *fictional* images so important" (113).

In *Iris Murdoch* (1987) Johnson, a feminist critic, also grounds her theorizing in Sage's essay, quoting the latter's claim that "'None of [Murdoch's] novels dwells exhaustively on its subjects, or on its own language. The imaginative curiosity that is always left over feeds into a new book.' Iris Murdoch's 'aesthetic of imperfection,' Sage goes on to say, 'is powerfully attractive because it mocks the critical demand for totalities, and makes fiction seem a living process'" (106). Johnson describes several ways in which Murdoch's inconsistencies unsettle "reader-expectations" (113), including the use of "deliberate lapses," drawing "attention to the makeshift quality of the structures" (105). To build her case Johnson quotes a review by Stephen Metcalf of *The Good Apprentice* as asserting that in Murdoch's fiction "'parable' has a way of turning into 'experiment'" (113). Johnson finds it quite appropriate for Murdoch to produce novels as if they were disposable, "for each novel, as it appears, is, for all its philosophical searchings and questionings, by no means the 'last word': it merely creates the illusion of finality by virtue of being the most recent" (106). For example, *The Good Apprentice* refuses "to sum anything up: it leaves the door open for all the different ways in which the characters within the novel and the audience outside the novel choose to read their human experience" (106). Johnson shows that the Murdoch reader is an important part of the mix, a participant who helps determine the outcome of the novel.

Final Critical Issues

The second critical issue that this study addresses is the degree to which Murdoch achieved her often-stated desire to write like the nineteenth-century realists. She helped to create this issue by discussing her goals in essays and interviews. Critics' definitions of *realism* and the extent to which they find Murdoch a realist often depend on their understanding of Murdoch's distrust of modernist perfection. Early critics Byatt and Baldanza both rely heavily on Murdoch's use of the term *transcendental realism* in her essays "Vision and Choice in Morality" (1956) and "Against Dryness" (1961). Byatt interprets the term in a more spiritual sense than Baldanza, who finds it difficult to categorize Murdoch's work. He adds, therefore, a caveat: accepting Murdoch as a traditional realist requires making an exception for a "fairly high dependence, in her novels, on classic theatrical devices of physical farce, surprise entrances, the importance of timing, and unforeseen twists of plot which turn out, on consideration, to be richly revelatory of character and of broad thematic meanings" (15). When Baldanza interprets Murdoch's reference in "Against Dryness" to "transcendence of reality" by using the term *transcendental realism,* he means that Murdoch "opens an early novel with all the accepted realistic conventions" and then, without warning, begins to use melodramatic elements so that the realistic scene becomes "outrageous, quirky, fantastic. . . . This eruption of the unexpected is a testimony to the richness of reality" (21). For him, Murdoch begins with the convention of nineteenth-century realism in order to transcend it. Byatt's and Baldanza's reliance on the term *transcendental realism* is further grounded in Murdoch's statement in "Against Dryness" that "we live in a world whose mystery transcends us and . . . morality is the exploration of that mystery in so far as it concerns each individual" (quoted, 47).

In *Iris Murdoch: Work for the Spirit* (1982) Dipple reviews the "original polemical statements of realism" (37) according to Balzac (the author is "merely a recorder or secretary of society") and Stendhal ("a mirror in the roadway") (38) before she tests them on Murdoch's fiction. She endows Murdoch with the understanding that "because no writer can be totally realist (there is no human mirror in the roadway) and still impose form, the whole realist idea is fraught with irony" (39). The convention of realism is, then, paradoxical. Moreover, central to such a tradition is its moral perspective. If to see reality clearly as a novelist is to be trained in the nineteenth-century realist tradition, a suggestion Murdoch makes, then being a novelist requires a moral outlook. Dipple and Murdoch agree that literature has a moral component that "involves the old Horatian *dolce-et-utile* idea of the ethical usefulness of literature" (40). Given her particular caveats, Dipple sees Murdoch as a moral realist.

The third and final section of this study focuses on the unanswered, open-ended questions critics have asked about the postmodernist strategies Murdoch employs in her fiction. Beginning with Sage's essay in 1977 it became clear not only that there were new questions about Murdoch's oeuvre but also that addressing such crucial issues required new discourses. The post-structuralist theories of the 1960s and 1970s supplied them. Critics began to list characteristics that define what theorists were calling "the postmodern," and Murdoch's novels obviously displayed these characteristics: "fragmentation," "elliptical" wordplay, indeterminate meaning, "indeterminate outcomes," "ambivalent evidence," and lack of "authenticity, autonomy or unity" (Heusel, 58). Readers have always known that Murdoch accomplished more in her novels than anyone had yet claimed. Critics recognized that in an effort to grasp aspects of the unnameable she was exploring what Johnson has called the fragility of "rigid systems" (111). Murdoch's first novel, *Under the Net*, uses Wittgenstein's image of the net as metaphor for a rigid system of theory that covers and restricts reality like a coarse net or tarpaulin. Playfulness also figures in several critics' analyses. Many of the critics I have cited in this introduction have repeatedly referred to Murdoch's habit of giving unabashedly of herself in each novel. Agreeing with Conradi that this abundance of "Murdoch's playfulness and her mystery" enriches the novels, Johnson acknowledges that other critics are less patient with what they consider a glut (105).

In *Patterned Aimlessness* (1995) Heusel spends much time on Murdoch's postmodernist point of view, tracing it to *Sartre, Romantic Rationalist* and examining it with Mikhail Bakhtinian strategies. She argues that "*Postmodernist* describes Murdoch at least insofar as her desire to escape the bounds of one way of looking matches the postmodernist impulse to get outside the mind to see the mind thinking. Murdoch's texts insist that in order to look outside oneself to see the self looking, one must first see the self in the other" (89). Dipple and Conradi laid the groundwork for Heusel's study by suggesting new ways of looking at Murdoch in relation to American experimentalists and to Dostoevsky, respectively.

By demonstrating that the most characteristic phenomenon in Murdoch's novels is the continual changing of the rules, the continual defamiliarization (making strange or "other"), Dipple has done much to help readers see that Murdoch's tactics are like those of the postmodernist novelists: "Fiction has an important task, that of disarming and alienating its readers from their sense of security in the world they perceive in habitual ways. Within Murdoch's particular agenda, the slippery presentation of narrators, of characters, of action reversing logical expectation, robs the reader of interpretative certainty" ("The Green Knight and Other Vagaries of the Spirit," 143–44). Such detachment calls for a responsible and responsive reader who is at once mesmerized and detached enough to be critical: "In an increasingly secular world, one central use of literature as practiced by Iris Murdoch is to detach us from the illusion of determinate meaning, in both fiction and the spiritual life" 144–45). Dipple warns that a Murdochian strategy such as "the page-turning impetus" (*Iris Murdoch: Work for the Spirit*, 157) distracts readers from Murdoch's conscious artistry and teases them into seeing her as a "simple tale-spinner" (5). She hazards a guess that Murdoch's reason for this intentional distraction is self-effacement, perhaps because of her shyness or her desire for old-fashioned objectivity.

Another closely related issue that is raised by Dipple and by other critics, such as Conradi in *Fyodor Dostoevsky* (1988), Johnson in *Iris Murdoch*, and Heusel in *Patterned Aimlessness*, is Murdoch's strategy of using multiple genres not only to defamiliarize the conventions familiar to readers but also to analyze certain questions pertaining to morality, psychology, history, and philosophy. In the August 1995 *Iris Murdoch News Letter* Dipple makes a cogent and revealing generalization in her review of *Jackson's Dilemma*, a novel generally considered weak: "Here we have the romantic Shakespearean source material brought wholesale and transported into the last few years of the twentieth century — just to see how we can look at it, if we can indeed see it in the latter days, and whether it can be dealt with within a new chronotopic experiment." Furthermore, she says that "Murdoch is writing a Shakespearean comedy for us, as a novel. In doing so, she parodies the technical demands of the genre . . ." (6). Johnson's reason for exploring genres is not so different from Dipple's: to deal with "the unsettling effect of the endings" that are "bound up with the formal problem of genre" (106).

This introduction has been recounting the effects of Iris Murdoch's novels on a group of her most devoted readers: her critics. They have told many conflicting stories of how she created her poetics over time, weaving strands from divergent sources. These students of Murdoch capture her meteoric rise as one of Britain's "angry young men" as she broke onto the scene in 1954 with *Under the Net*, her momentary fall in the 1960s when critics began to accuse her of "rewriting the same novel each year" (Begnal, xiv), and her place at the close of the century as a literary giant, philosophical intellect, and cultural figure. In addition, this study focuses on the changing attitudes of her critics during the last third of the century toward her unusual ideas and literary strategies — what John Haffenden calls "the mixture of apparent bizarrerie, excogitation and anagogical implication" (191).

For the reader's convenience the book organizes chronologically three phases through which the criticism has progressed: 1965 to 1976, 1977 to 1986, and 1987 to the late 1990s. What A. S. Byatt suggests about the critical process — that she wrote *Degrees of Freedom* to understand Murdoch's first seven novels — applies to all critics: their analyses represent their own stages or tests of understanding. Whatever the arguments of these critical voices, each struggles with three major questions about Murdoch as a creator of fiction. These questions — to what extent is Murdoch a philosophical novelist? Is she a realistic novelist? Is she a postmodern novelist? — form the three sections of this study. The study decries, as did Murdoch, the act of categorization; it remains an activity, albeit a dangerous one, which apparently all human beings learn in infancy and many use indiscriminately.

Notes

[1] For further information, see Schaefer, *The Great War: A Guide to the Service Records of All the World's Fighting Men and Volunteers*, and Fowler et al., *Army Service Records of the First World War*.

[2] Laraine Civin compiled *Iris Murdoch: A Bibliography* in 1968 as a requirement for a diploma from the University of the Witwatersrand.

Works Cited

Baldanza, Frank. *Iris Murdoch*. New York: Twayne, 1974.

Bayley, John. *Iris and Her Friends: A Memoir of Memory and Desire*. New York and London: Norton, 2000.

———. *Elegy for Iris*. New York: St. Martin's, 1999.

Begnal, Kate, ed. *Iris Murdoch: A Reference Guide*. Boston: G. K. Hall, 1987.

Bloom, Harold. Introduction to *Iris Murdoch: Modern Critical Views*. Ed. Bloom. New York: Chelsea House, 1986. 1–7.

Bove, Cheryl. "Iris Murdoch." *Dictionary of Literary Biography 194: British Novelists Since 1960, Second Series*. Ed. Merritt Moseley. Detroit: Gale, 1998. 220–43.

Byatt, A. S. *Degrees of Freedom: The Novels of Iris Murdoch*. New York: Barnes and Noble, 1965.

Chevalier, Jean-Louis, ed. *Rencontres avec Iris Murdoch*. Caen: Centre des Recherches de Littérature et Linguistique des Pays de Langue Anglaise, 1978.

Civin, Laraine. *Iris Murdoch: A Bibliography*. Johannesburg: University of the Witwatersrand, Department of Bibliography, Librarianship and Typography, 1968.

Conradi, Peter. *Fyodor Dostoevsky*. Macmillan Modern Novelists. London: Macmillan, 1988.

———. *Iris Murdoch: The Saint and the Artist*. New York: St. Martin's, 1986; rpt. 1989.

———. "Memoir, Festschrift, Biography." *The Iris Murdoch News Letter* 11 (Winter 1998): 8.

Dipple, Elizabeth. "Fragments of Iris Murdoch's Vision: *Jackson's Dilemma* as Interlude." *The Iris Murdoch News Letter* 9 (August 1995): 4–8.

———. "The Green Knight and Other Vagaries of the Spirit; or, Tricks and Images for the Human Soul; or, The Uses of Imaginative Literature." *Iris Murdoch and the Search for Human Goodness*. Ed. Maria Antonaccio and William Schweiker. Chicago and London: U of Chicago P, 1996. 138–68.

———. *Iris Murdoch: Work for the Spirit*. Chicago: U of Chicago P, 1982.

Fletcher, John. "The Birth of a Writer: Iris Murdoch before 1950." *The Iris Murdoch News Letter* 1 (July 1987): 1–3.

———. "Iris Murdoch." *Dictionary of Literary Biography 14: British Novelists Since 1960*. Ed. Jay L. Halio. Detroit: Gale, 1983. 546–61.

———, and Cheryl Bove. *Iris Murdoch: A Descriptive Primary and Annotated Secondary Bibliography*. New York and London: Garland, 1994.

Fowler, Simon, William Spencer, and Stuart Tamblin. *Army Service Records of the First World War*. London: Public Records Office, 1997.

Gordon, David J. *Iris Murdoch's Fables of Unselfing*. Columbia and London: U of Missouri P, 1995.

Haffenden, John. "In Conversation with Iris Murdoch." *Literary Review* 58 (April 1983): 31–35. Rpt. in *Novelists in Interview*. London and New York: Methuen, 1985. 191–209.

Hauptfuhrer, Fred. "The Lost Loves of Iris Murdoch." *People* (March 14, 1988): 17–18.

Heusel, Barbara Stevens. *Patterned Aimlessness: Iris Murdoch's Novels of the 1970s and 1980s*. Athens: U of Georgia P, 1995.

Johnson, Deborah. *Iris Murdoch*. London: Harvester P, 1987.

"Losing Her Mind to Gain the World." *Sunday Times* (London), July 26, 1998.

Murdoch, Iris. Letter to author, January 12, 1983.

———. "The Sublime and the Beautiful Revisited." *Yale Review* 49 (December 1960): 247–71.

Sage, Lorna. "The Pursuit of Imperfection." *Critical Quarterly* 19 (1977): 60–68. Rpt. as "The Pursuit of Imperfection: *Henry and Cato*." *Iris Murdoch*. Ed. Bloom. 111–19.

Schaefer, Christina K. *The Great War: A Guide to the Service Records of All The World's Fighting Men and Volunteers*. Baltimore: Genealogical Publishing, 1998.

Thompson, T. J. T. and E. P. T. *There Is a Spirit in Europe: A Memoir of Frank Thompson*. London: Gollancz, 1947.

Todd, Richard. *Iris Murdoch*. London and New York: Methuen. 1984.

———. *Iris Murdoch: The Shakespearian Interest*. London: Vision Press, 1979.

1: A Philosophical Novelist? Early Dialogues

MURDOCH'S READERS ARE FORTUNATE to have had as her early
critics fine scholars who researched and synthesized her philosophical texts, her interviews, and her fiction to help the readers com-
prehend the many layers of the complex controversy about whether she
is a philosophical novelist and what such a term might mean. Her critics have classified her structuring of the novel form over the last third of
the twentieth century into groups such as philosophical novel, realistic
novel, symbolist novel, comic metaphysical adventure, spiritual adventure story, religious fable, ethically controlled fantasy, and postmodernist novel. During the first phase of Murdoch criticism from 1965 to
1974 critics such as A. S. Byatt, Peter Wolfe, Frank Baldanza, and Rubin Rabinovitz laid an excellent groundwork for subsequent readers'
interpretations of Murdoch's novels. What I call the orthodox position
in Murdoch studies regarding the relationship of her philosophy to her
fiction grows out of their work. This position is that her philosophy reveals ideas that the novels illustrate directly. None of these critics is so
simplistic as, on the one hand, to claim that she is a philosophical novelist without employing any caveat or, on the other hand, to deny any
connection between her philosophy and her fiction; each demonstrates
how unsatisfactory the label *philosophical novelist* is in describing the
complexity of her novels, while, at the same time, each dwells over-
much on her philosophical statements.

These critics, being first, dealt with the most crucial issues. Generally they were sensitive to the nuances of Murdoch's definition of a
philosophical novelist and her attitudes toward analyses of philosophical
ideas in novels. On the other hand, they also understood that many
readers were what Rabinovitz calls "mystified" by the novels. He attempted to make such readers happy by filling in their gaps in regard to
her philosophy in the monograph *Iris Murdoch* (1968), which he wrote
for the Columbia Essays on Modern Writers series — the second significant American critique. What Rabinovitz could not have foreseen,
because Murdoch had not yet discussed the issue in interviews, was her
emphasis on mystification as an important task of literature. He expressed cogently in the second sentence of his essay what was to become the orthodox view: "A category — philosophical novelist —
seems ready-made for her, but Miss Murdoch does not feel that she is a

philosophical novelist in the sense that a writer like Sartre is" (3). But such a caveat did not stop him from summarizing a long list of philosophical sources with which a reader might well feel it necessary to become familiar as background to Murdoch's novels. Trying to be helpful, he overemphasized the need for such background when he suggested reading, among others, Simone Weil; Murdoch's critiques of Immanuel Kant; Georg Wilhelm Friedrich Hegel; Jean-Paul Sartre; Friedrich Wilhelm Nietzsche; Martin Heidegger; Søren Kierkegaard; Martin Buber; Gabriel Marcel; J. L. Austin; G. E. Moore; and Stuart Hampshire (40, 44). Paradoxically, even as these early critics explicate her novels via her philosophy, as Rabinovitz does in this study, they agree with her that the label *philosophical novelist* does not apply.

Degrees of Freedom: The Novels of Iris Murdoch

Then a young British novelist, now a well-known Booker Prize winner for her novel *Possession*, A. S. Byatt wrote the first book of criticism devoted to Murdoch's novels: *Degrees of Freedom: The Novels of Iris Murdoch* (1965). Because Murdoch enjoyed mentoring beginning British writers, Byatt had easy access to the older author's attention and soon became her friend. Byatt was perhaps more sensitive to the critical issues in Murdoch's earlier books than were most early critics, but she also had more help and more influence from Murdoch. She relied heavily on "Against Dryness" when she published her critique of Murdoch's first seven novels in Britain one year before Wolfe published his in the United States. Byatt and Murdoch were both relatively unknown when Byatt wrote the first bit of the Murdoch critical narrative and set up what became the conventional story about whether Murdoch was or was not a philosophical novelist. Byatt had an advantage over subsequent American critics: her "Acknowledgment" expresses gratitude for Murdoch's "many helpful suggestions for further reading and thought." Because Murdoch revealed some of her goals to Byatt, Byatt's book had the potential to be a more significant study than Wolfe's 1966 book. Actually, it proved to be only a stage through which the critical community had to pass — that of critics, admiring Murdoch and fearing to misrepresent her position, asking Murdoch for legitimation.

Subsequent critics have consulted Byatt's book-length study as the Ur-text in Murdoch studies. By relying heavily on Murdoch's aesthetic statements, Byatt helped determine their value to criticism. The number of items in Byatt's bibliography exposes her predicament: seven novels by Murdoch, seven books or articles by Murdoch, seven articles about Murdoch's work, and five other books cited by writers known to have influenced her. In comparison, Wolfe only one year later has seventy-eight secondary sources, as well as eight novels, fourteen articles, and one dramatic collaboration by Murdoch.

Being first inevitably lays one open to criticism when later scholars uncover more information or gain a broader perspective. That second-guessing of Byatt's interpretation of Murdoch's oeuvre is important to the present study. For example, Guy Backus's *Iris Murdoch: The Novelist as Philosopher, the Philosopher as Novelist* (1986) is quite skeptical of Murdoch's aesthetic, which was the basis for much of Byatt's interpretation; in fact, he bases his incisive study on calling Murdoch's aesthetic into question. In addition, he builds much of his case on the backs of Byatt's, Robert Scholes's, and Elizabeth Dipple's arguments in praise of Murdoch's aesthetic. Backus's critique of this orthodox position fuels the controversial issue. Most of Murdoch's critics neither deny that particulars in her novels may grow out of her philosophical ideas nor argue that that criterion alone makes them philosophical novels.

A Philosophical Novelist?

In attempting to gauge the degree to which Murdoch is a philosophical novelist, Byatt finds a unique relationship between Murdoch's fiction and her philosophy. After noting that she is not certain whether other readers use the label *philosophical novelist* to signify "praise or abuse," she points out that Murdoch seems to use the term pejoratively in *Sartre, Romantic Rationalist* when speaking of Sartre's novelistic practices. She infers from Murdoch's attitude that Murdoch would not attempt to be like Sartre. Also — to add another example of Murdoch's view on the extent to which philosophy is important to the reader's understanding of the novels — Byatt quotes from the interview in *The Times* (London) of February 13, 1964, in which Murdoch says: "I suppose I have certain philosophical ideas about human life and character, and that these must somehow find expression in my novels: but for the most part I am not conscious of this process and I think it would be destructive if I were. Certainly I am not a philosophical novelist in the sense that Sartre or Simone de Beauvoir is" (quoted, 184). Furthermore, Byatt interprets Murdoch to be arguing that Sartre reveals in his novels the pattern of his own ideas but does not reveal to the reader "the stuff of human life"; Byatt asks whether critics might say the same of Murdoch (quoted, 183).

Readers learn a great deal about the thrust of Byatt's book and her interest in philosophical issues on the first page. She explains immediately, using a quotation from "Against Dryness" — "we need to be enabled to think in terms of degrees of freedom, and to picture, in a non-metaphysical, non-totalitarian, and non-religious sense, the transcendence of reality" (quoted, 9) — that the word *transcendent* is often used in a special way in philosophy and that Murdoch uses it to mean comprehensiveness and ubiquity. This initiation into Murdoch's stance that reality is omnipresent establishes the focus of Byatt's book: each of Murdoch's characters experiences a certain degree of freedom to recognize reality. Byatt's positioning of information demonstrates that she considers next in importance Murdoch's aesthetic pronouncement in this article, which is in some ways Murdoch's reiteration of the argument against the modernist movement that she began in *Sartre, Romantic Rationalist*. Murdoch distinguishes herself from modernist writers, whom she sees as setting out aloofly to create in their texts perfect symbols that have no direct link to the messiness of everyday life. She describes two kinds of novels: the crystalline novel, which is "dry," "self-contained" (quoted, 210), full of "myth and symbol, precision and coherence," and the journalistic novel, which is "a large, shapeless quasi-documentary object" (quoted, 9), neither of which has a solid understanding of the human personality. Murdoch's ideal is a third kind of novel. For Byatt, Murdoch's position is significantly anti-modernist. Whereas Byatt argues that Murdoch is not a modernist and not a philosophical novelist in the sense that Sartre and Simone de Beauvoir are, she focuses heavily on philosophical matters, accepts Murdoch's stated aesthetic, and judges Murdoch's texts on the basis of modernist and formalistic criteria.

Byatt organizes her analysis of Murdoch's first seven novels on the basis of unity of theme. (She leaves out the 1964 novel *The Italian Girl*, which Wolfe would examine the following year.) Byatt argues that all the novels are studies of the "degrees of freedom" available to the characters (11); given her discussion of Murdoch's criticism of the Sartrean stance, this attention to the existential dilemma is conspicuous. As will be noted later in the present study, Dipple suggests that this emphasis gave readers a distorted idea of the evolution of Murdoch's novelistic development. Examining the whole of Murdoch's novel-writing process, Byatt discerns a "break in subject matter" after the second novel, *The Flight from the Enchanter*. In the third novel, *The Sandcastle*, Murdoch moves from an interest in the characters' jobs or "a social dimension" to "freedom within personal relationships, with Jamesian studies of one person's power over, or modification of another person — although both ideas are of course present in most of the novels" (11). Furthermore, Byatt recites a litany of ways in which these early novels — *Under the Net, The Sandcastle, The Bell,* and *An Unofficial Rose* — dwell on problems of economic freedom and the limits of freedom on the job, as well as how they attempt to develop characters who reveal their power struggles in the manner in which John Bayley says that Henry James's Maggie Verver does (13). That is, Murdoch wants to create the normal, conventional person, not what Bayley calls the "'lonely, self-contained individual,' who is seen as the analogue of the literary self-contained symbol" of the philosophers Hampshire and Sartre but "the real impenetrable human person" found in Shakespeare and in Russian writers such as Leo Tolstoy (quoted in Byatt, 10–11).

Creating "Impenetrable" Characters

Creating this "impenetrable" human being or ordinary person is a major part of Murdoch's aesthetic. Byatt not only establishes Murdoch's version of her aesthetic as gospel but, as she states in her acknowledgments, she asked Murdoch to read her manuscript before publication. Although this clearing of the draft with Murdoch may seem worshipful, Byatt's criticism seems to have been unaffected by Murdoch's favor. Because this courtesy apparently became customary as subsequent critics published books on Murdoch's fiction, future examinations of Murdoch criticism should ask how much control Murdoch had over her own criticism and whether there has been a tendency to take an official line. Central to Backus's challenge to the orthodox position is his implication that such a tendency exists. When Backus censures Byatt's acceptance of Murdoch's stated aesthetic intention, he is, apparently, alluding to the complex of ideas in "Against Dryness," such as: "to return to its imaginative power," the novel "must pit against 'the consolations of form, [or] the clear crystalline work, [and] the simplified fantasy-myth,' 'the now so unfashionable naturalistic idea of character'" (quoted in Byatt, 11).

Even though Byatt is hesitant about ascribing philosophical intentions to Murdoch's novels, she, like others holding the orthodox position, finds it necessary to use philosophers to discuss Murdoch's novels. Byatt thinks that her emphasis on Murdoch's aesthetic requires that she elaborate on Wittgenstein's use of "the net," the gridlike system under which one must crawl to look at particulars (15), and on Hampshire's and Sartre's picture of the human being (10). To develop Murdoch's crucial interest in the human personality Byatt demonstrates that the latter two philosophers' egocentric pictures of suffering man are totally unlike Murdoch's. She quotes Murdoch from in *Sartre, Romantic Rationalist:* "we should see man, as we no longer do 'against a background of values, of realities, which transcend him.' The concept of sincerity is 'self-centred,' the concept of truth 'other-centred'" (10). Murdoch is also emphatic about her belief in the impenetrability of persons; the artist's job is to depict the reality of the person in conjunction with the reality of the world outside the person. Murdoch argues that Sartre and those who wrote dry modernist texts left out the relatedness of people to the world. Using a metaphor from Simone Weil, a French mystic who never sentimentalized being an outsider, Murdoch wants "the novel to return to its imaginary roots" (quoted in Conradi, 13). The crystalline novel of modernist perfection fails to depict human beings in all their fullness and complexity.

The forcefulness of Murdoch's cry for the investigation of the individual personality convinces Byatt of Murdoch's moral interest in the mystery and value of the human spirit. In *Sartre, Romantic Rationalist* Murdoch documented Sartre's lack of respect for the individual; in his texts man is "stripped and made anonymous by extremity" (quoted in Byatt, 12–13). Demonstrating the connections in Murdoch's writing among the terms *individual, human,* and *normal,* Byatt quotes (13) from "Solidity of the Novel," in which G. S. Fraser demonstrates that for Murdoch the term *normal* captures the "mysterious transcendent reality" of human beings. It is interesting to speculate as to why Byatt found it necessary to explain that Murdoch's husband, Bayley, describes the concept *human* similarly: "to be human is to be virtually unknown"; for Murdoch, normality is an aspect of the "stuff of human life which contributes to the opacity of persons, to the mystery of freedom in relation to reality" (13). Byatt understands that Murdoch's aesthetic views are tied to her moral views: her "respect for the individual . . . as the centre of our moral thinking, is extended to her thinking about form" (189). Consequently, a corollary to this moral issue becomes the question of the degree to which form inhibits the play of a given Murdoch plot and enslaves the characters.

Byatt's Formalist Criticism

More interested in the strategies Murdoch borrows from formalist critics than in the moral issue, Byatt asks how different formal questions become relevant in judging each novel. She explores each of the first seven novels by investigating its form and the significance of the symbols to see if Murdoch achieved unity and if her theory of the novel is a key to success. Byatt discovers that her criticisms of Murdoch's novels "are partly a result of the developing complexity of Miss Murdoch's sense of the novel form" (208). Byatt realizes that as Murdoch challenged new ideas and forms, her books became less successfully unified, but that, at the same time, the evidence of Murdoch's growth as an artist is dramatic proof of "a continuing and powerful vitality" (208). Byatt's seeming detachment, as well as the awe she feels in regard to the uniqueness of Murdoch's project, are evident when she says: "no other novelist . . . sees the problem of form in the modern novel quite as she does; writers are, as she says, usually *simply* crystalline or simply naturalistic, and her attempt to explore the possibilities of a combination of the two seems to me intelligent and admirable, if at times a little nervous. . . . It is a question, as always in art, of how to fuse the intellectual sense of order with a passionate sense of real complexity and solidity, and Miss Murdoch seems to me at her best to have the equipment to do this if she has never quite struck the balance in a sustained way yet" (208). Byatt has a clear understanding of Murdoch's desire to mate form and the messiness of life.

Because Byatt cannot see clearly enough that the first seven novels do not fit nicely into preconceived categories, she has problems in explicating what she and the other early critics simplistically label Murdoch's symbols as if they were modernist symbols — what Murdoch calls "self-contained crystal[s]" (quoted, 210). Murdoch's oeuvre continually refused to fit into any one pigeonhole, or even a series of them: as soon as a slot such as Gothic novel seemed appropriate, Murdoch would try a new genre. Knowing that Murdoch's novels are critiques of classification, readers can enjoy the chagrin of Byatt and other early critics who struggled with the placement of Murdoch in the modernist school. Her resonant metaphors and symbols can no more be categorized than her novels can. Byatt explains that Murdoch, thinking in terms of the romantic ideal of "organic whole" in poetry, writes that a novel creates "a complete and unclassifiable image" that is diffuse but resounds and vibrates (210). Byatt seems to accept this largely Romantic notion of organic form, but she does not take into account Murdoch's opinion in "Against Dryness" that symbols belong in poetry rather than in prose fiction. She judges Murdoch's explanations and descriptions to be vague, saying that the "differences between 'self-contained crystal' (pejorative) and 'organically complete image, *sui generis*' (praise) may in practice be difficult to see, although the intellectual and emotional appeal of the ideas contained is easy enough to grasp" (210). While this analysis serves to rationalize Byatt's dissection of ostensible symbols, later critics agree that Murdoch does not really use symbols as the modernists saw them.

The Bell

The chapter on *The Bell* (1958), Murdoch's fourth novel, is a good one for studying Byatt's orthodox view of such ostensible symbols in Murdoch. Assuming the importance of the title, Byatt finds many connections in Murdoch's use of two church bells at an Anglican lay community: "a new bell . . . to be hung in the Abbey tower . . . [to] enter the gate like a postulant — here resembling Catherine Fawley" (73), also a postulant; and a cursed and fallen old bell accidentally brought up from the depths of the lake. Acknowledging G. S. Fraser's discussion of the bell as a "symbol of lost order and faith," Byatt sees its usefulness in connecting the complex concept she has been explaining: Murdoch's juxtaposing "the solidity of the normal, with the unutterably particular mystery" (76). In their sermons two men of the lay community make the new bell a symbol "for man's spiritual nature": "James sees the bell as a symbol of purity, clarity, candour and compares it explicitly with Catherine Fawley" (76). James also appreciates the voice of the bell, which will eventually be heard, while Michael, the leader of the community, "uses it as a symbol for man's spiritual energy" (76). Dora, a young, naïve artist who can be taken as the novel's protagonist, wants to raise the old bell, "a symbol for the involvement of spiritual energy in passion and ambiguous emotion" (74). Murdoch has Michael propose that individuals can increase their "spiritual energy" (quoted, 77); for Byatt, Murdoch is thinking in terms of Weil's idea of gravity, or the physical work it will take to pull up the medieval bell from the water, as opposed to spiritual grace, which is a supernatural gift. For Byatt the complex of references to the bells, even in the characters' dreams, demonstrates their importance to the novel's goal. The old bell, engraved "'Vox ego sum amoris' [I am the voice of love]," helps to symbolize, according to Byatt, "the ambiguity of love in the novel, where love is both a dangerous loss of purity and exercise of power, and a necessary part of humanity" (76). The novel's musical and sound imagery come together in the bell and reflect "the moral themes of purity and complexity, freedom and deliberate restriction" (78). Byatt develops these various levels of symbolism, no doubt, to show how well the novel works. Although finding her discussion useful, Peter Conradi adds what Byatt missed: that "the 'incompleteness' and, in a sense, even the clumsiness of the bell as symbolic device seem perfectly deliberate. Murdoch has consistently argued for a wariness in deploying symbol, so that the aesthetic centre it represents is resisted by a competing force within the characters" (120). He is noting a level of complexity in Murdoch's novels that critics in 1965 were not prepared to apprehend.

Although Byatt explicates what she considers the major symbols in the first two novels — the net in *Under the Net* and the fishbowl, symbolic of the systemic traps in *The Flight from the Enchanter* — she judges those novels as successful not because of symbolic devices but as a result of their appealing style and "unity of tone." She attributes the success of *Under the Net* to the "dead-pan curt style with carefully controlled romantic undertones which rarely (more often in *Flight*) get out of hand" (211). In the first novel the protagonist, Jake, is the controlling device; his language and behavior fit his personality. The later novels, revealing Murdoch's "natural fluctuations between washes of romantic feeling and a rather wry, rather dry wit," do not come off as well, because the characters have quite different problems from Jake's. A journalist and a somewhat "unscrupulous Bohemian, he indulges in amusing understatement and flat, effective jokes" (211). For him, then, the fluctuation from romance to witticism is genuinely his individual quirk and not his creator's. The character owes his success to his obsession: although he is "interested in purely philosophical problems," "knows philosophers, and even goes as far as writing, apologetically, a philosophical book, the philosophical language used does not jar, but adds precision" (211). This distancing between author and protagonist is parallel to the meticulous way Murdoch takes the symbol-making authority away from the author and gives it to characters.

Murdoch's Language

Formalism also helps Byatt to evaluate Murdoch's use of this protagonist's Romantic language. In the case of Jake, Byatt argues that it is "entirely in character, part of a picture, [these] sudden bursts of not entirely successful lyricism which are rather touching," because we are all — Jake, Murdoch, and the reader — "partially ashamed of them" for being excessive (211). Byatt finds that Murdoch does a superb job of capturing the movement of Jake's language: "reluctant to get off" the double-decker bus, Jake might resemble Milton's dove, because he is brooding on "the continual death of time, the lost meaning, the unrecaptured moment" (quoted, 212). The novel "hovers between the excellently vivid, idiosyncratic dialogue of thinkers, the description of events in themselves startling and economically told (Jake on the fire escape) and this kind of non-insistent Romantic brooding on Life" (212).

Byatt judges the first two novels to be more unified and more thoroughly well-crafted than the five that follow, because the prose of the latter falls less often into Romantic gracefulness. Emphasizing novelistic discourse more than other commentators do, she points out that the earliest reviewers said that Murdoch "wrote beautifully" (209); the stunning quality of these first two novels apparently surprised reviewers, who had heard so much about the death of the British novel, and made them gush. Then, she observes, other reviewers had to restore a balance. They criticized the next three novels — *The Sandcastle, The Bell,* and *A Severed Head* — especially the language, much more harshly. Byatt analyzes these problems as evolving from Murdoch's Romanticism and her attempt at eloquent prose and quotes some passages from Murdoch to bolster her argument. She thinks that one of Murdoch's aims is to work for "the strange eloquence of suggestion and rhythm" that Henry James mentions and that Murdoch quotes in "The Sublime and the Beautiful Revisited," and that another aim involves a point made in "Against Dryness": "prose must recover its former glory, eloquence and discourse must return. I would connect eloquence with the attempt to speak the truth" (quoted, 208).

As a result of her exploration of these texts, Byatt can react more wisely than more impatient critics who see Murdoch's prose as "too sloppy" and "too rhetorical" and often demonstrate somewhat mechanically that Murdoch can write badly and well on the same page (209). Byatt recognizes that Murdoch's lack of perfection demonstrates that she is searching for the answers to questions unknown to most novelists. Byatt sums up her own stance and shows how Murdoch's complexity has moved her to discover why these attempts are necessary: "I think [Murdoch's] sense of what prose *should be* has bedevilled her easy use of the kind of prose she naturally writes well. She is someone who is passionate or eloquent in bursts, and both when she is describing certain kinds of powerful feeling and when she is writing deliberately 'eloquent' descriptive prose, one senses a deliberate almost devil-may-care bursting out of a natural restraint, a natural reluctance to write so, combined with a strong feeling that something is lost if this *kind* of a thing cannot politely be done in prose" (209). Even though Byatt's descriptions come close to picturing a puritanical writer constraining a hedonistic one, the reality is that Murdoch often *was* more thoughtful than most people. Throughout her career Murdoch's craft had the flexibility to change and grow as the writer did.

Speaking in Puzzles

Byatt attributes to Murdoch both the nimbleness of a subtle modernist (she first labeled Murdoch a symbolist) and the humor of a nineteenth-century realist. In other words, while Murdoch's droll sense of humor is full-bodied — her sense of the incongruous is, after all, probably responsible for the immediate success of *Under the Net* — she also has the skill to use indirection, understatement, and irony, skills that Byatt thinks readers of the 1950s and 1960s valued. (American critics, especially, still used the formalist mode of interpretation.) Byatt's important contribution here is to attribute to Murdoch the aim of speaking in puzzles or riddles to get the reader to pay attention to semantics and definition: "Miss Murdoch's theory of eloquence could be made to argue perhaps that this is a limitation on what we can say. I would agree with this, and thus extend sympathy if not entire approval to Miss Murdoch's efforts to break the bonds of our mistrustful prose" (209). Demonstrating her formalist leanings, Byatt reveals her uneasiness about whether Murdoch's desire — if it is her desire — to "break" bonds or to teach readers by forcing them to pay attention to words is an artistic endeavor.

Again, Byatt cautions that a reader must always make sure that Murdoch has the same understanding of a word as the reader does. The following passage in which Murdoch disagrees with Sartre explains Byatt's view of Murdoch's goals of perfection that cannot be achieved ("Against Dryness") but also unintentionally shows, more broadly, that Murdoch's and Mikhail Bakhtin's ideas about language and art are similar: "Miss Murdoch's use of the three terms, journalism, poetry and eloquence to describe what prose can do, taken in conjunction with her feeling that Sartre is misled when he states simply that whereas poetry creates a thing 'outside language' prose is 'simply for communication,' seems to me a good way of coming at the area in which a novel through its language moves us. It should, she says, 'create a complete and unclassifiable image'" (209–10). Byatt's analysis prepares the reader for some of the repeated criticism of Murdoch's parodies of banality and melodrama. Byatt thinks that Murdoch has a special gift for noticing the "banalities of ordinary conversation and ordinary thought" and the ability to "'place' these [so] that they have a resonance beyond themselves" (210). Byatt sounds like Bakhtin when she says that Murdoch has captured "the eloquence of things vividly seen and accurately described (connected to our sense of the density of our lives); there is the eloquence of 'extra-ordinary' conversation and thought, precisely trapped and juxtaposed with each other; there is that deliberately serious, deliberately 'worked' description of high emotion or complex feeling, that most of us normally think of when we speak of eloquence of rhetoric" (210). Byatt says that critics find fault with Murdoch's attempt at this kind of sensibility: "It is easier in French; it is significant that it is Camus whom she singles out for praise" (210). One recalls that Samuel Beckett eventually switched from English to French in order to write more effectively about twentieth-century banality.

The Flight from the Enchanter

While not criticizing Murdoch's far-ranging intentions, Byatt does criticize her results, particularly her language. Byatt judges *The Flight from the Enchanter* a successful novel but finds it more mechanical than its predecessor. Ironically, however, looking at the novel from a formalistic perspective, Byatt has to admit that the tone and style do fit the content; the novel is about the mechanism of systems and networks (i.e., factories and social organizations). Thus, the evocative prose of *Under the Net* will not work in *The Flight from the Enchanter,* and the more mechanical prose is fitting. The systems Murdoch depicts in the novel inevitably create power figures, or enchanters, and powerless victims; although this category of suffering victims includes many of the characters, the most poignant is Nina, a refugee dressmaker whose country has disappeared in the Second World War. Nevertheless, Byatt finds language to criticize, prose that jolts the reader: "embarrassed perfunctory use of emotional language, not as precise as Jake's self-conscious perceptions" (212). On the basis alone of what Byatt admits to the reader — that the two novels are in no way similar — comparing the language of Jake, who has the potential to become an artist, to that of Nina is inappropriate. Why would a poor illegal-immigrant seamstress have the self-conscious perception of a potentially good writer? Furthermore, writing only a decade after the end of the Second World War, Murdoch might well have felt more emotional about this subject matter; Nina's predicament reflects Murdoch's experiences from 1944 through 1946 as an administrative officer with the United Nations Relief and Rehabilitation Administration in England, Belgium, and Austria.

In evoking that wartime experience Byatt introduces Murdoch's readers to Weil, an introduction Backus will later call superficial and distorting. Byatt explains that Weil's *L'Enracinement* "is a study of the need of the community to provide a place for people to live and be someone, to have roots and not to be anonymous. (It is concerned precisely with the re-establishment of France after the war.)" (46). Nina is the first example of Murdoch's suffering refugee; she continued to create such characters, who are similar to the people Weil saw — as did Murdoch — to be "suddenly deprived of home, family, identity, self-respect, as well as food" (46). Murdoch, like Weil, is interested in the social and personal effects the experiences of such people cause. One social effect is the rise of power figures who take advantage of the chaotic breakdown in order. Captivated by the maneuvers of power figures, Murdoch lets them proliferate in many variations and incarnations and to dominate many kinds of victims in subsequent novels. For example, *The Unicorn*, which critics generally agree is Murdoch's most philosophical novel, not only explores victimization but also defines the conflict Weil saw between the imagination and self-effacement. Weil says, according to Byatt, that the imagination is "something which precludes an apprehension of reality in us" (69) and that "the acceptance of injustice, the acceptance of suffering," is "an apprehension of reality . . . and therefore we must pay attention to it" (161). Byatt understands that the theme of victimization, which begins with Nina and her cohorts in *The Flight from the Enchanter*, is basic to *The Unicorn*, a novel about such suffering.

The Unicorn

Of the seven novels she discusses, Byatt spends the most space, thirty-four pages, on *The Unicorn*. It is revealing to look at some of her discussion of this novel vis-à-vis Weil, both because of her belief that *Under the Net* is more successful than the seventh novel and because of Backus's subsequent attacks on Byatt's analysis of *The Unicorn* for its emphasis on Weil's concept of suffering. Byatt argues that in *Under the Net* "the philosophical language can be understood in terms of what is in the book and refers to it, whereas with *The Unicorn* the language is too often a dead reference to some thought outside the book with which we are not properly in touch" (211). In 1986 Backus, rather than criticizing the novel, criticizes Byatt's handling of it. He indicates that partly because of her unwillingness to focus on philosophical issues Byatt was not prepared to deal with the complexity of *The Unicorn*, a gothic story in which a young schoolmistress, Marian, sets out to tutor Hannah, a woman entrapped in an Irish country home by the homosexual power figure Gerald Scottow.

Byatt enumerates the ways in which the novel is successful at the beginning, when Murdoch is simply storytelling: "the sinister aspects of the landscape, Marian's unreasonable fear, the slight repulsion she feels from Hannah's oddity . . . the slow change in Scottow from the pleasant burly countryman to something indefinably horrible and cruel . . .

the moment . . . when he touches Jamesie's cheek with his whip, the whole monotonous strangeness of country, house, society" (205). For Byatt the best part of *The Unicorn* is its drama and mystery, not its basis in "philosophic patterns" that assume that "Hannah's suffering is . . . real in Simone Weil's sense" (205). Byatt proposes that Murdoch equates the French mystic with Hannah the unicorn (a symbol of Christ). Gordon goes further, suggesting that Weil and Hannah have "a moral passion for an image of suffering unsentimental and severe enough to be called an 'unselfing'" (5). Byatt regrets that this information is outside the book and unavailable to most readers, but she also argues that Weil's suffering is much different in kind.

Comparing the novel to *A Severed Head* in its ability to generate "intellectual excitement," Byatt says that perhaps Murdoch was asking herself which interpretation of Hannah "was 'correct' in terms . . . of actions which might ambiguously be called either obsessional neurosis or religious redemptive suffering" (205). The obsessional neuroses in *A Severed Head* address similar anthropological and mythological suggestions about a broad range of sexualities: adulterous, homosexual, and incestuous. Finding, instead, Murdoch's ability to dramatize "spiritual progress" limited, because the spiritual epiphanies are not dramatic enough in "the contemplative life" she investigates, Byatt insists that only Dostoevsky, whose life and insights were violent, could make such problems live on the page (206). The weakness in Byatt's analysis is her description of the novel as a great puzzle that can only be "'solved' with Freudian/mythical references" (205). Such a conclusion diminishes the novel by implying that it is structured on Freudianisms, a novelistic ploy that Murdoch makes fun of, especially in *The Black Prince*.

Byatt grants that *The Unicorn* creates "a private myth, a private religious symbolism" to gauge human attitudes and reactions to religious suffering in general, but she thinks that the emphasis on Weil's concept of suffering is not appropriate in a novel about "wealthy Anglo-Irish" (206). Weil's world is too far from the one Murdoch creates: Weil dealt with the suffering of extremely poor, deprived individuals, based on her having "worked in a factory and lived on the dole," and she "died partially of privation"; her knowledge and her experiences were so different from Murdoch's that they cannot be compared to suffering of a Romantic kind, involving a "magic garden and beautiful lady" (206). Weil based her theories on refugees who were more like the prostitutes and criminals she wanted to study. Arguing that the symbols do not fit the religious reality of Murdoch's novel, Byatt also criticizes its lack of balance and harmony and unity. Byatt is apparently so intent on judging the form of the novel and "the relationship of the symbols to the ideas" that it never occurs to her that Murdoch might be striving deliberately to generate "artistic discomfort and uncertainty" (207) in the reader, not modernist symbols. Backus criticizes her for avoiding issues he thinks are obvious.

Often referred to by other early critics as one of Murdoch's most perceptive readers, Byatt seems to have had a blind spot regarding Weil's texts. No doubt Murdoch had suggested that Byatt read Weil for background, and Byatt had the confidence to tackle the French philosopher's ideas before many of her works had been translated into English. Rather than giving her credit for having initiated this line of inquiry, Backus excoriates Byatt for a lack of critical rigor in ignoring much of Weil's work.

The Disciplined Heart: Iris Murdoch and Her Novels

While Byatt benefited from Murdoch's solicitous critical help, American critics had to rely on the available texts, such as Byatt's *Degrees of Freedom*. Byatt's American contemporary Peter Wolfe published the second critical book, the first book-length analysis of Murdoch's novels in the United States: *The Disciplined Heart: Iris Murdoch and Her Novels* (1966). Wolfe's point of departure is that Murdoch's philosophical essays are always the first line of interpretation for critics who want to understand the complex depth of her novels. His argument is that "the thematic dovetailing in her work of philosophy and social comedy justifies a theoretical-descriptive approach" (4). Such an attitude prevailed in the early criticism. Moreover, reading Wolfe's analysis sensitizes a present-day reader to Murdoch's relative anonymity in the U.S. at the time and the necessity for identifying her. As a professor, he believed that for English departments "to continue neglecting postwar literature is to deprive . . . students of an inspiration grounded in *their* world" (vii). Such a forward-looking view was as helpful to the scholarly community's acceptance of Murdoch's novels as were the discussions of early criticism of Murdoch's fiction in the bibliographical studies *Iris Murdoch and Muriel Spark: A Bibliography* (1976), by Thomas T. Tominaga and Wilma Schneidermeyer, and *Iris Murdoch: A Reference Guide* (1987), by Kate Begnal.

Wolfe was well aware that the worldview Murdoch reflected in her social comedies arose out of a dynamic philosophical outlook. According to Wolfe, "The distance between man's inner life and the ways in which his needs and convictions are externalized creates a variety of social criticism [in her novels] rooted deeply in both irony and philosophy" (4). He characterizes the struggles within Murdoch's social critique as being between "the amorphous, non-reflective world and man's responsibility as a creator of values. Her belief that private standards of conduct cannot be validated until they are tested in social experience places great narrative and philosophical emphasis upon particular situations" (4). Wolfe qualifies his definition of *philosophical novelist* as it applies to Murdoch: "Unlike L. H. Myers or Thomas Mann in *The Magic Mountain*, she does not openly discuss philosophical ideas in her fiction. When her characters consider problems in ethics and morals, the problems are never presented as abstract doctrine. Her philosophical interest is always social morality rather than a moral code or set of principles that the reader is invited to apply to action and plot" (6). Wolfe contends that Murdoch does not "sacrifice the individual to a principle or a universal" and that by refusing to do so she has expanded what Lionel Trilling (among others) calls "the great tradition." Her philosophical essays, like Plato's Socratic dialogues, argue that seeing reality without illusion and being aware of one's own thought pattern is crucial to maturity. Wolfe's view is that these essays admit the obvious: theory is inevitable to anyone who thinks or has a view of reality: "without theory there can be no morality. . . . This theoretical bias gains expression in the novels in the form of closely observed character interaction. . . . The final test of any professed morality is direct social experience. Life is not a thought system, and any attempt to reduce it to one involves a falsification. But by dramatizing concrete situations, the novelist shows personal conduct fortifying and even creating moral value" (6). Perceptively, he moves toward Murdoch's later position that her novels reflect a "moral psychology" (quoted in Conradi, [1]) rather than a philosophy by emphasizing that according to her, there can be no morality without theory. Moreover, Wolfe is not averse to placing her in the great nineteenth-century "novel tradition." (Conradi further explores Murdoch's writing in terms of both moral psychology and this novelistic tradition.)

A Paradoxically Philosophical Novelist

Wolfe demonstrates that a critic's way of defining a term determines the conclusions to which he or she comes. In his discussion of Murdoch's complex exploration of theory in her novels, Wolfe proposes that she can be called a philosophical novelist because her texts take a position on the morality of certain human behaviors. To her, he says, "Myth and philosophy . . . are not secondary interests: we live in them all the time and must perpetually clarify and reconstruct them to illuminate our changing predicament. Her world is rich and ebullient. The

role of the perceiving self as an active moral agent prevents the surrounding social frame from chilling into lifeless materialism" (209).
Murdoch's celebration of human beings' ability to situate their lives in
the material world and, at the same time, to think about what is and
what ought to be (that is, the relation of fact and value) without becoming solipsistic leads Wolfe to focus on Murdoch's belief that ideas
and theories make life comprehensible: "as Hume and Wittgenstein insist, raw experience is something that merely occurs, containing in itself
no positive values." Unfortunately, "traditional metaphysics" is incapable of solving the problem because, "by frequently overlooking the distinction between *is* and *ought*, [it] is not close enough to finite
experience to convey the reality of individuals. She preserves the dignity
and substance of the phenomenal world by 'theorizing away,' to use
her expression, all theory, including the existential antitheoretical
method of describing reality" (209). Furthermore, she does not simply
accept the "human-centered interpretation of reality" but eschews any
scientific obligation to the law of reason (210). Here is a critic, then,
who instinctively focuses on the paradoxical in Murdoch's statements
— a critic who had read "Against Dryness," which is still considered a
crucial statement of Murdoch's aesthetic. His book inspired a growing
number of American scholars: by 1966 Kate Begnal could list fifty
pages of "Writings about Iris Murdoch" in her *Iris Murdoch: a Reference Guide*.

Rabinovitz's *Iris Murdoch*

Rabinovitz accomplishes a great deal in a few pages. He depends on
Byatt's analysis as the Ur-text, drawing some of the same parallels she
does between earlier works of literature and *The Unicorn*. Like Byatt,
Rabinovitz — and, later, Baldanza and, particularly, Conradi — carry
forward what they see as the necessary explication of Murdoch's use of
Weil's ideals about love (to love is to pay attention to an individual reality) and suffering (to resist evil, one must refuse to pass on suffering
to another). Rabinovitz writes that Murdoch employs these allusions to
Weil's texts to create "fantasy and enchantment" (35). He explains that
the characters in *The Unicorn* do not suffer quietly and selflessly; on the
contrary, they pass on their suffering to those around them. He compares one of Murdoch's philosophical statements — "suffering, in the
context of self-examination, can masquerade as purification" and
sometimes "leads to more evil" (quoted, 35–36) — with that of a character in this gothic novel. In the twelfth chapter Max Lejour, a pure
Platonist, discusses the concept of *Até:* "an evil act does not end after a

single person has been victimized; the victim finds his own victim and passes the evil on, so that a long chain of evil is created" (quoted, 36). Rabinovitz attributes these ideas to Weil's *Gravity and Grace,* in which she says that "suffering usually leads to self-hatred or to violence" (quoted, 35).

Rabinovitz worries that too focused or rigid an interest in moral issues, especially in the danger of solipsism, leads Murdoch to become dogmatic. Such intensity has already allowed her to employ the tautology "loving concern is necessary to achieve love" (45). Furthermore, he thinks that she constantly denies in interviews that she is a philosophical novelist because she fears and is guarding against "her own tendency to be dogmatic" (45). Such moral intensity might lead to an old-fashioned didacticism, a characteristic disdained by modernist critics in 1968. Rabinovitz thinks that the best way to avoid "the dangers of mythologizing, of didacticism, or of *la littérature engagée*" is to express ideas openly and to argue the opposing side (43).

Murdoch's Strategies

Rabinovitz assumes that Murdoch shortens her analysis of necessary concepts to control her own philosophical tendencies. Her strategies are "to introduce the ideas in subtle forms, to provide alternatives for the ideas, to introduce her own ideas through a minor or unsympathetic character, and even to leave the reader with problems that cannot be solved rationally, a sort of mysticism in fiction" (43–44). His criticisms here come quite close to those of Backus. He also comes close to critics who find postmodernist strategies in Murdoch's novels. His conclusion is, however, that it is futile for Murdoch to mask "the ideas in her novels," to deny "that she is a philosophical novelist"; he finds that these realities are evident to "the reader who has managed to get through the necessary background material" (45).

Such criticism of what he sees as questionable literary strategies leads Rabinovitz to recount Murdoch's weaknesses. In addition to his supposition about her fear of being dogmatic and subjective, he says that she fails to explain the differences between "loving concern and mere curiosity" about others (45). Other faults are a general "puzzling quality," "a drabness which permeates some of her inferior novels," and "a desire to fool the reader with sudden and unexpected twists of plot" (46). Rabinovitz gives his position away when he appears unconsciously to admit that readers primarily read novels for consolation: general readers, he says, want to put "down the novel with a sense of satisfaction and not irritation" (46). He clearly appreciates what was in 1968

Murdoch's most recent novel, *The Nice and the Good*, for its optimism and the way the characters "conform to the 'ordinary morality' of the linguistic analysts" (43). At the time he published his study readers of Murdoch's first eleven novels had not had the opportunity to recognize her use of unusual strategies to teach her readers about the realities of the world; the lesson is definitely not consolation.

Important moral issues that Rabinovitz finds Murdoch dramatizing are "the self-involvement which prevents a person from looking objectively at another" (37) and the relationship between loving someone and such "looking objectively": "If love is the actual recognition of otherness, freedom is one's capacity for this recognition" (32). Many characters in Murdoch's novels appear to be loving but are actually subtle "representatives of neurosis and convention" (25). For example, in regard to *The Bell* Rabinovitz agrees with Byatt, who sees Michael Meade as "similar to the neurotic Sartrean hero" and James Tayper Pace as living by "the ordinary moral rules of the logical empiricists"; instead of preaching, this novel demonstrates "the failures of the respective ideologies" (25).

Rabinovitz praises Murdoch "for her thoughtful characterizations, for her unpredictable inventiveness, and for her intelligent and compassionate ideas"; for these attributes "she deserves the reader's attention and respect" (46). Concluding that Murdoch "somehow misses being of the first rank" as a novelist, he gives reasons that now appear naïve: he suggests that this shortcoming can partly "be attributed to her own modest ambitions; she does not seem to want to write the great novel which deals with universal themes, perhaps because she does not want to risk the great failure" (46). Readers can see here how little Rabinovitz understands Murdoch's Platonism. Her fiction continually challenges "universal themes" — most obviously, the ubiquitous struggle of good and evil; she does not view risk and failure the way the modernists did. Rabinovitz is stuck in his own 1968 worldview. He read but apparently did not recall a line Richard Todd quotes from "The Sublime and the Beautiful Revisited" (1959): "Almost every work of art is a failure" (Todd, 44). As will be shown at the end of this chapter, Todd is the first critic to answer these criticisms of Murdoch's lack of perfection.

Baldanza's *Iris Murdoch*

The third major book of Murdoch criticism appeared in the U.S. in 1974. Frank Baldanza presents a complex, contradictory, and paradoxical view of Murdoch's novelistic perspective. He sees it as his professional obligation to review the earlier criticism, put it in context, and analyze the directions it has taken. Apparently reacting to critics who used the label *philosophical novelist* disparagingly, and qualifying his categorization more stringently than Byatt, Wolfe, and Rabinovitz, Baldanza writes: "Miss Murdoch is 'philosophical' only in the sense that she is a serious novelist interested in coming to terms, by means of her fiction, with real experiential aspects of ideas like power, freedom, and love; but she always does so in terms of a totally realized narrative which makes its primary appeal entirely as narration" (14). Though Baldanza deemphasizes the importance of philosophy, he assumes that the reader needs a thumbnail version of Murdoch's philosophy based on her philosophical writings. He boils her philosophy "down to its essence," and his short, simple, and accurate summary has proved to be a useful model for the critical community. He says that Murdoch's view of the problem in fiction in the 1970s is "the result of a line of Romantic philosophy stemming from Immanuel Kant through Friedrich Hegel to the existentialists (Søren Kierkegaard and Jean-Paul Sartre) and the Linguistic Analysts (G. E. Moore and Ludwig Wittgenstein). . . . modern man inherits in Sartrean Totalitarian Man (the lonely, anguished individual) and the Linguistic Analysts' Ordinary Language Man the twin wills of Neurosis and Convention, 'the enemies of love.'" For Murdoch, Baldanza emphasizes, "both philosophies tend toward solipsism. Neither pictures virtue as concerned with anything real outside ourselves. Neither provides us with a standpoint for considering real human beings in their variety, and neither presents us with any technique for exploring and controlling our own spiritual energy. Ordinary Language Man is too abstract, too conventional: he incarnated the commonest and vaguest network of conventional moral thought; and Totalitarian Man is too concrete, too neurotic: he is simply the center of an extreme decision, man stripped and made anonymous by extremity'" (24–25).

Baldanza's Estimate of Fifteen Novels

Baldanza's assessment of Murdoch in 1974, after fifteen novels in nineteen years, is that she "certainly ranks among the top five novelists writing in England today" (174). Baldanza apparently sees the theme of love growing out of Murdoch's philosophy of the other, for he writes that "convention, and neurosis are the enemies of love, because both dull one's perception of others" (26). For proof of her disagreement with Kant he recommends "The Sublime and the Good," from which he quotes a passage on love: "Art and morals are, with certain provisos . . . one. Their essence is the same. The essence of both of them is love. Love is the perception of individuals. Love is the extremely difficult realization that something other than oneself is real. Love, and so art and morals, is the discovery of reality (51)" (26). Baldanza is confident that, having read the philosophy, he can summarize and evaluate its significance in relationship to the novels.

He distinguishes Murdoch's thinking from that of the behaviorists, existentialists, and empiricists by quoting from a paper she read in 1956: "There are people whose fundamental moral belief is that we all live in the same empirical and rationally comprehensible world and that morality is the adoption of universal and openly defensible rules of conduct. There are other people whose fundamental belief is that we live in a world whose mystery transcends us and that morality is the exploration of that mystery in so far as it concerns each individual" (quoted, 27). Juxtaposing with that passage a paper she delivered in 1967 as the Leslie Stephen Lecture at Cambridge University, which became the essay "The Sovereignty of Good Over Other Concepts," Baldanza explains: "Within a decidedly agnostic context, she establishes Good as the most pervasive and unifying of moral concepts but as also one of the most difficult of definition. After a demonstration of how the concept of Good can be approached by means of the beauties of nature and art, and the disciplines of study and intellectual effort, she concludes — perhaps a bit regretfully, even — that love itself is a subordinate concept to that of the Good" (27–28). Backus and Alasdair MacIntyre will speak to this issue and will disagree with Baldanza and Murdoch.

Baldanza is interested in the effect of Murdoch's philosophy on her novel writing, and his summaries of her philosophical texts are useful to readers who want to be able to understand Backus's arguments without reading Murdoch's philosophy: "Murdoch is more interested in certain subjective moral processes, and in the value-language in which these processes are couched, than is the current British empirical philosophy which has prevailed at Oxford. That philosophy has confined itself to analysis of simple terms like 'good,' whereas she maintains that the rich inner processes of attention occur in a context of very subtle and rich linguistic distinctions" (27). Baldanza was answering in 1974, when few readers knew much about Murdoch's philosophical outlook, questions they would have been asking after reading *A Fairly Honourable Defeat* (1970), *An Accidental Man* (1971), and *The Black Prince* (1973). Readers now have the opportunity to read Baldanza's summary before comparing Backus's arguments with the philosophically professional analyses collected by Marie Antonaccio and William Schweiker in their *Iris Murdoch and the Search for Human Goodness* (1996).

Even so, Murdoch's early readers could see her disagreement with Kant about whether knowledge or will is the basis of morality and could see that she preferred a Platonic knowledge, a preference that never changed. Eschewing much of British empirical philosophy, she opted for Weil's "'active moral agent' . . . 'attention,'" Murdoch's experience during The Second World War having revealed to her a non-Romantic morality (quoted, 26). Baldanza saw that Murdoch had always been interested in the ways people think about moral behavior and the language they use to discuss it. He explains that Murdoch sees art and morals as performing not different but the same task: the task of attention, or seeing. For Murdoch, "the idea of choice, under this inner attention, comes closer to a matter of necessity or obedience rather than of will," showing art and morals "'to be two aspects of a single struggle. . . . Goodness and beauty are not to be contrasted, but are largely part of the same structure'" (quoted, 27). People behave as they do either because they perceive their own blind spots and move beyond their illusions; or because they fail to recognize their illusions, which become unconscious controlling and enslaving determinants.

The Artist-Saint Dichotomy

Baldanza's exploration of Murdoch's use of the artist-saint dichotomy began a trend that Conradi captured in his groundbreaking *Iris Murdoch: The Saint and the Artist* (1986). The idea first appeared in Murdoch's philosophy in articles in *The Adelphi* in 1943 and 1944; evolved in the dialectic in *Under the Net*, with Jake's expression versus Hugo's silence (Jake, a failed artist, usurps and exploits the ideas of the idealistic, beneficent, and voiceless Hugo); and continued in *The Sandcastle* with Mor's sensual nature coming in conflict with Bledyard's moral nature. The middle-aged Mor and the mature artist Bledyard struggle over the soul of the young painter Rain Carter. In *The Adelphi* Murdoch had written that the artist "sees the earth freshly and strangely but he is ultimately part of it" (quoted in Conradi, 14). Rain's experience dramatizes this observation. Her ability to create dissipates when adulterous love distracts her from her craft. Baldanza says that in addition to plotting, "the dichotomy also relates to Miss Murdoch's tension as a writer between Dickensian insouciance (saint — goodness) and Jamesian patterning (artist — beauty)" (23). He captures the gist of this theme in his analysis of the disagreement between the two leaders of the Christian religious community in *The Bell*. James Tayper Pace, who appears to be the "saint-figure," and Michael Meade, who is not saintly, may change places when it is clear "that James's sermon is antithetical to the implied values of the novel and of the author. . . . he opposes the very idea of personality"; and Catherine's saintliness may be masking a "maladjusted personality" (77). Baldanza admits that, just as in real life, the reader is left with unanswered questions.

Baldanza's book is an especially good source for analyses of Murdoch's elaborate patterning. Because it appeared almost ten years after Byatt's, it was able to include eight more novels — *The Italian Girl* (1964), *The Red and the Green* (1965), *The Time of the Angels* (1966), *The Nice and the Good* (1968), *Bruno's Dream* (1969), *A Fairly Honourable Defeat* (1970), *An Accidental Man* (1971), and *The Black Prince* (1973) — and, more important, was able to include analyses of the relationships among the novels. For example, Baldanza not only elucidates the intricacies of *The Black Prince* by demonstrating how "carefully [Murdoch] stitched together" patterns of repetition within a single novel but also relates Murdoch's experimentation in that novel and *An Accidental Man* to expectations she had set up in the earlier novels, tracing consistent links and helpful echoes (170). Moreover, he traces the theme of the alien-god figure, which links *Under the Net, The Flight from the Enchanter, The Sandcastle, The Bell,* and *An Unofficial Rose;* and he counters with good evidence Byatt's judgments about the early novels, such as her belief that *Under the Net* is better than *The Flight from the Enchanter.*

This chapter has explored the critical arguments published between 1965 and 1974. Byatt, Wolfe, Rabinovitz, and Baldanza set the scene for Murdoch criticism and established the first orthodox position. The following chapter tells the story of the second phase of Murdoch studies.

Works Cited

Antonaccio, Maria. "Form and Contingency in Iris Murdoch's Ethics." *Iris Murdoch and the Search for Human Goodness.* Ed. Antonaccio and William Schweiker. Chicago and London: U of Chicago P, 1996. 110–37.

Backus, Guy. *Iris Murdoch: The Novelist as Philosopher, The Philosopher as Novelist, "The Unicorn" as a Philosophical Novel.* Bern and New York: Peter Lang, 1986.

Baldanza, Frank. *Iris Murdoch.* New York: Twayne, 1974.

Begnal, Kate, ed. *Iris Murdoch: A Reference Guide.* Boston: G. K. Hall, 1987.

Byatt, A. S. *Degrees of Freedom: The Novels of Iris Murdoch.* New York: Barnes and Noble, 1965.

Conradi, Peter. *Iris Murdoch: The Saint and the Artist.* New York: St. Martin's, 1986; rpt. 1989.

Gordon, David J. *Iris Murdoch's Fables of Unselfing.* Columbia and London: U of Missouri P, 1995.

Murdoch, Iris. "Against Dryness: A Polemical Sketch." *Encounter* 16 (1961): 16–20. Rpt. in *Iris Murdoch: Modern Critical Views.* Ed. Harold Bloom. New York: Chelsea House, 1986. 9–16.

———. "The Sublime and the Beautiful Revisited." *Yale Review* 49 (December 1960): 247–71.

Rabinovitz, Rubin. *Iris Murdoch.* New York: Columbia UP, 1968. Rpt. in *Six Contemporary British Novelists.* Ed. George Stade. New York: Columbia UP, 1976. 271–332.

Todd, Richard. *Iris Murdoch.* London and New York: Methuen, 1984.

Wolfe, Peter. *The Disciplined Heart: Iris Murdoch and Her Novels.* Columbia: U of Missouri P, 1966.

2: A Philosophical Novelist? A Range of Perspectives

FIVE IMPORTANT BOOKS — one published in 1979, one in 1984, and three in 1986 — capture the passing of the orthodox position, or early phase in Murdoch criticism (1965–1978), and prepare the way for a new orthodoxy. The critic who helped lay the groundwork for these metamorphoses was Richard Todd. The international perspective he brought to Murdoch criticism in his groundbreaking texts *Iris Murdoch: The Shakespearian Interest* (1979) and *Iris Murdoch* (1984) has helped critics rethink the early responses to Murdoch's novels. Cheryl Bove's *Character Index and Guide to the Fiction of Iris Murdoch* (1986), a reiteration of the orthodox position that Murdoch is a philosophical novelist, proved that Murdoch had achieved academic popularity; Guy Backus's *The Novelist as Philosopher, The Philosopher as Novelist* (1986) questioned the most sacred tenets of the orthodox critical position; and Peter Conradi's *Iris Murdoch: The Saint and the Artist* (1986) identified what was to become the second orthodox position — that Murdoch is a moral psychologist. These five books encapsulate the movement in the criticism from 1979 to 1986. This chapter explores the critical approaches of Todd and Bove; the following two chapters focus on those of Backus and Conradi, respectively.

Todd's *Iris Murdoch: The Shakespearian Interest*

More critical of the label *philosophical novelist* than were the early critics, Todd not only added a new perspective to this critical mix but prepared Murdoch studies to move into a new period, preparing for the large and impressive critical texts of Elizabeth Dipple and Conradi and the generally unknown text of Backus. Todd's *Iris Murdoch: The Shakespearian Interest* is the first important book that finds it unnecessary to explain Murdoch's philosophy per se. Like Dipple, he insists on the uniqueness of Murdoch's aesthetic and on the misapprehension of peripheral critics who had labeled her a philosophical novelist but also called her prose careless, hurried, slovenly, and melodramatic. He does acknowledge inconsistencies, which he assumes have a purpose. Her novels challenge him, as they would Dipple, to grapple with these perceived inconsistencies in Murdoch's theory and practice that were baffling earlier scholars.

In his first book Todd investigates Murdoch's oeuvre from a literary, not a philosophical, standpoint, posing scores of new questions to be explored by critics. He agrees with Lorna Sage that "something of 'the peculiar kind of illusion the books are after' . . . has to do with Murdoch's deployment, in the novels since *The Nice and the Good* [1968], of 'a confident formula which stresses both the richness of detail and its disposability'" (quoted, 19). He insists that Murdoch's strategy is "contemplative of the Shakespearian interest," the novels being her meditations on plausibility as Shakespeare employed it (19). The new interest in "Shakespearian form counters the interest in Jamesian style," as Todd observes in his later study *Iris Murdoch* (53). Todd's tolerance in this area and his insights, along with those of Dipple, opened up the space for Mikhail Bakhtin to be introduced into the Murdoch critical mix. (Barbara Stevens Heusel's *Patterned Aimlessness: Iris Murdoch's Novels of the 1970s and 1980s* [1995] argues, for example, that Murdoch gains not only a freedom from staid, formal realism through her Shakespearian interest but a problem-solving strategy and a carnivalesque style.)

Todd's *Iris Murdoch*

In *Iris Murdoch* Todd takes up the popular issue of whether Murdoch is a philosophical novelist. Using Murdoch's 1957 review of Simone de Beauvoir's *The Mandarins*, which Murdoch criticizes for its lack of "restraint about the relationship between politically committed and creative fictional writing" (22), Todd shows that Murdoch revealed openly that she had no intention of fulfilling her early readers' expectation that she would be a philosophical novelist. She was, perhaps, peeved at their ignorance of information that was explicitly available in *Sartre, Romantic Rationalist*. In her review Murdoch says that Beauvoir cheats the reader of "the novelist's traditional furniture: social institutions, customs, the moral virtues," just as Murdoch had complained of Sartre's giving the reader "ideology and abstraction" (quoted in Todd, 21). Todd shows that Murdoch calls for "the novelist as philosopher, but not the philosophical novelist" (21) — a remark that, perhaps, gave Backus the idea for the title of his work. She says, according to Todd, that the lesson that Sartre did not learn is "that the human person is precious and unique" (21). Todd finds little political commitment in her novels, showing that Murdoch has a "very clear sense of restraint about the relationship between politically committed and creative fictional writing": "the *engagé* novel is not explicitly her aim or purpose" (22–23). He interprets Murdoch as insisting that "philosophy and fiction writing are separate activities, and that in her case the former is subordinate to the latter. Indeed her theory of fiction itself takes issue with the philosophical novel, at any rate that of Sartre's type, where poetry alone is free for the imagination, but prose is committed irrevocably to history" (23–24).

Todd's Stages of Development of Novels

Todd divides Murdoch's novels into stages of development that are different from those of Byatt. Finding it necessary to end Murdoch's first stage after the first four novels, he thinks that it is significant that her concentration on her literary and philosophical essays comes at this point. Like Rabinovitz and Byatt, he points to "The Sublime and the Good" (1959), "The Sublime and the Beautiful Revisited" (1959), and "Against Dryness" (1961) as major keys to understanding the thorny philosophical and literary issues in her novels. The major concepts she explores in these essays are the particularity of nature — but not according to Kant — and "its formlessness which should excite our *Achtung* (attention)" (43). Todd ties together better than the other critics Murdoch's point that "developments in the history of western European thought, . . . expressed both in linguistic empiricism and existentialism, both of which make man, in effect, his own measure, . . . too readily push literary conceptions of man in the direction of either 'convention' or 'neurosis.' The former leads to a version of the literary hero she refers to as 'Ordinary Language Man' and the latter to 'Totalitarian Man'"; this binary dichotomy cannot explain "that sense of human nature which is found in the greatest literary art of Tolstoy or Shakespeare" (43–44). Moreover, both Murdoch and Bayley comment on how often fiction employs conventions and neuroses "as instruments for the exploration of character and motive" (44). Since Murdoch's major interest is such exploration, her theory of love and attention, although not clear to the public at the time she published *Under the Net,* is already nascent in Jake and his one experience outside himself. Although Todd proposes that the protagonist's "driving compulsiveness seems less Jake's than Murdoch's own" (31), he allows that Jake's "urgency of 'otherness'" — his focus on Anna's reality — "is perhaps the book's basic premise": "It seemed as if, for the first time, Anna really existed now as a separate being" (32). Todd's analysis helps move Murdoch criticism away from seeing Murdoch "as Britain's version of the French philosophical novelist" (20).

Artistic Strategies

In regard to artistic strategies, Todd moves the reader beyond the analysis of Murdoch's symbolism that Byatt had presented in 1965. He explains that the author's symbolism operates "in a subordinate and undominating way" (39) to reveal character, not "in terms of the kind of dominant symbol which acts as a piece of currency with the same significance to all characters and readers" (40). The characters, not the author, create the symbols in the novels. Murdoch's characters attach value to objects and events; she shows that such behavior is not the exclusive prerogative of the artist. Furthermore, Murdoch captures the characters' various processes of making symbols. Todd seems to have a special tolerance for Murdoch's "distinctive balancing of the strange and the realistic"; he refers to her second novel, *The Flight from the Enchanter*, where the "gods and demons who make their appearance . . . need not be inconsistent with realism, for they are 'there' in the novel in so far as they are seen to be created by the characters, not by the perverse imagination of the author — so that the author simply, so to speak, 'observes' them in action" (34). Todd's analysis opened the door to other explorations of Murdoch's unique method of dealing with characters. In addition, he has a new answer to two questions the present study explores: is she a philosophical novelist, and is she a realist? His answer is that both questions are irrelevant.

The Flight from the Enchanter is significant for its development of the "power figure" that later inhabits so much of Murdoch's fiction. This form, in general, and the character Micha Fox, a "magical pattern maker" much like the artist, in particular, give Murdoch the freedom "to conceive of her characters as individuals within a patterned whole without denying them each their aspect of freedom" (32–33). Todd argues that such occasional switching of form from a first-person narration to what Murdoch "calls a 'peripheral' novel, one that is not overwhelmed by a 'magical pattern' and which is attentive to characters who cannot be regarded as at the centre of the plot or pattern" (33), helps her depict the "secret fantasy" of people "to bestow structure by allocating roles" (32). Murdoch continued to use this strategy so that she could explore the tendencies of institutions, like families, to play obsessive compulsive scenarios without having to make authorial judgments (36).

What Todd says about *The Sandcastle* reveals the complexity of his analysis of Murdoch's fear of coercing her characters. By mentioning her regret at not "making [the wife, Nan] somebody with quite extraordinary ideas of her own" (38), he demonstrates that Murdoch works hard at her craft, varies her strategies to perfect her aims, and learns from past mistakes. He also shows that one of her aims is to make the characters independent of her. Murdoch suggests that she could have done so with Nan by imagining her as a complex human being and giving her a larger role in the making of illusions: "not letting her just play the part of this rather tiresome wife but . . . [play] some quite different game, perhaps, having some dream life of her own" (quoted, 38–39). Speaking to Heide Zeigler and Christopher Bigsby, Murdoch judged her mistake as having "coerced" Nan in the way D. H. Lawrence sometimes compelled his characters (38).

Todd opens the way for other critics to explore Murdoch's use of strategies to play with formal constraints. Taking an unusual position on *An Unofficial Rose,* which is generally ignored by critics, Todd describes it as "a formally very beautiful work with a number of contingent graces which tend to mask the form, so that the reader's overall response is one of subdued, aesthetic pleasure at the blend" (50). Murdoch, he says, employs here a "more mannered form of the drama of a repeated action" and makes it representative in "successive generations" (51). At the same time he complains that some strategies in the novel can be provocative or, at least, annoying: "The chain of unrequited affections, for instance, seems here, as implicitly in *A Severed Head,* almost willfully self-parodic" (50). Without proffering any reasons why Murdoch would want to parody her own writing, he suggests that such use of parody is worthy of investigation. Other criticisms are occasional authorial intrusion, "telling without showing," and reworking former themes, which results in "the grasp on stylistic freshness becom[ing] less secure" (51). This reworking is especially egregious in *The Italian Girl* and *The Red and the Green.*

Admitting that any division of an author's work into phases is arbitrary, Todd argues — evoking the thrust of his earlier book — that the novels Murdoch published between 1968 and 1975 came "out of the 'doldrums'" at the same time they began to use more obvious references to "Shakespearian comic form" (62). In *The Nice and the Good* the protagonist, John Ducane, is similar to the artist not only in being omniscient but also in having the power "to round off a situation" so that the outcome could be nice but not necessarily morally good. Ducane makes the choice of the good artist. Asked to investigate a suicide that has occurred in the Whitehall hierarchy, Ducane is unwilling "to take the professionally correct course," which would inevitably bring about the destruction of the person responsible. Ducane could easily destroy Biranne's career and fulfill his mission responsibly, but, instead, he "agrees to present his report incomplete, in the sense that he will demonstrate the satisfactory" and moral closure (64). Todd explores Murdoch's advance in narrative omniscience in this novel: he sees a "new, authoritative stylistic confidence" (62).

Todd's two books stand between the early critics, who often tend to see her "elusiveness" as a flaw, and later ones who see it as an asset, an effective storytelling device that helps her simulate the mystery of reality. He sees that her philosophy might well outline the perimeters of her literary strategies.

Bove's *Character Index and Guide to the Fiction of Iris Murdoch*

In her *Character Index and Guide to the Fiction of Iris Murdoch* Cheryl Bove takes a position that is closely aligned to those of Peter Wolfe and Frank Baldanza. The book is a sign that Murdoch criticism had come of age by the mid-1980s, that the critical community needed a character index to keep track of her expanding and complex novelistic world, which was a kind of British Yoknapatawpha — a world, that is, comparable to Faulkner's novelistic world of the southern United States. Summing up the original orthodox position that readers will misapprehend Murdoch's vision if they ignore the author's theoretical statements, Bove's introductory essay is a helpful review of Murdoch's philosophical and critical statements that relate to her novels. Using Murdoch's works of philosophical and critical theory and her interviews, Bove lays out the author's aesthetic and philosophical goals. She insists that understanding the issues to which Murdoch attends in her nonfiction helps the reader to see more of the density of Murdoch's fiction. Bove suggests that readers contemplate Murdoch's philosophical statements about human nature and the possibility of moral advancement, since Murdoch advances such truths in her novels. Referring to *The Sovereignty of Good,* Bove quotes and paraphrases Murdoch's argument: human beings are "'transient mortal creatures subject to necessity and chance.' While Murdoch admits that, in a traditional sense, religion has its value and that moral philosophy and religion have shared ends, her concern in moral philosophy is with right action in a manner not connected with pleasing an outer omnipotent being. She has stated that she believes human life to have no external meaning; that is, there is 'no God in the traditional sense of that term'; and she believes that the 'various metaphysical substitutes for God — Reason, Science, History — are false deities'" (4). Bove finds philosophical statements in the novels and proposes that Murdoch thinks of them as truths.

The Importance of a Knowledge of Theory

Bove insists that Murdoch's "concept of characterization . . . is her greatest contribution to the development of the novel" and that understanding this concept "requires a knowledge of her philosophical heritage, its metaphysics, and consideration of the resulting theory of man with his capacity for reason, for communication, and for approaching truth; all of these are interrelated with aesthetics and moral philosophy, her main areas of concern in characterization" (3). Bove, like Wolfe, attempts to see the philosophical problems from the point of view of a hypothetical student. She reviews Murdoch's disagreements with "utilitarianism, linguistic behaviorism, and current existentialism" (8). Murdoch's first book, *Sartre, Romantic Rationalist,* foreshadows these philosophical interests. Murdoch's other philosophical essays, Bove demonstrates, focus first on an exploration of human consciousness, move on to moral philosophy, and then apply her views to literature.

Explaining Murdoch's philosophical essays, Bove groups all philosophies that emphasize action rather than vision into a category she labels "existential." For the existentialist, Murdoch says in *Sovereignty of Good,* freedom is not "the sudden jumping of the isolated will in and out of an impersonal logical complex; it is a function of the progressive attempt to see a particular object clearly" (quoted, 4). Existentialists find the essential human self in the will "accompanied by 'the void,' or 'the sense of not being determined by reasons'" (quoted, 5). For British philosophies and others that insist on reasons, the reasons are impersonal. These philosophies "believe man 'freely chooses his reasons in terms of, and often surveying, the ordinary facts which lie open to everyone: and he acts.' It is the action itself which is the exercise of freedom. . . . [Murdoch] would place vision as a determining factor of action, with 'attention' as contributory to our particular vision. . . . Freedom 'is a small piece meal business which goes on all the time and not a grandiose leaping about unimpeded at important moments'" (quoted, 5). Bove bases her analysis more on the freedom one experiences by means of morality; Baldanza emphasizes the concept of existential freedom.

Bove describes Murdoch, then, as one who believes that the artist is morally responsible for discovering and telling the truth. Murdoch understands that twentieth-century novels cannot be like nineteenth-century novels because of a "loss of common background" in the philosophical concept of the nature of language — the naïve view that language simply names reality (6). The break with the old view resulted partly from a focus on scientific theory. In her essays and in *Sartre, Romantic Rationalist* Murdoch reacts strongly to the behaviorist view of scientific language "as a way of delimiting, interpreting and predicting sense experience." She uses her philosophy to argue against this view; she uses her philosophy, her criticism, and her fiction to argue against the other cause of the break with the old view: "the discovery that rational men can have different 'natures' and see the world with radical difference" (quoted, 6). Murdoch struggled — as do all writers — with the consequences of these changing views of humans and their language. Bove says that Murdoch "deplores the surrealist-impressionist impact on the modern novel" (7). Specifically, she disagrees with the two symbolist reactions to this shift in perspective: "Rimbaud's overloading of referents leads to confusion by the reader, and Mallarmé attempts the impossible task of making language exist without referring" (6). Although Murdoch celebrates the awareness that the language revolution has brought, she is unwilling, according to Bove, to lose the referential and communicative quality of language; she wants to hold on to its ability to describe reality. She continues to assume, as Wittgenstein did, that language refers to the world. Perhaps this is why she is continually suspicious of the use of symbols in prose fiction for emotive purposes.

Claiming that the Good, for Murdoch, has a "unifying nature," Bove discusses its indefinable quality and three virtues that help readers identify it in her novels: "freedom, love, and humility" (14). Recognizing the ways in which Murdoch agrees and disagrees with Plato can also make it easier to understand her characters. Murdoch's emphasis is to "attend to virtuous people, great art, and the idea of goodness itself" (17). Murdoch insists that great art has ethical and educational purposes, pointing toward the Good: "the artist has a moral responsibility to reveal the truth. . . . Art . . . has an active and integral part in . . . [the] improvement of morals" (17). People have lost confidence in morality as a result of "the removal of our belief in God," a sign of our living in an "untheological time" (18). As Murdoch says in "Existentialists and Mystics," the modern novel is "a great sensitive mirror, or screen, or field of forces . . . still one of the most articulate expressions of dilemma of its age " (quoted, 18). Because of the modern novel's value to our culture, its creators, Murdoch thinks, must get beyond the "existential novel" and the "mystical novel" and find a way to convey truths about life in a non-Romantic novel form, using "real and various characters" (21). This new novel, Murdoch explains in "Against Dryness," must leave the symbol where it belongs: in poetry, "the proper home of the symbol" (quoted, 22). Although formation of symbols, in the novel and elsewhere, is integral to language, the process tends to be overdone, revealing the author's fear of contingency and her intolerance of individual differences. Murdoch criticizes her own excessive use of symbolism in *The Unicorn* and *The Italian Girl*. Bove sees Murdoch as living in two worlds and logically combining the knowledge she gains from each. For this critic, Murdoch is tolerant of "the imperfect and egocentric nature of man" but expects the artist to "overcome his selfish tendencies and to present the world in a loving and compassionate manner" (25). She suggests that the reader not detach Murdoch's "theory from the fabric of her voice" (3).

This chapter has outlined the arguments of Todd and Bove. The two chapters that follow serve as a symposium in which Backus and Conradi review Murdoch's philosophical and literary statements about her texts and what it means to be an artist and test these statements against the evidence in her novels. These critics' contradictory critical reactions to Murdoch's oeuvre demonstrate that no other novelist could ever fill Murdoch's place in literature.

Works Cited

Bove, Cheryl Browning. *A Character Index and Guide to the Fiction of Iris Murdoch*. New York: Garland, 1986.

Murdoch, Iris. "Existentialists and Mystics: A Note on the Novel in the New Utilitarian Age." *Essays and Poems Presented to Lord David Cecil*. Ed. W. W. Robson. London: Constable, 1970, 169–83.

———. *Sartre, Romantic Rationalist*. London: Bowes and Bowes, 1953. Rpt. New Haven: Yale UP, 1967.

———. *The Sovereignty of Good*. New York: Schocken Books, 1970.

Todd, Richard. *Iris Murdoch*. London and New York: Methuen, 1984.

———. *Iris Murdoch: The Shakespearian Interest*. London: Vision Press, 1979.

3: A Philosophical Novelist?
Questioning of the Earlier Criticism

O F THE BOOKS CRUCIAL TO THE CRITICAL ACCLAIM of Murdoch's
novels, two appeared — in London and in Bern, Switzerland, respectively — in 1986: Peter Conradi's *Iris Murdoch: The Saint and the
Artist* and Guy Backus's *Iris Murdoch: The Novelist as Philosopher, The
Philosopher as Novelist, "The Unicorn" as a Philosophical Novel.* Backus's
little-known literary analysis reveals him to be the most extreme propo-
nent of the Murdoch-as-philosophical-novelist position; in fact, he implies that she is more philosopher than novelist. He has brought to the
Murdoch discussion outrageous but interesting issues, such as whether
Murdoch is a neo-Platonist mystic (referring to her influence by Simone Weil) and whether there is a meta-Murdoch (suggesting that
Murdoch's readers need a code to unlock her ideas).

Unfortunately, Backus's exhaustive analysis of *The Unicorn* has yet
to enter into the critical debate in the United States. Published by Peter
Lang, it has not been reprinted by a major university press so that the
critical community might absorb its provocative conclusions and respond to them as part of a broader dialogue. Backus is the most negative and controversial of the critics who have written substantial studies
of Murdoch's work; it is time for his cogent ideas to become part of the
discussion. His knowledge of philosophy has enabled him to raise provocative issues regarding Murdoch's philosophy and aesthetic, ideas
that are useful in analyzing Murdoch's novels.

Conradi's book is different in almost every way. Published by St.
Martin's Press, and soon to be issued by HarperCollins in a third edition, it is known worldwide as a basic source for any Murdoch reader.
Conradi has also become the authorized Murdoch biographer, suggesting an analogy between his writings and those of Richard Ellmann,
whose biography and criticism are fundamental to James Joyce scholarship. On a literal level, one should read Conradi's title, *Iris Murdoch:
The Saint and the Artist,* as a reference to her many statements to interviewers such as Ruth Heyd, Malcolm Bradbury, and Michael O. Bel-
lamy about "the conflict" between saint and artist and what it "had to
do with the ways in which the temptation to impose form existed in life
as much as in art" (15). Conradi paraphrases Murdoch's understanding
of the terms, which first began to appear in essays in *The Adelphi*: "The

saint is unconsciously good, silent, and for him it is action that counts. The artist is consciously, aesthetically creating his life" (15). On a metaphorical level, Murdoch herself is being referred to as saint and artist; Ved Mehta says that in some British circles she "has the reputation of being a saint, and she has no enemies" (quoted in Conradi, 15).

Presumably, Conradi knew Murdoch better personally than did any other critic treated in the present study. With such knowledge comes power but also potential problems of distance. He asserts that much more is going on in Murdoch's novels than a philosopher might notice — or, if a philosopher did notice, he or she might not call Murdoch's literary playfulness "philosophy." Rather than talking about Murdoch as a philosophical novelist, Conradi takes his cue from the author and speaks of her philosophy as *moral psychology,* a term that emphasizes her focus on the mysteriousness of human difference. His best argument for adopting this term is that "it holds the idea of conceptual mastery in such suspicion[;] her philosophy is in a sense an 'anti-philosophy.'" He says that critics should read her entire canon in the light of her later novels, in which she ably combines "myth with psychology." Her philosophical development, he argues, began with existentialism and moved toward a more religious view similar to Buddhism. He says that "in this process a Neoplatonic view of Eros, which brilliantly marries Freud to Plato, is central. The idea of the purification of undifferentiated desire lies at the heart of her moral psychology and of her view of the artist's endeavour alike." He demonstrates that "the tension between a spiritual and a secular or worldly view of the moral agent animates her work from the beginning." Conradi and Backus agree that Murdoch's critiques border on what Conradi calls the "anti-philosophical" (x).

Whereas Conradi's book has been reviewed widely since it was first published, the most readily available critique in the United States of Backus's book is the entry by Cheryl Bove in her and John Fletcher's *Iris Murdoch: a Descriptive Primary and Annotated Secondary Bibliography* (1994): it is a "detailed and thorough study (in English) of the correlation between Murdoch's fiction and philosophy as seen in *The Unicorn.* The work includes an extensive analysis of *The Unicorn* and its literary sources" (237). About Conradi's book she says: "An outstanding and comprehensive guide to Iris Murdoch's works, this volume provides a detailed analysis of the characterization, myths, allusions, and themes in Murdoch's fiction and drama and relates her aesthetics and philosophy to her novels" (240). These two references sum up the attitude of the critical community surrounding Murdoch's novels: Conradi's book has been much more widely read and appreciated.

Murdoch criticism has reached the stage when what Backus calls the "detractors" should be heard, so that readers might discover areas of Murdoch's fiction that have not been sufficiently scrutinized. Of major importance in Backus's work is his jousting with A. S. Byatt, Elizabeth Dipple, Robert Scholes, and Richard Todd about the effect and value of Murdoch's novels, especially *The Unicorn*; about the veracity of her philosophical conclusions; and about his definition of the philosophical novel and its impact. Backus asks scores of important questions that no critic had previously asked about Murdoch's philosophical stances, and these points could foment more creative dialogue about Murdoch's oeuvre. The need for dialogue is a reason why the multidisciplinary Iris Murdoch Conference at the School of Divinity of the University of Chicago in 1994, and the essays that resulted from it, have been such a boon to Murdoch scholars. The 1996 collection of those essays, *Iris Murdoch and the Search for Human Goodness,* edited by Maria Antonaccio and William Schweiker, provides philosophical views that balance Backus's complex professional one. Subsequent scholars will not be able to ignore the benefits of a multidisciplinary approach to Murdoch's writing. Since Backus's overemphasis on philosophy has the potential of diminishing readers' respect for her philosophical output and for her novels, they need to see his ideas in relationship to other philosophical arguments.

Backus's is the most challenging book to Murdoch's readers who are not professionally trained philosophers. Summarizing a broad range of critical discourses that were available in 1986 and that are rarely discussed, Backus has opened up many avenues for exploring Murdoch's contradictions. Though his analysis focuses on one novel, it tackles some major questions about all of Murdoch's fiction: what is a philosophical novel? What is its value to the novel tradition? Is Murdoch her own best judge? Might she have been overly influenced by the Oxford atmosphere and by her husband, Bayley? Might some critics be overly influenced by comments from Murdoch?

Backus Assumes Early Supporters Are Naïve

Though Backus paraphrases Murdoch to explain that interest in literature drew her into philosophy — "it was not . . . the Greek philosophy component of the Greats course that persuaded her to become a professional philosopher. It was rather, she asserts, her enthusiastic discovery of Sartre" that propelled her into her career — he labels Murdoch "a philosophical novelist" in the opening paragraph of his introduction (11); such a stance solves many critical problems for him. Discussing

The Unicorn, he argues that Dipple and Byatt, like Murdoch in her 1977 interview with Bryan Magee, exclude "the possibility of a novel which might be called 'philosophical' in that it presents material which teases in the same way as philosophical problems" because they believe that Murdoch produces the kind of work she holds up as an ideal in her literary essays (22). Backus, consequently, makes an important contribution to Murdoch criticism by opening up the possibility of alternatives beyond the question of whether she is or is not a philosophical novelist. He claims that these critics are naïve in believing that Murdoch achieves her stated objectives in her novels. Neither Dipple nor Byatt, Backus points out, has a grounding in philosophy; his implication is that they cannot see the complexity of the philosophical issues. He reminds readers that one cannot necessarily believe the artist, because her job is not to analyze her own work. He cites Martin Heidegger: "the author's own belief that he is sovereign with respect to the location of intention, blinds him to a crucial conception of his text" (13). Backus informs the reader that his book will expose the irreconcilable inconsistencies in Murdoch's work.

The only way the present short study can come to grips with Backus's 325-page text is by focusing on general philosophical questions that arise from his critiques and on the ways he constructs his case by arguing with other critics, so that readers of Murdoch can locate where to begin searching for answers to their questions. He finds three camps in Murdoch criticism: "Murdoch, her detractors, her supporters"; unfortunately, he says, none "does justice to the real merits and defects of Murdoch's fiction" (13). His contributions to the criticism are his energetic descriptions of these "merits and defects" and his responses to them. A major part of his complaint is that "according to Murdoch, her own maturation has paralleled that of the Good Artist," developing "art and philosophy . . . [that] lead away from day-dream to hard fact" (11–12). Apparently misunderstanding the extent of her Platonic goals, he jests that she moves from hard fact to daydream. He also complains that "politically, while remaining within the liberal orbit, Murdoch moved further and further to the right. She can, at present, attack comprehensive education while pleading for tolerance towards homosexuals" (11). Readers must resist such oversimplification and define for themselves what Murdoch means by "the Good Artist" and analyze for themselves Murdoch's aesthetic statements and political behavior. It is, however, well known that, being unusually self-deprecating, she never pretended to be the Good Artist.

Criticizing Murdoch for Vagueness

Grouping together criticisms by detractors such as Alasdair MacIntyre, Irving Howe, William Van O'Connor, and Gabriel Pearson, Backus points to Pearson's 1962 reaction to Murdoch's aesthetics as illustrating what he sees as readers' general lack of admiration for her aesthetics. The passage he quotes from Pearson also serves as an example of Murdoch's purported habit of not defining her terms (such as *attention*) carefully and fully, as a philosopher must, but referring to them in a casual and general way: "In calling for a new liberal picture of personality to be achieved by a new vocabulary of attention I can't see that she is saying much. I wished she could have conveyed what a new vocabulary of attention would be like. It sounds to me very much like a piece of half-baked rhetoric. What could it contain over and above sensitivity, an ear for nuance and a compassionate and alert eye?" (12). Pearson is censuring Murdoch's critical vocabulary, not her artistic creation. Backus suggests that Murdoch's unphilosophical use of definition has discouraged scholars from writing "serious studies of Murdoch's work. It is impossible to find, for example, a substantial account of her view of metaphor" (12). He says that her stance on metaphor is that "words and the world are one thing not two. Metaphor is king because a 'sort of idealism cannot be avoided'" (109). This kind of investigation is necessary, and Backus's call for more analysis is crucial to Murdoch scholarship.

Murdoch's Critical Imperialism

Backus accuses Murdoch of "critical imperialism" and says that her aesthetic is problematic in two ways: "it appears surprisingly rigid and unfruitful for a thinker whose emphasis falls always upon the 'uncomputability' of the real," and it has determined the way critics read her novels. He attributes the latter effect to Murdoch's openness in explaining her writing process: "it is as if a trained philosopher must be right about the theoretical space in which her own novels are situated" (12). Most artists, including Murdoch, would agree that they have a problem in distancing themselves from the work of art and need critics to critique it. She expressed such an understanding of the relationship between the artist and the critic in a 1988 interview: "I'm just a novelist and critics are critics. If people want to explain something by saying that it is like something else then okay. Anyway we can't stop them, so they will" (Heusel, 8).

Although Murdoch's position as a moral philosopher was out of favor most of her adult life, Backus says that it had come back into vogue by the mid-1980s. Philosophers such as Richard Rorty, he notes, applauded *The Sovereignty of Good* in 1986 "for its determined rejection of appeals (in ethics) to foundational principles, rules or axioms" (12). Backus lists philosophical issues that Murdoch's work has helped make popular: not only "the severance of moral predicates from needs, wants or interests; virtue as central to morality; the rejection of verificationism in semantics" (12) but also "Intuitionism," which he glosses as "moral characteristics . . . known non-inferentially in a way which parallels perceptual ones" (86). In addition to pointing out that the newfound attention from philosophers has not led to serious philosophical studies of Murdoch's neo-Platonism or of the relationship between her "arguments against Stuart Hampshire and her fiction" (15), Backus contends that her ideas here contradict her ideas in earlier essays, such as "Vision and Choice in Morality" (1956). Discerning that Murdoch's ideas had changed by the time she wrote *The Sovereignty of Good*, Backus maintains that in *The Unicorn* "we have moved from a morality of 'visions' to an avowedly Platonic mysticism about Good. We have moved from the claim that fundamentally different moral pictures should exist to the claim that the Image of the Good is our best picture of moral life" (107). Backus describes that collection of philosophical essays as "an aggressive identification of virtue with knowledge" (165): "We have moved from naturalism [in "Vision and Choice in Morality"] to intuitionism ["she denies that moral judgements, although cognitive, are entailed by nonmoral ones"] . . . and from a theological view structured by concepts like sin and love being one possible morality to its being the only correct one" (107). He says that her stance changed from what she called "inconclusive non-dogmatic naturalism" in "Idea of Perfection" (1962) and "Vision and Choice in Morality" (1956) to utilitarianism in "Existentialists and Mystics" (1970) to neo-Platonism in *The Fire and the Sun* in 1977 (107). Another possibility is that Murdoch was simply testing out her new ideas and comparing them to her old ones before deciding whether to adopt them.

Backus makes a conspicuous blunder when he remarks that Murdoch says that because life is so "hopelessly evil," living in fantasy is better (165). Such a claim contradicts not only what readers understand about her worldview but also the majority of her public statements. Backus judges that "Murdoch's awareness of the informal nature of her 'proofs' . . . clashes with her apparently doctrinaire conclusions"; he also has no patience with her "description of herself as having been strongly influenced by Plato *and* Wittgenstein [which] highlights all her *volte-faces* and contradictions regarding form" (165). He is not the first to argue that she is doctrinaire, but the reader might wonder whether he is listening to everything she says. How can he determine her influences? Clearly unhappy with her growing conservatism, Backus appears to see himself as the first philosopher to have been challenged to perform a serious analysis of Murdoch's philosophical thought process (12). He chooses to write an entire book on one of her novels because the important points Murdoch makes in her philosophical texts "The Sublime and the Beautiful Revisited," "The Sublime and the Good," and *The Fire and the Sun* "are more evident when outlined against *The Unicorn*" (75). For him this novel is, therefore, critical to an understanding of Murdoch's inconsistent philosophy, and his aim is decidedly philosophical.

Furthermore, he claims that because Murdoch has tried to justify her development as "the Good Artist" (11), she has confused her critics by leading them to think that her pronouncements about art, rather than being her ideal, are achieved in her novels. To reconcile these issues that Backus considers contradictions in Murdoch's philosophy, readers will find it beneficial to compare his discussion with literary analyses such as Baldanza's of 1974 and philosophical analyses such as Antonaccio's of 1996 and 2000, *Picturing the Human*.[1]

Backus's genuine contribution to criticism is that "Murdoch's novels aim at relaxing tensions existing in her moral philosophy" (15), a point he admits having "intuited." Perhaps here he comes closest to understanding Murdoch or listening to her voice. He use the term *intuition* to indicate that his study is "no inductive argument based on a survey of Murdoch's 22 novels" (15). He illustrates his propositions with one novel; using the Anglo-Saxon philosophical mode, he argues that Murdoch employs both philosophical solutions and parody in her novels to tease the threads of tension within her theories (15). Certainly, there is a grain of truth to this claim.

The Unicorn as Philosophical Novel

Backus itemizes the reasons why he chose *The Unicorn* for analysis. A statement Murdoch made in a 1963 interview in *Partisan Review* led him to use this novel to discover "tensions which her theory masks" (17). Speaking of *The Unicorn*, Murdoch explained to Frank Kermode "that something about the structure of the work itself, the myth as it were of the work, has drawn all these (characters) into a sort of spiral, or into a kind of form which ultimately is the form of one's own mind" (quoted, 17). In response, Backus delineates *The Unicorn* as "that chameleon-like creature, a philosophical novel" (17), that is likely to display the patterns of Murdoch's thinking. Backus concludes that the author was able to achieve her aesthetic ideal in this novel, but that, ironically, she has never claimed this achievement.

Useless Taxonomy

According to Backus, certain critics make the mistake of thinking that Murdoch puts her aesthetic into practice in all her novels. Since his focus is on "the overlap between Murdoch's fiction and her philosophy," he specifically criticizes Byatt and Dipple for putting too much faith in Murdoch's division of novels into binary oppositions such as crystalline versus documentary or open versus closed and, particularly, in her polemics against the crystalline, or philosophical, novel (15). (He would, no doubt, criticize the same tendency in Conradi's text.) Backus argues, instead, that the taxonomy Murdoch has explained to interviewers is unnecessarily binary and oversimple and that, furthermore, she supplies no criteria or authority. He favors her thinking in the early "Vision and Choice in Morality" (1956), calling her voice there "sane" and labeling it "Procrustean" in the 1961 essay "Against Dryness" (19). *The Unicorn* would be a more appreciated novel, he thinks, if she had not changed the attitude she expressed in "Vision and Choice in Morality." With these philosophical arguments in mind, the reader can evaluate Backus's opinions about *The Unicorn* and other critics' views of it. Ultimately, the reader must decide whether Murdoch's ideal is more than binary or whether she exchanged a multidimensional ideal for a binary one.

Use of MacIntyre's Objections

Before examining *The Unicorn,* the novel Backus uses to illustrate his argument about Murdoch's unorthodox use of philosophical strategies, the reader will want to evaluate Backus's critical strategies. Backus employs Alasdair MacIntyre's criticism of Murdoch's philosophical practice to set up his own partial defense of her method. He explains that he takes advantage of MacIntyre's philosophical objections because MacIntyre "provides the most interesting short review of Murdoch's novels[;] he has also a powerful theory of the virtues which somewhat resembles Murdoch's theory." Backus says that most of MacIntyre's objections have "stemmed from Murdoch's refusal or inability to say why or how 'the good attracts'" (102). MacIntyre thinks that virtue is beneficial to society, and he, like Murdoch, distinguishes between internal good and external good. Murdoch and MacIntyre emphasize that "the virtues are always a potential stumbling block to being rich, famous and powerful," and both value humility (102). It seems that the virtuous people Murdoch cites in *The Sovereignty of Good* are not good enough for MacIntyre; he apparently wants more references to particular people and their occupations.

Backus and MacIntyre complain that Murdoch's word choice lacks precision and specificity in her explanation of the "idea of a virtue." One might gloss their argument: if Murdoch cannot describe a virtuous individual in her philosophy, how can the reader recognize such an individual in the novels or understand the point she is making about virtue? MacIntyre writes that for her, "humility is 'not the name of a particular virtue . . . but of virtue as such'" (quoted in Backus, 99). In other words, for her, humility is a necessary aspect of virtue or goodness; good people are humble. MacIntyre says that instead of citing a clear and precise example of a virtuous man, she cites Søren Kierkegaard's tax collector, who, according to Kierkegaard, "does not betray the merest 'heterogeneous fractional telegraphic message from the infinite'" (quoted in Backus, 99). One might ask why she or her reader must expect the virtuous person to have a telegraphic connection to God. Her "identifying the aim of the virtues with an indeterminate reality and . . . refusing to anchor them in man's nature or any form of social life" is not philosophically acceptable, Backus argues (99). If virtue cannot be easily categorized, how can a reader determine whether Hannah Crean-Smith, the heroine of *The Unicorn* and supposedly a Christ figure, is virtuous? Most critics, remembering Murdoch's proposal in *The Sovereignty of Good* that good is for nothing, would assume that one point she is making is that someone who is truly good does not expect good in return. She writes that although the humble man is not yet good, he is "the kind of man who is most likely of all to become good" (104). It is because this man can see "himself as nothing" that he "can see other things as they are" (103–4). Even more specifically, she cites a unique example of a good and courageous man: one who acts "unselfishly in a concentration camp" (57), when there is nothing to gain.

Not reluctant to manipulate MacIntyre's argument, Backus says that he will focus on MacIntyre again, "this time to present a supposed defect in *S. of G*. Murdoch's moral theory is, according to MacIntyre, 'ineffable'"; her view of moral truth can escape "theoretical expression" (99). One of MacIntyre's arguments that supposedly proves Murdoch's puzzling stance is that "characters who espouse Murdochian ethics fare badly": MacIntyre cites Marcus Fisher in *The Time of the Angels* (99). One wonders at MacIntyre's grievance here; as he knows, being a good person has never earned anyone earthly rewards, so why should characters adopting Murdoch's theory of the good fare well? Furthermore, Murdoch does, of course, give several examples of virtuous people in *The Sovereignty of Good*. If the humble man has not yet reached the Good, his virtue has allowed him to make a few steps toward it. Others who are "candidates for goodness," Murdoch writes, are "simple people — inarticulate, unselfish mothers of large families" and "the virtuous peasant" (52–53). In addition, the mother who loves "the retarded child or . . . the tiresome elderly relation" is good (103). Murdoch also demonstrates the cognitive processes of the hypothetical M as she attempts to be good to her daughter-in-law (17–23).

Moreover, for MacIntyre, Murdoch's novels "embody a theory about theories: viz., all theories, including those expressed in *S. of G.* are misleading" (100). Murdoch indicts philosophy in all of her texts. Even so, it is hard to understand why MacIntyre insists that her philosophy plays any significant part in her novels. Having set up this MacIntyre-Murdoch controversy, Backus defends Murdoch. He finds no statements by her that cast doubt on all philosophy. He points to her Wittgensteinian anti-philosophy, of which he says MacIntyre is aware, to show how she uses the Wittgensteinian "associated theme of 'showing' and 'saying' . . . in *Under the Net*" (100). Rather than indicting all philosophy, according to Backus, Murdoch makes a distinction between distrusting philosophy and distrusting "one quasi-scientific" kind of philosophy (100). Pointing out further distinctions, Backus shows that MacIntyre over-generalizes — or, even worse, misreads — when he complains that Murdoch believes that "what makes utterances true or false is not the same as what makes statements true or false" (100). Backus responds: "She suggests that all language can 'lie,' not that it does. Philosophy has to be read sympathetically: and the living dialogue between 'live minds' is even better" (100). At the heart of Murdoch criticism is the consensus among philosophical critics like MacIntyre and Backus and literary critics such as Lorna Sage and Deborah Johnson that Murdoch leaves her own philosophy open to question. These critics come to similar conclusions from different directions. The reasons MacIntyre and Backus hypothesize for Murdoch's choosing such strategies are weaker and less demonstrable than those Sage and Johnson hypothesize. Moreover, it is hardly surprising that Murdoch, who always had such high regard for Wittgenstein, would incorporate his ideas into her own; both treat philosophy as a useful, but disposable, discipline. Backus makes one thing certain: readers must read Murdoch with devoted attention.

Backus employs his critical dialogue with MacIntyre to search for and point out problems. He asks: "Is it self-evident that 'a theory which is to some degree against all theory — including itself — could never have received adequate expression merely at the level of theory'?" (100–101). He responds that no one knows why Murdoch would use her novels "to cast doubt on philosophy" and that MacIntyre contradicts himself because he has already implied that her novels are philosophy. Explaining that he is critiquing MacIntyre's problematic — "the characters who appear to deprive Murdoch's views of credibility by the circumstances in which they utter them" — Backus pursues a more "plausible" answer. He asks why, in her novels, Murdoch criticizes characters who are clothed in her own beliefs. In citing examples from the novels he focuses, like MacIntyre, on Murdoch's "preoccupation with bourgeois society" (101). MacIntyre is somewhat personal and petty, arguing that many British readers "who wish their 'Bloomsbury' or 'North Oxford' values ratified" have stock responses to Murdoch's novels, the novels reinforcing their delusions (101). Why would Murdoch want these people to sustain their bourgeois illusions, puffing themselves up with ideas from *The Sovereignty of Good?* My answer is that the novels are comedies riddled with jokes of all kinds, some deprecating. Backus's answer is that "Murdoch surveys her philosophy from those points where it is the weakest. And where she is not underlining her philosophy's defects she is parodying them" (101).

Both of these philosophers search for the source of Murdoch's skepticism. Disagreeing with MacIntyre, according to whom "the meta-Murdoch" is "one who believes that (ultimately) morality is ineffable" (101), Backus works much harder at discovering reasons for her seeming inconsistencies. MacIntyre paints Murdoch with too broad a brush. For him, Murdoch, being "a sort of neo-Platonistic mystic," takes a "meta-philosophical position"; for Backus, who seems to have contemplated her stance more attentively, she makes the "'negative movement' in a positive discourse which is so characteristic of mysticism" (101). Backus's explanation is in this way similar to Conradi's claim that Murdoch often assumes a mediating position, a kind of negative sublime, that resembles a Buddhist stance.

Having agreed with her view in "Vision and Choice in Morality," Backus is most disturbed by Murdoch's "notion of the 'empty good'" in *The Sovereignty of Good,* where she says that "virtue is for nothing" (102) and "attack[s] the idea that moral visions can be unified" (101). He criticizes her for having fought against false universality in the early essay and later adhering to the idea when she argues for complete objectivity. He does not find adequate proof for her conclusions. He questions her assumption that "complete objectivity provides the goal of the moral agent. . . . Life is always lived partly from the inside: the notion of a single objective impersonal point of view which structures all moral lives is an instance of the false universalisibility Murdoch fought in 'Vision and Choice in Morality'" (95). Perhaps this is a blind spot caused by her neutrality, which she calls "detachment." Perhaps she fights so hard against what she calls "absolutist theories," such as Jacques Derrida's, that she never succeeds in disposing of this one or in explaining exactly where she stands on the issue of objectivity.

Murdoch Attempts the Impossible

Moreover, Backus says that her "description of herself as a 'Wittgensteinian neo-Platonist' refers to the tension in Murdoch's work" (102). Backus concludes that three certainties have led Murdoch to try to achieve the impossible or make claims that cannot be argued, which he calls "whistl[ing] what can't be said": (1) "the desire, in the novels, to give fictional body to the doctrines of *S. of G.*," (2) "the awareness, in the novels, of the difficulties of *S. of G.*," and (3) "moves to remove these difficulties by non-Platonic means" (102). Backus says that these three certainties are factors but asks whether they are not interpretations. Sometimes Backus seems to see Murdoch clearly; sometimes he seems to be too caught up in his own argument to see that Murdoch finds paradoxes to be true and often employs several perspectives at the same time. Why should she not have the freedom to do as she wishes in her novels? With these philosophical arguments in mind, the reader can evaluate Backus's opinions about *The Unicorn* along with other critics' views of it.

One of Backus's major disagreements with Byatt and Dipple is his belief that Murdoch's novels are analytical and that she employs conservative methods in a disciplined way. He points out that her "enthusiasm for analytic methods is expressed" in *Rencontres* (1988–89) and exhibited in *Sartre, Romantic Rationalist* (1953). For these reasons, he regrets Dipple's failure to define what she and Murdoch mean by their "hatred of the 'tag' of 'philosophical novelist'" (20). He supplies several examples of Dipple's naiveté in regard to philosophy — her failure to tell the reader, or simply to understand, that "Ayer's theory of meaning is the target not only of Murdoch's early 'Nostalgia for the Particular' but, under the guise of the 'genetic theory of meaning,' also of *The Sovereignty of Good*" (20). Assuming that Wittgenstein, R. M.

Hare, and Gilbert Ryle and their respective analytical methods are as important to Murdoch as are Kierkegaard and Weil, Backus argues that "her elaboration of a set of terms in which the novel can be discussed, is resolutely conservative in that the terms could be incorporated into the work of a literary critic like John Bayley without discomfort being felt" (15). For Backus, it would be implausible to ignore links between Murdoch's analytical concerns and *The Unicorn* or, for that matter, links between Murdoch's ideas and Bayley's. Backus is unusual among Murdoch's critics in taking these positions.

Criticism of Dipple

Finding her concerns artistic and literary rather than analytical, Byatt and Dipple value Murdoch's stated intentions. Each of them justifies her philosophical views and her aesthetic, exploring her novels in light of her philosophical statements. Dipple judges *The Unicorn* to be content-laden (*Iris Murdoch: Work for the Spirit*, 266), but she does not see Murdoch conversing with other philosophers or using philosophical language in her novels. Unfortunately, Dipple did not foresee that a critic such as Backus would focus on such generalizations of hers as "There is complete consistency of idea in Murdoch; once the thought patterns are worked out the reader can watch the technical expertise with which she plays them" (6), while ignoring the context. If Dipple ever heard of Backus's complaint about this statement in her introduction, she no doubt wished that she had qualified it. Clearly, Backus was looking for such generalizations to prove his case against what he saw as an orthodox view of Murdoch's novels. It is ironic that Backus should criticize Dipple, who broke so much new ground in Murdoch scholarship, for a mindless acceptance of what he implied to be the Murdoch party line. Dipple has perhaps uncovered as much as any critic about the novelist's inconsistencies but has also evaluated their implications in relation to the novels and found just cause for them, or at least registered thoughtful hypotheses. It is characteristic of Dipple that, instead of guarding against criticism such as Backus's, she describes in her introduction the stages of a reader's encounter with a Murdoch novel. She encourages readers to realize that Murdoch creates new characters in each novel to work on a new problem that has age-old roots and challenges them to use the novel to search for such "knowledge and experience" (6).

Contextualizing *The Unicorn*

Byatt is an equally keen judge. She assumes that Murdoch selects the plot of *The Unicorn* for dramatic reasons — to take characters away from a "background of normality into a world of necessity and physical intractability," an "irreducible reality which we cannot absorb or conquer" (147). Being gothic, *The Unicorn* is resplendent with meaningful allusions to a hidden world. To achieve such a fantastic other world, Murdoch revitalizes Sheridan "Le Fanu's ghosts . . . the most disquieting of all ghosts," according to V. S. Pritchett, "the ghosts that can be traced, blobs of the unconscious that have floated up to the surface of the mind" (148–49). Byatt sees the importance of Murdoch's use of Freud and of Le Fanu's *Carmilla:* "There are pointers enough in *The Unicorn* for it to be certain that Hannah's passive suffering, her religion of guilt and withdrawal, can be seen, not as a 'real' religious act, but as an obsessional neurotic fantasy"; for Byatt, Murdoch's novel is "a case history of Hannah in purely Freudian terms" (153). Backus, on the other hand, argues that *Carmilla* "instantiates, in pure form, the means to signal weaknesses in Murdoch's philosophy" (147). He contends that Murdoch is using a combination of "the Gothic, Medieval and Detective conventions" to parody and "to criticise some of her own philosophical themes" (153). This conclusion seems obvious; why would such an activity on Murdoch's part not be worthwhile?

Other critics, however, agree with Byatt and Dipple that the novel is about storytelling. For example, in *Iris Murdoch* (1968) Rubin Rabinovitz, relying heavily on Murdoch's allusions in *The Unicorn*, treats the novel as literary history and unearths deep veins of influence and multiple literary echoes. Murdoch employs not only the "medieval writers of romances" but also other writers who modeled their stories on these romances: "Structurally, *The Unicorn* bears a resemblance to Jane Austen's parody of the Gothic novel, *Northanger Abbey*" (34). Furthermore, its mood is reminiscent of the mood in novels by Hardy and the Brontës: Murdoch reproduced "the vampire-like qualities" from *Carmilla* in Hannah, the suffering, enchanted figure locked in the castle (35). According to Rabinovitz, the characters in this novel, as in many of Murdoch's others, "govern their lives by myths, till they are prisoners of their own fantasies" (35). His emphasis on literary significance and creative play is certainly close to most readers' reactions to *The Unicorn*.

Rabinovitz's insight that one of Murdoch's major interests is the modern courtly lover (34) has proved a significant contribution. Citing the courtly-love theme in *An Unofficial Rose* and *The Bell*, he makes clear that Murdoch's literary critical stance is to attack Romanticism and parody it in Sartrean neurotic heroes; parody of such gothic excesses is crucial to the development of many of her novels. Dipple continued this discussion and moved it in a new and unorthodox direction when she argued that *Jackson's Dilemma* (1996) is the testing of the courtly love metaphor at the end of the twentieth century ("Fragments of Iris Murdoch's Vision," 6). Perhaps such parodying looks like philosophy to Backus.

Using formalist theory, as Rabinovitz does, Byatt criticizes Murdoch's philosophical ideas from a different perspective, asking whether they are necessary to further the story; philosophy works for Murdoch, but when any author employs untransformed ideas, the particular novel does not work well. Comparing *Under the Net* and *The Unicorn*, Byatt writes that Murdoch's tackling a problem makes the ideas and approaches of these novels "self-consciously philosophical" (183–84). The difference between them is that the former uses philosophical language that "does not jar," for Jake Donaghue, the protagonist, is "interested in purely philosophical problems," and that the latter uses too "often a dead reference to some thought outside the book" with which the reader is not familiar (211). Revealing her understanding of Murdoch's Wittgensteinian net-pattern in *Under the Net,* Byatt explains that Hugo has the characteristics of a philosophical thinker with a "non-classifying vision of life which sees everything as 'unutterably particular'" (14). For Hugo, the saint figure, "things cannot be arranged finally in patterns by the organizing intellect" (15). Murdoch is playing with Wittgenstein's net and showing that human beings are "rational animals in the sense of theory-making animals" (quoted, 16). Byatt describes well what might be occurring in the disagreements between Backus and the other critics: Murdoch would, I think, take Hugo's position that, because "things cannot be arranged finally in patterns," the artists require the freedom to study the potential of "things" in their novels. Backus takes the position of the man who must classify everything; he has difficulty in getting beneath the net to envision the reality in the novels.

Backus argues that Byatt and other critics search blindly for the key to *The Unicorn;* of course, such a key does not exist, so he is pointing out the obvious. He proves that Byatt is looking for a "solution" to a "puzzle" by referring to her word choice, such as "Once one has solved the Freudian mythical references" and "It . . . is as though Miss Murdoch had set herself here the problem of seeing which interpretation was 'correct'" (quoted, 117). Byatt decides that the key is "Weilian philosophy." Furthermore, Backus suggests that *The Unicorn* is not complete in itself but should be treated in the way publishers have treated *The Waste Land,* because it, like T. S. Eliot's poem, has "an esoteric centre which can be reached only by the use of material external to the work" (117). He believes that Eliot's footnotes "seem an integral part of the poem rather than a gloss" and argues that "Murdoch's 'glosses' rather than being 'keys' to her fiction become integral parts of it" (117); Backus is correct in concluding that Murdoch's novels are stories about the artistic process. The "esoteric centre," or undisclosed center, of *The Unicorn* and other Murdoch novels is an issue Dipple and Johnson will explain further in the final chapter of this study.

The issue in regard to *The Unicorn* comes down to whether readers can understand the intricacies of the novel without a gloss. Backus argues that the gloss must be Murdoch's philosophical essays. Critics should not read the novel as if it is relativistic and should impose "no Jastrow-diagram which can be read now as a duck, now as a rabbit" onto the novel (119). This analogy gives critics the opportunity to question whether Murdoch might have wanted to write a novel patterned on a Jastrow-diagram. All in all, Backus imposes more significa- tion on *The Unicorn* than it can possibly bear. Unless one is a trained philosopher, perhaps it is safer to rely on earlier analyses of the novel, which see it as less complex but also see it in a more balanced way, sim- ply as an historical text.

Backus argues that Murdoch's project is to answer "the staid exami- nation question: can we have knowledge of the Good? Or is 'all vanity' (*S. of G.*, pp. 72, 73) with morality and great art, in a 'serious' sense, 'an ephemeral illusion'?" (121). This is the same question that Conradi says Murdoch poses more explicitly in *Bruno's Dream*. Backus divides his question into two parts: "(1) can one be moral and remain self- deceived? and (2) what is the connection between knowing and estab- lishing that one knows? And further that any excursions into the social sciences or metaphysics are subservient to this end" (121). Backus's study focuses on these issues, which are reasonable ones to raise. His interpretation that these goals are Murdoch's and his avoidance of her storytelling put him squarely in the Murdoch-is-a-philosophical- novelist camp. Nevertheless, the reader cannot fault him with missing Murdoch's jokes and paradoxes, for he says, "Murdoch . . . is fond of using her fiction to make sly references to her philosophy. Can we ex- pect Murdoch's philosophy to provide 'notes' for *The Unicorn?*" (146). Backus assumes that the novel is a *reductio ad absurdum* of some kind. The most concise statement of his thesis is that "*The Unicorn* tests to destruction, sometimes to the point of parody, Murdoch's philosophical ideas" (147). But for him, the parody is difficult to analyze and does not make one laugh: "At best *The Unicorn*'s half-formed and protean fear and anxiety offer a sporadic foothold for the burlesque and the ridiculous" (152).

On the other hand, Backus knows that he has a work of great magnitude in *The Unicorn*. Recounting all of Murdoch's sources, he calls them an "*embarras de richesses*" (141); this phrase alone is a significant contribution to the criticism. Echoing the too-much-of-a-muchness statements made by Conradi and Howard German and recognizing the embarrassing riches that a single Murdoch novel can encompass, Backus identifies the conventions of three different genres she uses to criticize her philosophical themes: not only the obvious gothic form but also "Medieval and Detective conventions" (153). He reveals his reactions to the novel in his comparison of Hannah, the potential unicorn of the novel, with Sheridan Le Fanu's Carmilla: Hannah is "beautiful," with "long reddish-gold hair," "reticent," "morbidly metaphysical," "languorous," and hysterical. She comes from an "ancient and noble" family whose past is strewn with blood (145). He says that all of these features and Murdoch's Platonic ideas in *The Sovereignty of Good* interlock in the novel. The plot is an archetypal journey of two outsiders, Effingham Cooper and Marian Taylor, to Gaze Castle in the West of Ireland, a moral pilgrim's progress and also the movement of Plato's prisoners working their way out of the dark cave. Marian, a governess, has been hired ostensibly to teach French to an isolated woman, Hannah. Backus considers Effingham and Marian liberals "exposed to this world which robs them of their moral background because it poses them an ethical problem of great difficulty"; their morality has to compete with the moral codes of a feudal system and with a "mystical Platonism" (167). The moral question for them is whether they should awaken Hannah from her sleep, that is, her illusions; the cognitive problem is to decide whether she a "fantasist" or a "scape-goat" (167).

Murdoch's use of mirrors suggests that Hannah, the "sleeping princess," the unicorn, is "the unknowable endpoint of moral concepts" and that she is also "*La Belle Dame* . . . the enchantress whose sadomasochistic wiles produce false images of the good" (152). Backus writes that "the 'fatal woman' of both the medieval and detective *genres* coalesces . . . with the image of the vampire." Murdoch uses these images to move through various realms: "life to death . . . error to truth . . . natural to supernatural" (152). Finally, manipulating the struggle of individuals to be good through perceiving good or through knowing good, Murdoch, Backus assumes, is suggesting that "Hannah is killed by being known" (133). In this interpretation the adolescent Marion is

"sleeping sexuality" (144). The detectives — she and the other outsider, Effingham — "are never directly privy to main actions," so they
cannot see or know Hannah (146). The experience at "Gaze is an idealistic dream which depends on Hannah for its realisation" (135) and is
never accomplished.

Backus reviews several critics' analyses of the analogues for *The Unicorn*, including the work of German and Peter Wolfe. But one of the
most interesting developments in the criticism, he says, is Z. T. Sullivan's idea that "Murdoch has deepened her moral vocabulary by
aligning it with another vocabulary, the Gothic, which better suits
contemporary man" (143). In other words, "Murdoch uses the Gothic
form as a *reductio*," as if to say to R. N. Hare and Stuart Hampshire:
"'Look how well your theories, once enlarged a little, fit the Gothic'"
(143). This significant contribution by Sullivan corroborates an argument about Murdoch's writing strategies made not only by Backus but
also by Conradi and Maria Antonaccio: that Murdoch is mediating
ideas.

Conflicts "Oblique" but "Powerful"

Backus says that he has chosen *The Unicorn* for his analysis because it
has an unusual number of conflicts that are "oblique" but "powerful."
While all of Murdoch's novels are complicated, *The Unicorn* is complex
at several levels because "Murdoch is both didactic and unsure about
her philosophical conclusions" (165). For Backus *The Unicorn*, "by
casting a light on Murdoch's philosophy, becomes philosophical." An
explanation of the conflicts demonstrates that Murdoch "identifies
knowledge, virtue and perception. Knowing is tied into seeing via the
idea of accurate representation or privileged standpoint" (165). His account is accurate but not complete.

Whereas Byatt accepts that Murdoch knows what she is attempting
to accomplish in her novels, Backus judges it unfortunate that the early
critics of Murdoch assumed that *her* reading of her novels was "'crite-
rial,' or at least of overwhelming importance, for their correct reading"
(13). Among Backus's most creditable arguments are those that disagree with Byatt and Scholes. His problematizing of their assurance
that the reader can hope to find a key that will unlock the allegory of
The Unicorn will be valuable to future Murdoch criticism. His examination, however, being philosophical rather than formalistic, is overly
esoteric. He explains that Byatt's key to the novel — a reading of Weil
— does not work for many reasons, one of which is Byatt's inability at
the time to read the Weilian texts that had most captured Murdoch's

imagination. Murdoch makes clear in "Knowing the Void," a review of *The Notebooks of Simone Weil,* that the texts Byatt discusses in her book are not the ones that were of particular interest to Murdoch. Byatt may have been misled by Murdoch, who told Ruth Heyd that "many of the views expressed on sacrifice, guilt and essential goodness . . . originated in 'Weilian philosophy'" (quoted, 117). Backus cites a statement by Murdoch in the Rose interview that may have led Byatt astray: "*The Unicorn* . . . is about the ambiguity of (relationships formed by mechanical love-making) when they get mixed up with notions on redemption and other religious notions. In a way it is about the ambiguity of the spiritual world itself, the curious connections there are between spirituality and sex" (quoted, 118). Backus interprets Murdoch's glossing of her text to refer to "the connections there are between spirituality [Weil's concepts] and sex [Freud's concepts]," and, on the other hand, the way "the ambiguity of spirituality infects that of sex" (118). Backus is annoyed that Dipple is negligent in excusing "herself from considering the influence of Weil on Murdoch" (20), because the real work had not already been done by Byatt. He admits that Byatt had no intention of explicating the Weil material; according to Backus, she simply "offers a series of parallels" (120). Nevertheless, critics such as Todd and Dipple have felt it unnecessary to question Byatt's use of the Weil material.

The Lens of Formalism

Byatt and Scholes have applied the lens of formalism to *The Unicorn,* attempting to solve the puzzle at the center of the text by using external source material. Such an approach may have overemphasized the bifurcations Murdoch is so fond of manipulating. Backus is bothered by the binary dilemmas early critics such as Byatt set up: for example, Hannah, the scapegoat figure, is either a "'compulsive neurotic' or a saint" (117). Obviously, such a position is oversimple. Backus introduces Scholes's interpretation for a similar reason: to complain that it is too ingenious; he insists that Scholes's "machinery does not illuminate *this* novel" and that there is too much "material which is recalcitrant to Scholes's theory" (126).

According to Backus, Scholes does address the relationship between fiction and philosophy in *The Unicorn* and describes it as a process: Murdoch "submit[ting] philosophy to fiction" (23). Backus, who also sees the novel as a process, agrees with him and further suggests that Murdoch uses her literature to parody her philosophy. For Backus, Scholes's theorizing is not only too binary but also too relativistic. Although he credits Scholes with a "bold and original theory" (122) and agrees with his argument that as readers of Murdoch "we must sharpen up our hermeneutical skills" (121), Backus criticizes him for lack of clarity in such statements as: "For Iris Murdoch is teaching us to read allegorically in *The Unicorn*, teasing us into this lost way of reading by imperceptibly moving from conventional mysteries to philosophy. . . . The book itself is seen as fulfilling the purifying function of the traditional scapegoat, by providing a ritual purgation for those initiated into its mysteries" (quoted, 121). Whereas learning to read allegorically would seem to be valuable, Backus questions the extent to which readers have to rely on their own interpretation of the characters. Backus considers Scholes too much an advocate of reader response theory and, therefore, as too relativistic.

On the other hand, Backus praises Scholes's insights: "Scholes by his emphasis on 'relativity,' recognises the displacement of symbolism in *The Unicorn*" (126). But the idea that the novel is "a primer for allegorical reading obscures his insight" (126). The two scholars agree about the form of the novel, "the use of an allegorical or parabolic form to deepen or change our moral concepts by means of storytelling. This story links, in new ways, old situations" to create a new moral pattern (126). But Backus asks whether it is possible to tell the same story when moving toward a new goal: "can the principle which governs the continuation of a mathematical series be expressed in the same way as the series itself?" (126). This kind of philosophical analogy is too elliptical to be of use to the Murdoch reader who is not a trained philosopher.

Backus Criticizes Todd's Analysis

Backus's response to Todd's analysis of *The Unicorn* is more critical. He assumes that Todd's dismissal of the novel results from the latter's accepting at face value Byatt's argument that understanding certain Weilian and Freudian texts is necessary for understanding the novel. Backus says that when Todd writes that "'special interests' obtrude to the detriment of the novel" (120), he must be following Byatt, and the special interests to which he refers must be Weil and Freud. Backus faults Todd with failing to question Byatt's evaluations; Backus does not find her book particularly insightful. Although Backus disagrees with Scholes, he comes off better in the end than do Todd and Byatt. Todd, on the other hand, praises Scholes's discussion of *The Unicorn* for showing that "among the many levels on which it operates is that whereby Marian creates for herself a myth (the myth of the novel's title?)" (56).

Because Backus's rendering of Murdoch's literary project could diminish respect for her philosophy and her novels, it is useful to analyze his arguments in relation to other philosophical arguments. The multidisciplinary essays in *Iris Murdoch and the Search for Human Goodness* judge Murdoch's moral philosophy as groundbreaking, several considering it, as well as her novels, polyvocal. Two important critics who respond to issues this chapter has addressed are David Tracy and Cora Diamond. There is no evidence that these Murdoch supporters have read Backus, but they answer his complaints obliquely in their essays. Backus, of course, bases his arguments on the texts Murdoch had written up to 1986; Tracy and Diamond have the advantage of many more texts and, most important, Murdoch's last book of philosophy, *Metaphysics as a Guide to Morals* (1992).

In his essay "The Many Faces of Platonism" Tracy supplies the information that readers need to balance Backus's negative comments about Murdoch's philosophy. He has great respect for all of her philosophical work, especially the often-criticized *Metaphysics as a Guide to Morals*. Tracy finds this final version of Murdoch's Gifford Lectures both ambitious and subtle, and his emphasis on her Platonism (66) corroborates Backus's analysis of her move toward Platonism, as do literary analyses such as Conradi's. Tracy confirms MacIntyre's conclusion that Murdoch is a philosophical novelist, while demonstrating that not only Murdoch's novels but also her philosophy cast doubt on her own philosophy. He says that her readers cannot distinguish literature from philosophy or either from art in the texts; one presumes that he means that she has liberated herself from the bonds of genre. Nevertheless, the structure Murdoch employs for "rendering a Platonic theory of the Good in the late twentieth century, that is, the century that has read not only Plato and the great Platonists but also Freud and feminists and such powerful philosophical critics of Plato as Nietzsche, Heidegger, and Derrida," perfectly fits the content of contemporary reality (66). Tracy characterizes *Metaphysics as a Guide to Morals* as similar to the Platonic dialogues: "From the beginning of this strange and attractive book one finds oneself in the midst of a wider and unhurried conversation on unities and forms, on the Good and the search for the good, on illusion and the ego, on art and love and death and the Void" (66). Comparing Murdoch's philosophical opus to her novels, he says that they work in similar ways: philosophical voices, like characters keep returning. The text is Bakhtinian in that it is multivoiced, working "like the ancient mimes, that is, rather like ordinary life and its conversations. . . . The complex, again often meandering, sometimes self-disrupting order of Iris Murdoch's novels seems to suggest that any ordinary realist ordering of both experience and understanding in a novel as in life and thought is, in fact, a falsification" (67–68).

Tracy agrees with Backus on a minor point and with MacIntyre on a major one when he argues that "MacIntyre is right to insist 'Iris Murdoch's novels are philosophy but they are philosophy which casts doubt on all philosophy, including her own.'" He adds to MacIntyre's argument that the reader will have a "glimpse of the Good in the midst of actual human life" when her philosophy's "mime-like form, its modern novel-like genre replacing the mime-like dialogues of the ancients, is taken as the signal clue to the philosophical content of her philosophy" (69). Tracy says that she is Wittgensteinian in casting doubt on her own philosophy, and he points out that when the ideas of a culture change, the change is reflected in its philosophical form, which is instrumental in determining the content; and, of course, it would be likely to occur immediately in the popular form of the novel. Tracy's comment that "the multi-voiced (one might also say Bakhtinian) character of her novels rejects any single narrative voice in favor of many" (68) corroborates the contention of Dipple, Johnson, and Heusel that Murdoch's work is multivalent.

Another philosopher, Cora Diamond, suggests in "'We are Perpetually Moralists': Iris Murdoch, Fact, and Value" the connection between Murdoch's philosophical view and her novels and calls into question MacIntyre's analyses of Murdoch's fact-versus-value argument. Contextualizing Murdoch's challenge to philosophers to return to moral philosophy, Diamond explains that Murdoch and her contemporaries in analytical philosophy were far apart in 1956 on the issue of "the 'gap' between fact and value. Analytical philosophy has moved in the direction of the better ground she then pointed out . . . [but has] not moved to the right place. . . . The philosophical idea of a separation of fact and value goes, she says, with an unrealistic understanding of consciousness. For consciousness is always morally colored; moral activity is present in all cognitive awareness" (105–6). Diamond insists that all of Murdoch's writing, including the novels, argues against the division of fact and value.

Diamond explains that according to Murdoch, the artist who separates fact and value as Kant does cannot give the reader "a realistic representation of consciousness" (104). Diamond makes a strong connection between Murdoch's view of fact and value and her realism. For Murdoch, a realistic novel strives to portray character and, consequently, "the mode of awareness of its characters. Since awareness is morally colored, every realistic novel is in a sense an argument against the separation of fact and value. A character cannot be represented as a living human being unless his awareness of facts has internal to it his mode of moral responsiveness" (104). This observation introduces another of the critical problems with Murdoch's novels: her realistic dilemma. Out of these kinds of controversies has emerged a new openness about Murdoch's oeuvre, one that celebrates her experimentation and her use of the novel form to work out literary problems, such as how much mystery or psychological realism one can incorporate and still call the text realistic.

Backus's statement that "Murdoch has never troubled herself with working out her own moral epistemology" (107) seems to be a key to both his understanding and his misunderstanding of her project. He apparently needs to define her as a philosopher and then argue that she must think like a philosopher when she is writing fiction. Backus's project has the potential to enliven Murdoch criticism by raising unending and difficult questions for critics to explore. His book also has the potential inadvertently to diminish the reputations of certain critics who understood by instinct some of the targets at which Murdoch was aiming but for which she could not, early in her career, cite strong evidence. Finally, the book also has the potential to confuse readers who might draw conclusions too early. Backus deserves, however, detailed and disciplined answers to the questions he has raised and will no doubt receive them from trained philosophers — perhaps from some of the contributors to *Iris Murdoch and the Search for Human Goodness*.

Notes

1 *Picturing the Human: The Moral Thought of Iris Murdoch.*

Works Cited

Antonaccio, Maria. "Form and Contingency in Iris Murdoch's Ethics." *Iris Murdoch and the Search for Human Goodness*. Ed. Antonaccio and William Schweiker. Chicago and London: U of Chicago P, 1996. 110–37.

———. *Picturing the Human: The Moral Thought of Iris Murdoch*. New York: Oxford UP, 2000.

Backus, Guy. *Iris Murdoch: The Novelist as Philosopher, The Philosopher as Novelist, "The Unicorn" as a Philosophical Novel*. Bern and New York: Peter Lang, 1986.

Baldanza, Frank. *Iris Murdoch*. New York: Twayne, 1974.

Byatt, A. S. *Degrees of Freedom: The Novels of Iris Murdoch.* New York: Barnes and Noble, 1965.

Conradi, Peter. *Iris Murdoch: The Saint and the Artist.* New York: St. Martin's, 1986; rpt. 1989.

Diamond, Cora. "We Are Perpetually Moralists: Iris Murdoch, Fact, and Value." *Iris Murdoch and the Search for Human Goodness,* 79–109.

Dipple, Elizabeth. "Fragments of Iris Murdoch's Vision: *Jackson's Dilemma* as Interlude." *Iris Murdoch News Letter* 9 (August 1995): 4–8.

———. *Iris Murdoch: Work for the Spirit.* Chicago: U of Chicago P, 1982.

Fletcher, John, and Cheryl Bove. *Iris Murdoch: A Descriptive Primary and Annotated Secondary Bibliography.* New York and London: Garland, 1994.

Heusel, Barbara Stevens. "A Dialogue with Iris Murdoch." *University of Windsor Review* 21:1 (1988): 1–13.

Johnson, Deborah. *Iris Murdoch.* London: Harvester Press, 1987.

Magee, Bryan. "Bryan Magee Talked to Iris Murdoch." Modern Philosophy: Philosophy and Literature, BBC *Men of Ideas* series, no. 14: Iris Murdoch, October 28, 1977. National Sound Archives, London.

———. "Philosophy and Literature: Dialogue with Iris Murdoch." In his *Men of Ideas: Some Creators of Contemporary Philosophy.* New York: Viking, 1978, 264–84.

Murdoch, Iris. *Metaphysics as a Guide to Morals.* New York: Viking, 1993.

———. *The Sovereignty of Good.* New York: Schocken Books, 1970.

———. *The Unicorn.* New York: Viking, 1963.

Rabinovitz, Rubin. *Iris Murdoch.* New York: Columbia UP, 1968. Rpt. in *Six Contemporary British Novelists.* Ed. George Stade. New York: Columbia UP, 1976. 271–332.

Sage, Lorna. "The Pursuit of Imperfection." *Critical Quarterly* 19 (1977): 60–68. Rpt. as "The Pursuit of Imperfection: *Henry and Cato.*" *Iris Murdoch.* Ed. Harold Bloom. New York: Chelsea House, 1986. 111–19.

Todd, Richard. *Iris Murdoch: The Shakespearian Interest.* London: Vision Press, 1979.

Tracy, David. "Iris Murdoch and the Many Faces of Platonism," *Iris Murdoch and the Search for Human Goodness,* 54–75.

4: Murdoch's Moral Psychology

G UY BACKUS JUDGES MURDOCH'S unconventional combination of Platonism and empiricism as not only unique but also peculiarly inconsistent for a philosopher. His stance provokes important questions, and many of his conclusions seem to be intuitively accurate but turn out to be wrong. Perhaps more understanding of Murdoch's spirituality would have leavened his conclusions. This chapter explores two responses, one exclusively literary and the other both literary and philosophical, to Backus's arguments about Murdoch's lack of consistency and his explanations of her inconsistency; neither of these writers cites Backus or each other.

The most significant literary response to Backus's negative reading of Murdoch's project is Peter Conradi's. Conradi is concerned with her public statements about the relationship between her philosophy and her novels, because such statements reflect her worldview. Furthermore, his experience as a personal friend of Murdoch's and John Bayley's has allowed him to compare her private comments about her spirituality and her aesthetic aims with her public statements. Finally, his status as Murdoch's authorized biographer shows the family's trust in his judgment.

The philosophical and literary response that counters Backus's position is that of Maria Antonaccio, a professor of religious ethics who has captured Murdoch's far-reaching ethical views in her essay "Form and Contingency in Iris Murdoch's Ethics." Antonaccio conveys more concretely than other critics Murdoch's view of the relationship between human beings and the world. She asks the same question Murdoch asks in the 1992 philosophy book *Metaphysics as a Guide to Morals:* "how can metaphysics be a guide to morals?" (quoted, 110). Antonaccio's answer is a useful demonstration of Murdoch's consistency in both her novels and her philosophy: her novels are metaphysics as a guide to morals. In other words, Antonaccio makes a convincing case that the philosophical and novelistic sides of Murdoch are one and the same, and she demonstrates the apparent overlap with an effective explanation of the moral theory Murdoch developed over her forty years as a philosopher and novelist. Antonaccio includes her essay in the 1996 collection she coedited, *Iris Murdoch and the Search for Human Goodness.* Conradi's and Antonaccio's analyses show that Murdoch employs her novels to search for truth and to mediate between extreme assumptions in Western culture.

Insight into Being Human

Conradi's commonsensical stance, outlined in the previous chapter, begins by agreeing with Murdoch's careful choice of terminology for her viewpoint — moral psychology — which she described in her 1978 interview in Caen, France. He suggests that after admitting that all individuals have their own philosophies of life, she wanted to be more precise and to distinguish her own moral philosophy, a professional system of beliefs, from her general worldview, on which she based the various settings for her fiction. She preferred to call the latter "moral psychology" because of its focus on the interaction of human beings and the interaction of their voices. Conradi defines moral psychology as "a complex mass of living insight into what being human is like" (75). Obviously, Conradi's perspective on Murdoch's novels and the novel as a form is broader than that of Backus, who has failed to examine any alternative possibilities between the either-or of being a philosophical novelist or not being one.

Conradi, however, understands that the primary goal of the novels is to grapple with the mysteriousness of life and explains that they make "the strange seem familiar . . . and the familiar seem strange" (47), a narrative strategy that might well be confusing to casual readers. One habit, then, of this speculative writer was to use literary strategies that defamiliarize readers so that they, too, can experience mystery. In addition to focusing on literary technique, Conradi challenges other critics' emphasis on Murdoch's philosophy by shifting to theology and asserting that Murdoch was more comfortable with "a Buddhist world-picture" (86) than a Christian one: "Religion, in Murdoch's view, is a recent invention. Spirituality and nihilism alike are ancient" (85–86). Conradi argues convincingly that her texts, especially the later novels, come out of the great European tradition of dark comedy; they are not philosophical tracts. He views Murdoch as a writer whose mind constantly developed, who might well have agreed with Emerson that consistency is the hobgoblin of little minds, and whose moral psychology is brilliantly complex enough to put into play Hegelian dialectics, conundrums, and paradoxes for her own and the reader's pleasure.

Conradi chooses the subtitle *The Saint and the Artist* from an early review Murdoch wrote in *The Adelphi*, in which "she compares the detachment of the artist and that of the saint. The artist, she argues, is not 'apart' as the saint is. 'He sees the earth freshly and strangely but he is ultimately part of it, he is inside the things he sees and speaks of as well as outside them'" (14). In his preface Conradi explains why he divided his book into discussions of Murdoch's moral psychology, her oscillation between open and closed novel form, and her mediation of the warring virtues of these forms beginning in 1970. In his 1987 essay, "Canonizing Iris Murdoch," John Burke criticizes Conradi's book on the basis that it does not do what Conradi promises in the title: analyze "the recurring pattern of saint and artist" (487). In expressing his disappointment that sections two and three pay scant attention to the saint/artist dichotomy, Burke finds it unfortunate that Conradi makes "the key to the enormous, disorderly merits" of Murdoch's mature novels "the notion of open and closed forms" (487). Conradi does, however, address the issue briefly, listing some representative saints — characters who are "unconsciously good" and who act: "Belfounder, Tayper Pace, Ann Peronett" — and some would-be artists who "consciously aesthetically" create their lives: "Donaghue, Mead, Randall Peronett" (15).

Contextualizing Murdoch's Moral Psychology

One of Conradi's major purposes is to explain and contextualize Murdoch's moral psychology. He shows that she has woven her own psychology from her struggles to make light what is dark: her early influence by Plato; Simone Weil's theory of unselfing; Sigmund Freud's theories, which are grounded in Plato's;[1] and, finally, Buddhism. The influence of Buddhism is the new ingredient Conradi brings to the discussion. Understanding Buddhism himself, and having discussed it often with Murdoch, Conradi may be able to judge how much Buddhist mysticism Murdoch is summoning up when writing a particular novel. He shows that it develops from her internalizing, to some extent, the concepts of Buddhism and of the early-twentieth-century French mystic Simone Weil. As a beginning writer, Murdoch discovered in Weil's texts the vocabulary she needed and the conceptual connections her developing insight required. Not having experienced The Second World War and its horrific displacement of human beings, many late-twentieth-century readers, including Backus, find Murdoch's interest in Weil's concept of "unselfing" or "loss of self" (112) masochistic and, therefore, unfathomable. Conradi says that Murdoch found in Weil what she could not find in Sartre: evidence for the unsentimental historical-religious argument she wanted to make, an argument that confirmed her experience "that the affliction and degradation caused by the destruction of roots was such that it deprived all but the saintly person of the capacity to change or 'unself' from inside. The uprooted hurt and uproot others" (13). Weil treated the outsider with love but never with mawkish romanticism or sentimentality. Furthermore, Murdoch's "warnings about the dangers of moral over-reaching" have been influenced by Weil's philosophy that "a spirituality inadequately rooted in the deep structure of personality" will not survive (71–72). Conradi finds that "morality depends, for Weil, on the slow attenuation or destruction of the ego, which itself requires a quiet environment. Sudden or violent deracination can mean complete or demonic demoralisation" (13). Murdoch recognized in Weil's discussion of "unselfing" the strategies and vocabulary for putting her feelings into words. Conradi ties together this influence of Weil and Buddhism, arguing that "the Buddhist attack on the fictionality of the ego is more profound, for both Weil and Murdoch, because it is based on a realistic assessment of the limited capacity of the ego to decentre itself, and because it is nonetheless designed to alter perception and behaviour" (13). These ideas helped Murdoch to express her view of the human struggle, and in *The Sovereignty of Good* she states her own view in a more positive way than Weil did: unselfing, or ascesis, occurs when an "active moral agent" focuses "a just and loving gaze . . . upon an individual reality" (34).

In Conradi's estimation, Murdoch embodies a paradox: "the most other-worldly *and* the most worldly of our novelists" (68). She made a point tangential to Conradi's in an interview with Haffenden in 1983: "Buddhism is not at all an other-worldly religion[;] it's absolutely this-worldly, here and now: this is where it's all happening and there isn't anywhere else" (quoted in Conradi, 86). Human beings and characters in novels who are able to "unself" must do it in this world. That is why her characters must ultimately "give up the temptation to allegorise and must forego the pleasure of 'interpretation'" (86). The unconscious mind is a machine filled with myth and symbol. To mature is to learn to pay attention to what is outside oneself and to see the world without blinders, recognizing that "life-myths," which Freud calls "the family romance," cause people to get caught in a particular pattern of emotions that are "laid down early" (83). Conradi cites Northrop Frye to show that in maturity an individual can transfer energy and affection "from the Oedipal incestuous family situation outwards to outsiders" to shatter the romance (83). To grow is to see these survival myths as provisional and to override them with what is outside oneself in order to let them go. Murdoch's grounding in these patterns from Freudian psychology is an additional reason for calling her view a moral psychology.

Under the Net

Conradi finds evidence for all these influences as early as *Under the Net,* whose theme is, for him, a "Buddhist quest to get beyond the duality of self and world" (38). Characteristically, the narrator, Jake Donaghue, the would-be artist-quester, perpetually bumbles in his effort to report reality, illustrating Plato's and Murdoch's fear that the artist's version of the world is seldom accurate. The conversations between Jake and Hugo Belfounder, the philosopher, that Jake records in his book, *The Silencer,* become "a flowery philosophical dialogue" (38). He gives his readers only touched-up versions of what actually occurred. Because Murdoch makes the conversations "an 'artistic' conflation of many weeks" (38), the reader understands Hugo's point that "the language just won't let you present [an experience] as it really was. The whole language is a machine for making falsehoods" (quoted, 37). Conradi finds that Murdoch links "Jake's habitual carelessness with truth and his working-up of Hugo and his talks into a stylish, shapely, pretentious dialogue" (42). In the novels characters who are truthful have trouble writing. Characters mention that Finn, Jake's Irish cousin, "never tells lies, he never even exaggerates," (quoted, 42), and Jake wonders if Finn can write. Like many good characters in Murdoch, Hugo has a hard time communicating "on paper at all" (42). The author is playing dialectically with the evaluative Platonic difference between speaking and writing, speaking traditionally being considered closer to reality and, therefore, more truthful. Moreover, Murdoch reveals the dilemma such a stance causes in the plot. Good characters all tend to be the same — uninteresting. Conradi explains that these characters are "like Socrates, Christ and Buddha, who never wrote anything at all[;] the good man here is inarticulate on paper. Hugo notes that 'when I really speak the truth the words fall from my mouth completely dead'" (42).

At the beginning of her career, then, Murdoch explored her major theme: the engagement of the saint and the artist who writes about the distortion and the provisionality of art. Conradi says that Hugo, perhaps speaking for Murdoch, recognizes that the evanescence of fireworks recommends them: "It was . . . an ephemeral spurt of beauty of which in a moment nothing more was left. 'That's what all art is really'" (quoted, 37). (Hugo reminds the reader of the two philosopher-artist figures in George Bernard Shaw's *Major Barbara:* the title character's father, a munitions manufacturer, and her lover, a professor who becomes a munitions manufacturer.) Examining "the ancient quarrel . . . between art and truth," the novel sets up what is to become a familiar albeit ambiguous dichotomy between philosophers and artists: "Jake is an artist who writes philosophy of a sort, a translator who has written and had torn up an epic poem, and who ends the book ready to write a novel" (38–39).

The themes that attract Murdoch are the historical struggles of the human experience: the ways in which human beings are responsible for the morals of the society in which they live; their attempts to see God and the Good and to distinguish between them; good persons losing their way and bad persons finding a path to the Good; and the engagement of artist and philosopher. Murdoch no doubt loved art and respected morality, but as Conradi suggests, in her novels she takes a common-sense view, not an idealistic one. Speaking of the characters in *Under the Net*, Conradi distinguishes between the good and bad man in terms of their attitudes to art: to the latter "art does not matter much because nothing apart from himself matters at all; whereas Hugo devalues art because, for the good man, art is second-best and matters only to the extent that something else (religion, reality, morals, other people) matters more. The bad man evacuates meaning from art because the world is without sense, the good man because the sense of art depends upon and serves a larger sense outside it" (88). It is important to recognize Murdoch's anti-Romantic view of art, her rejection of the hubris evident in the art-for-art's-sake movement. As an artist, she knows that art is not perfect. As a realist, she knows that humans, not being gods, can accomplish only human feats.

The Provisionality of Art

Conradi reinforces his point by referring to the criticism of Lorna Sage, who has noted the number of "books or manuscripts" that are destroyed or unfinished in Murdoch's novels: "It is precisely the hypothetical quality of fictional images, Sage argues, the fact that they are in their nature 'obsolescent, provisional, imperfect' that makes them, for the Platonist, so important" (87). Sage attributes this tendency to a desire not only to demonstrate Plato's belief that art is provisional and unfinished but also to project "a hostility to the Moderns' scriptural pretensions to conceptual dominion" (quoted, 88). Conradi points out another way in which the early novel *Under the Net* illustrates provisionality: Murdoch employs the theatrical device of "rapidly changing and collapsing scenery" in the plot line. Sage proposes that Loxias's statement in *The Black Prince* mirrors Murdoch's belief; just as Murdoch suggests that family myths should be discarded after one has survived childhood, she prefers that the metaphors used to make stories or myths be discarded after a brief use; or, as Loxias says, "To purify Eros is to learn about the provisionality of myth" (quoted, 87). Because it is a truism that metaphors eventually become clichés, one can imagine that Murdoch is proposing that the Christian story has become clichéd and needs renewal when, in *Nuns and Soldiers,* she has Anne Cavidge, an ex-nun, experience a vision of Christ. Since Christianity does not treat its figures playfully, as some Eastern religions do, Murdoch no doubt annoyed many conventional readers. Her play in this novel reminds one of the flavor of holy play one finds, for example, in the Hindu celebration of the birth of God in Book III of E. M. Forster's *A Passage to India.*

Reminding other critics that Murdoch's art is "pure play," albeit serious play, Conradi implies that the reading public is too steeped in formalism to recognize this simple truth. Pointing to some of Murdoch's jokes that are local and meant to illustrate the provisionality and reality of art, Conradi compares them to the jokes of more solipsistic writers: Murdoch's "small and teasing joke is not permitted the vain and gleeful expansion a more portentous or formalist writer — Nabokov or Fowles perhaps — might have given it. It is 'pure play'" (86–87). As one discovers in *The Bell,* the major joke is often "spiritual pride": "To try to be holy may be mere play and escapism" (quoted, 115).

In light of his focus on the provisionality of art in *Under the Net,* Conradi's responses to other critics are invaluable. His argument with Byatt is simple: annoyed that Byatt makes this novel sound portentous, he works to convince the reader that it is Murdoch's most unphilosophical novel. Murdoch, he says, has a right to resent critics' attempts to "allegorise the books as if they were merely philosophy-in-disguise, preferring to be thought a reflective, religious or speculative novelist like Dostoevski, than, like Sartre, directly a philosophical one" (31). In 1975 Donna Gerstenberger argued this same point in her monograph *Iris Murdoch:* that it is a mistake to judge novels "as if they were mere demonstrations of Murdoch's critical theories" when they are actually "disturbing visions of a disturbed world" (16).

Conradi is also disturbed by critics who read into some of Murdoch's novels a liberalism and a closure that he insists is not present. He says that she takes the commonsensical position, which some critics miss because they "insufficiently see the open-endedness even of her most apparently 'closed' novels" (50). For example, Rubin Rabinovitz finds that at the end of *Under the Net* Jake "has now learned 'to accept contingency.' A. S. Byatt writes that Jake 'is free of his own net of fantasy' and describes his 'final enlightenment.' Malcolm Bradbury speaks of his 'learning a fresh truth' and of 'true vision'" (50). These views of the novel as having closure do not fit Murdoch's theoretical statements, nor do they reflect her story's plot line: in *The Sovereignty of Good*, Conradi says, Murdoch writes of "the effort toward reality as 'infinitely perfectible,' an 'endless task,' [and] emphasises 'inevitable imperfection' and 'necessary fallibility.' Again and again she has attacked the liberal belief in fast change as false and magical and opposed to it a truer picture of moral change as piecemeal, unending and in some sense goalless" (50).

Mediating between Moral Extremes

In conjunction with this kind of moral ambiguity, Conradi explains that often in her novels Murdoch employs a strategy, similar to Buddhism, of mediating between moral extremes, "a dynamic and cheerful philosophy of the Middle Way. It is dynamic in that it insists on moral effort, but a mediation in that anything but a temperate self-denial turns out to reinforce what you already are" (68), a truth that Stephen Dedalus in Chapter III of James Joyce's *A Portrait of the Artist as a Young Man* illustrates. Conradi says that while Murdoch does not like moral compromise in art, she knows that it is necessary and often sets it in motion as a theme. In *The Philosopher's Pupil* she juxtaposes the philosopher Rozanov, who is an "absolutist in ways she has disavowed," and George, "his mad, demonic, third-rate pupil," to explore perfectionism (73–74). Rozanov answers the ultimate question Murdoch is pursuing in the novel: "What do you fear most?" Murdoch's answer, according to Conradi, is Rozanov's: "To find out that morality is unreal" (74). For her, this question is crucial. One might apply Conradi's point more broadly by arguing that Murdoch's experience with Plato's dialogues might have encouraged her to employ the dichotomies, or binaries, of Western culture, often noticeable in her titles, so that she could mediate between them.

As an empiricist, Murdoch was open to testing and changing her opinions: she was a speculative novelist. But Conradi says that she was certain about perfection's being an illusion: "Murdoch's own work with its rapid supercession of one book by its successor, its throw-away imagery and migrating themes and motifs, feels in this sense Platonic and, since the Good itself is indefinable and cannot be inscribed, in pursuit of imperfection" (87). For her, Western Christian art is not so illusion-free. She censures "its false concreteness since, in instinctively materialising God and the religious life, 'What should be a mediating agency becomes a non-stop barrier' (FS [*The Fire and the Sun*] 70), an obstacle to the pursuit of the whole truth" (87). On the other hand, she commends "the deliberate incompleteness of Zen anti-art. 'Zen emphasises skill but favours throwaway products. Plato (*Laws* 956b) says that artifacts offered to the gods should be such as can be made in a single day' (FS 71)" (87). Murdoch's interest in the mediator figure apparently grew out of her study of the ancient Greek Eros. In *The Fire and the Sun* she writes that "Eros . . . is the ambiguous spiritual mediator and moving spirit of mankind. Eros is the desire for good and joy which is active in all levels of the soul" and through which a spiritual quester can move toward reality (34).

Conradi's focus on the illusion of perfectionism and the provisionality of art is meant to contextualize Murdoch's worldview and help explain her reasons for naming her view as she did. One reason she called it "moral psychology" instead of moral *philosophy* was that she, unlike the discipline of philosophy, held "the idea of conceptual mastery in such suspicion" (x). Referring to her view as "anti-philosophy," as Wittgenstein did his philosophy, Conradi argues that it is a "marriage" of Freudian and Platonic ideas. Highlighting her focus on the differences among human beings, he explains that "the shape of her career is towards a use of myth that is consciously disposable and provisional, subordinated to the moral psychology of the characters" (75). He means that by disposing of myths, such as Apollo and Marsyas, she depends less on classical myths for structure as she begins to write longer, less rigid novels in the 1980s. In addition to jettisoning neo-Platonic themes, "she becomes less absolute, more dialectical and playful, patient, comprehensive and open" (75). She deals with Eros, always her subject, in a new way. Conradi describes that use "in its higher manifestations — desire for knowledge, desire for God — the force that can release the prisoners from the Cave; but in its lower — desire for power and possession — precisely the mechanical repetitive force which binds them there in the first place" (84–85). Charles Arrowby in *The Sea, The Sea* illustrates the confusion and disorientation a character can experience if he ignores reality and reads his own "dream-test" (86).

Creating Eros

Conradi is explicit about the role love and sex play in Murdoch's moral psychology. Celebrating her wisdom as a creator of Eros, its "symptoms, pathology and . . . phenomenology — the changes it induces in consciousness" when one falls in love — he supports his point with John Bayley's distinction between love and sex. Bayley says in *Characters in Love* that sex is a "conservative instinct" evoking stock responses: "We desire in obedience to the fixed patterns of our sexual imagination, but we fall in love when we are really seeing another person" (quoted in Conradi, 85). Conradi fills in the cultural background by referring to F. M. Cornford's explanation of the difference between the Eros of Freud and that of Plato. For Freud, "the upward effort towards the higher manifestations of consciousness can be unmasked as a disguised version of the rude and primitive instincts of our animal ancestry." Such transformation of "love energy" Freud calls "sublimation." On the other hand, Plato sees that "this energy has an originally 'high' source and sublimation is conceived of as a home-coming, rather than an aberrant form of exile" (quoted, 85). Murdoch's texts weave together the two views of sublimation, valuing "the idea of a spiritualised sexuality, and the unconditional love which is its ultimate if unreachable goal" (85).

Bruno's Dream — no other critic's favorite book — is the novel Conradi chooses to illustrate her moral psychology and the process of slowly unselfing. What makes the novel persuasive from his point of view is its passionate focus on death. He says that there are few convincing analyses of death in literature, and that perhaps the best are the deaths of Ivan Ilyich, Patroclus, Cordelia, and Petya Rostov. This subject is important to Murdoch's novels, which illustrate Plato's and Weil's views on death as well as the Renaissance truism that focusing on death renews life. This novel gathers a small group of characters around Bruno Greensleave, who is dying; Murdoch employs this strategy again in *Nuns and Soldiers*. At the conclusion of *Bruno's Dream* the saintlike Diana Watkins Greensleave helps the suffering Bruno to complete his dying: "She tried to think about herself but there seemed to be nothing there. Things can't matter very much, she thought, because one isn't anything. Yet one loves people, this matters" (310). An experienced Murdoch reader can interpret that Diana has become unselfish enough to pay attention to someone else. Experiencing Bruno's dying, Diana becomes a selfless pilgrim as she moves "toward the sun" (Conradi, 101). Another pilgrim somewhere on the path toward the Good, Conradi estimates, is Nigel Boase, Bruno's nurse, who is mature enough to explain to Diana that many people create dreamlike "fantasms" of others that they pretend are real. But the novel makes abundantly clear that "trying to live out the philosophy of unconditional love with its attendant dangers of masochism and muddle" is a huge challenge (100). Bruno, who begins to see his head as similar to that of one of his spiders, is such a character and realizes just before his death that his solipsism has destroyed his efforts to love. Murdoch's characters who have been working to become unselfish for mysterious, perhaps Freudian, reasons often go off on emotional tangents, losing their way. Lisa

Watkins, a former nun, is an example in this novel of a character who has had a vision of the Good but chooses sexual love instead. Often, what seem to be efforts to unself turn out to be manifestations of solipsism, Freudian at base. In this tragicomedy some characters come to a comic end as a result of their "futile self-sacrificing altruism," as when Danby Odell's wife Gwen "died diving off Battersea Bridge to save a young girl, who then swam safely ashore" (100).

The Sublime

Conradi proposes that what a reader often misses when reading a Murdoch novel is that the sublime is at the heart of her moral psychology. It is "a central organising metaphor"; the reader can see it in "her plotting, her ethics, her aesthetics, and her use of ordeals by love and water" (112). All of these realities participate in and are related to Murdoch's concept of "the Good itself, which acts both as an inexhaustible fund 'elsewhere' from which we draw energy, and also as a quality here which we dimly and always incompletely intuit in good art and good neighbours" (76). In one sense, the sublime is the overabundance of Good in the world. The reader not only feels "rapture" and "transport" when reading one of Murdoch's novels but also experiences with the characters their individual pilgrimages as they trudge throughout the course of each story. The abundance of plot Murdoch always provides "offers itself," Conradi says, "as a small hermeneutic sublime to the reader, who may feel like one reviewer that 'there is a central, large, and simple meaning which one has somehow, just missed'" (112).

In *Sartre: Romantic Rationalist* Murdoch disagrees both ethically and aesthetically with Sartre's horror at "the contingent overabundance of the world"; she finds it celebratory, while he finds it nauseating. She attributes his lack of wonder to his "defensive egocentricity" (quoted in Conradi, 106), for "the sublime has at its heart the disharmony between mind and world, and the futility on the part of the imagination of the effort to grasp and represent the formless" (110). Being realistic and knowing that contingency is inevitable, Murdoch has no problem in grasping chaos and the fear that attends it or in representing chaos. In fact, she is a genius at re-creating it in novels; psychological hyperactivity is her forte, but she is also an expert at dramatizing excessive muddle. She creates Bradley Pearson not only to argue that an artist's job is to capture chaos and that contingency is the stuff of art but also to show that being finicky about order is comically neurotic. No doubt her moral goals, different from Sartre's, and her direct focus on people would have been unfathomable to the French existentialist.

For historical background Conradi refers to Samuel Holt Monk's *The Sublime*, agreeing that Immanuel Kant's sublime is "both the advance-guard of a new individualism, since its affective theory of art (involving 'transport,' 'rapture') moves the locus of aesthetics away from the artwork to the reader, and also an authoritarian concept putting a high value on anything that suggests man's relative weakness" (110). Murdoch, according to Conradi, agreed with Kant that the sublime includes "respect for the moral law" but disagreed with his "natural sublime," arguing instead for a "humanist sublime" (110). Murdoch wanted to reform the Romantic and existentialist aspect of this view of the sublime, because such a view led to solipsism and elitism. Citing the metamorphosis of Romanticism into existentialism and then into poststructuralism (particularly deconstruction), Conradi proposes that social and intellectual conditions in the late twentieth century have proved that the analyses of both Monk and Murdoch are correct. Conradi suggests that Derrida is Socrates' descendant: "Socrates' *aporias* (moments of undecidability) are dimly echoed by today's post-structuralists when they place the highest emphasis on those moments in reading when we know we are baffled." Socrates, however, reveals the false pretensions and punctures the pomposity of his listeners: "in the name of a Beyond whose sublimities he points to but which must remain nameless[;] Derrida's negative sublime of undecidability is gleefully self-sufficing" (111). Murdoch subsequently argues in *Metaphysics as a Guide to Morals* that Derrida's deconstruction is "plausible amoralistic determinism" (198).

Weaving into her moral point of view the component of love, Conradi says, Murdoch believes that individuals learn to know themselves "not by explaining the world but by loving it" (107). They must love reality in order to see it: such love occurs "through acts of selfless attention" like watching a bird in flight. Individuals can, like Effingham Cooper in *The Unicorn*, experience a sublime vision and then lose it. Because life is a comedy, "even the most piercing sense of revelation accompanying a greater awareness of one's moral position is likely to be nine-tenths illusion," Murdoch argues; "it would be hard to overestimate the amount of illusion in any given soul" (interview quoted in Conradi, 107). Conradi stresses that the sublime, being two-faced — or positive and negative — is both special and ordinary. He says that even though Murdoch creates characters who undergo the same kind of negative visions as Sartre's, their experience is not "elevated into a despotic metaphysical truth" as in his texts (107). Furthermore, Murdoch insists that all human beings experience such positive and negative states of mind.

In his examination of Murdoch's use of the ordeals of love and water, Conradi points out that for her, to swim "is almost to possess moral competence. Both [swimming and loving] depend on 'one's willingness to surrender a rigid nervous attachment to the upright position' (UN 107) and to feel like Jake at the end of *Under the Net*, 'like a fish which swims calmly in deep water . . . [buoyed by] the secure supporting pressure of my own life' (UN 250)" (109). In Murdoch's work, devils cannot swim. Conradi proposes that immersion in the particularity of the world, represented by a substance like water, is the first stage in unselfing. Furthermore, this immersion does not equal inoculation from disaster or contingency. In *A Fairly Honourable Defeat* a character who cannot swim says, "I propose to give myself to the situation like a swimmer to the sea" (203), an example of Murdoch's ubiquitous irony. She had great respect for the ocean, having almost drowned in it, and she incorporated this metaphor for morality into most of her novels. Conradi gives a partial list of drownings and near-drownings, of which perhaps the most memorable example is suggested in *Nuns and Soldiers*.

Like swimming, loving for Murdoch is a positive sublime that can quickly become negative. Both swimming well and loving well require unselfing, giving oneself to the elements. Just as a reader can view Murdoch's characters along a spectrum of sublime experiences from positive to negative, so the reader can view her characters along a similar spectrum of love. The two extremes of this spectrum are varying degrees of selfless love as opposed to degrees of false ascesis, or false loss of self. Conradi gives examples of good characters who at the extreme of their unselfing have relinquished their personalities: "Tallis in *A Fairly Honourable Defeat* is seen as an 'unperson' (145), Lisa during her saintly phase in *Bruno's Dream* wishes to be 'nothinged' (93). Kathleen in *The Red and the Green* has to her husband the quality of 'unlife' (189) [and] . . . James in *The Sea, The Sea* could be said to take marginality and ascesis to the extremest point when he spookily renounces life itself and stops his own heart" (112). For Murdoch such loss of personality is good, but the reader still must distinguish points at which characters such as James are obsessive-compulsive from others at which they achieve unselfishness. The ideal is mediation between selflessness and masochism.

Referring to Murdoch's "comedies of inveteracy," Conradi highlights the importance of the good person's unselfing slowly and patiently. In other words, the novels emphasize that the process of unlearning old family habits is not just slow but almost impossible. In regard to the artist's problem with habit or the controlling of behavior, Murdoch said to Magee in 1978: "Creative imagination and obsessive fantasy may be very close, almost indistinguishable forces in the mind of the writer" (quoted in Conradi, 50). Conradi interprets her to mean that what seem to be opposites, "self-flattering fantasy and an imagination which links us to the world," may actually be parts of a continuum and not, as one would expect, discontinuous. He cites Jake in *Under the Net*, who experiences "the morning of the first day," or the wonder that causes people to create or change (50). Conradi says that the end of the novel demonstrates Murdoch's understanding "that the world is most apprehensible at those moments when we are calmest about submitting to its inexhaustibility. . . . Once you can admit you don't fully know, you can begin, a little, to see" (51), suggesting again that concept of giving oneself to the elements.

The Unicorn

All that Conradi has explored in *The Saint and the Artist* helps to explain his view of *The Unicorn*, which is notably different from Backus's in its emphasis on poetry and not philosophy, mystery and not analysis. His examination makes one wonder whether Backus missed the beauty entirely, whereas Conradi argues that the gothic novels are speculative, being "*about* the mythopoetic and magical powers of the imagination, and about the limits of those powers. . . . They are the most poetic of her novels: their truth is in their poetry" (121). Moreover, the novels also make fun of "romanticism, in the form of an apocalyptic yearning for redemption" (121). Although Backus acknowledges Murdoch's subtle jokes at serious moments in the texts, one wonders whether he appreciates all the incarnations of humor that Murdoch includes in even the darkest of her novels.

Perhaps being a better reader of modernist literature (e.g., Beckett), Conradi sees that *The Unicorn* playfully uses "the stage props and scenery of the Romantic sublime. It is set in a prototypical 'horrid' province of European Romanticism, a wilderness in West Ireland. . . . The houses neighbour a sea which kills people, rocks with carnivorous plants, an unfeatured bog. . . . It is a 'very ancient land' with megaliths, one of them 'seemingly pointless yet dreadfully significant'" (121–22). This last phrase is a typical Murdochian paradox, a playful reference to ancient stones, long treasured by her, perhaps like those making up the Giant's Causeway in Ireland, pointless and yet significant. There seem to be at least two layers here. She is no doubt evoking the concept found in ancient Eastern religions such as Hinduism and Buddhism that pointlessness and significance are the same. For example, E. M. Forster's novel *A Passage to India* argues that the ancient stone caves of Marabar are both meaningless and meaningful. Murdoch's use of ancient land and megaliths in *The Unicorn* foreshadows her carnivalesque use of them in later novels, e.g., the Druid celebration at a place like Stonehenge, called "the Ring" (380) in *The Philosopher's Pupil* and a similar meeting at "the Stone" in *The Message to the Planet* (278). Backus and Conradi would enjoy the paradox and irony Murdoch employs here.

Conradi argues that Murdoch has made the unicorn symbol empty: "the imagery is disposable, and the absent centre perhaps points to Murdoch's own negative theology or secular mysticism in which the Good can be described only in terms of what it is not, and any attempt to incarnate or define it must finally be vain" (123). Hannah, the searchers discover, does not fit her role as suffering Christ figure, and the discovery invites the reader to participate in re-creating a reasonable view of this world. Murdoch's discussion of suffering in *The Sovereignty of Good* proposes that Romanticism wants to "buy back evil by suffering in the embrace of good." Such a "satisfying" and "thrilling" compromise leads to what Conradi calls a "romantic degeneration of the Good," echoing "an earlier analysis of sado-masochism, an enemy to clarity of vision in art or morals. . . . Purgatory, in this vision, is the realm of sado-masochistic compromise, in which the second-best masquerades as the Good" (124–25). Hannah is, however, "the source and repository of the idea of the ambiguity of Eros, but in needing her to play the roles both of Christ and tainted enchantress, they collude. Spirituality, sex, and power are throughout the story richly confused" (123). Conradi says that Murdoch's term "Sexual feudalism," not Robert Scholes's "Christian feudalism," describes the relationships in the novel (123). Murdoch is explicit about Hannah's embodiment of "an impure parodic and romantic attempt on virtue"; Hannah's fictional world is evil, not good (125). For Murdoch, art shows its audience that "daemonic energies" are hidden in the secular "here and now": "The unmasking of this strange power occurs, in the Gothic romances, through a playful *rapprochement* with the commonplaces of Romanticism, a paradox partly neutralised here by the fact that Effingham refers to the tale *as* a story" (126).

Metaphysics as a Guide to Morals

Another moral argument that demonstrates the weakness of Backus's philosophical one is Antonaccio's. Backus and Conradi constructed their arguments with the use of Murdoch's pre-1986 texts; while Conradi lists in his index the Gifford Lectures — the basis of *Metaphysics as a Guide to Morals,* the book central to Antonaccio's essay — Backus may or may not have been familiar with them. Backus's biased rendering of Murdoch's philosophical project has the potential to diminish readers' respect both for her philosophical output and for her fiction. Readers need to see his argument in relationship to comments by the other philosophers in this volume coedited by Antonaccio, for Antonaccio's argument in *Iris Murdoch and the Search for Human Goodness* helps one to envisage Murdoch's place in philosophy. Antonaccio explains in her introduction to the volume ways in which Murdoch foresaw and molded issues basic to contemporary ethics, "including the relation between human identity and ideas of the good, the effect of the modern critique of religion on moral life and thought, the relation between ethics and literature, and the contemporary debate about liberalism. Over the past forty years Murdoch's diverse writings have influenced a generation of moral and religious thinkers" (xi-xii).

Art as Formalizing Life's Contingency

Antonaccio has made an extremely useful contribution to Murdoch criticism not only by editing this volume but also by writing a concise and effective explanation of Murdoch's moral theory. While capturing Murdoch's far-reaching ethical views, Antonaccio focuses on answering a question Murdoch herself asks in her final book of philosophy: "how can metaphysics be a guide to morals?" (110). Answers come in Antonaccio's discussion of the connection between Murdoch's philosophy and fiction and in her exploration of the complex mediating Murdoch manages to effect between the tensions of form and contingency in the novel and between the tensions of metaphysics and empiricism in her philosophy. She points out that even though Murdoch called for "a retrieval of metaphysical theorizing as essential to moral reflection on human life, her work also shows a persistent suspicion of theory and indeed of all forms of discourse by which we try to capture truth, or to fix knowledge in rigid forms" (111). Such speculations might seem contradictory to some critics. It is important that readers study the novels conscientiously and give Murdoch room to explore and to play before coming up with rigid answers to explain what she is doing. Her first novel, *Under the Net,* illustrates and analyzes this very point but does not force a rigid answer on any character. Antonaccio says that in *Metaphysics as a Guide to Morals* Murdoch meditates on the reality that life is contingent and that philosophy and art formalize that contingency. Distinguishing metaphysics from other kinds of philosophical inquiry by its never-ending search for unity, Antonaccio says that metaphysicians want to find the deep structure of life. Murdoch calls this desire "the urge to prove that where we intuit unity there really is unity" (*Metaphysics as a Guide to Morals,* 1). In their search for truth and subsequent constructions of systems, metaphysicians console human beings who "fear plurality, diffusion, senseless accident, chaos" (*Metaphysics as a Guide to Morals,* 1).

Most important is that while Murdoch accepts theory as necessary, she does not tolerate any totalizing theories. Antonaccio shows Murdoch's strategies for creating "a type of metaphysical theorizing which remembers the contingent and mocks the idea of totality from within" (112), the kind of paradox Backus sees but to which he refuses to attend long or intently enough to discover the reasons behind it. Murdoch as philosopher wants to juxtapose "contrasting impulses": she wants to envision an orderly system of human life, but she must admit such a life is "chancy and complete" (111). Antonaccio concludes that although her discipline demands systematic unity, Murdoch as philosopher must insist on holding the contingent before her and demand that the individual and the particular not get lost or suffocated under the net of theory. Murdoch perceives that the "abstract theorizing of metaphysics must be challenged by empiricism" (111) and determines not to allow the particular to be absorbed into any totalizing system.

Antonaccio's claim is that Murdoch constructs her "theory of art and her theory of morals . . . by parallel tensions: the tension between form and contingency, in the novel; and the tension between metaphysics and empiricism, in moral theory" (124). Using *Metaphysics as a Guide to Morals* as an "exercise in metaphysics," she characterizes as innovative Murdoch's "two-way movement in philosophy": in style and in subject matter. Throughout her career Murdoch worked to mark a place for the individual within the formal unity of philosophy or literature, and here the individual is the crux of her moral theory (112). Antonaccio explains that Murdoch in the crucial 1957 essay "Metaphysics and Ethics" contrasts the liberal view of morality, associated with Kant and Jean-Paul Sartre, to the Natural Law view, which she associates with "Thomists, Hegelians, and Marxists" (115). Disagreeing with Sartre and Kant, who suggest that "the moral agent is responsible for endowing this [metaphysical] totality with value" (114–15), Murdoch argues that freedom cannot be achieved apart from one's relationship to others and to reality. The liberal or Romantic "view tends towards solipsism," Antonaccio explains, "because it pictures the individual and morality as self-contained. Freedom is conceived as a detachment or leap of the will in the face of duty or moral choice, rather than a continuous interaction of the agent with a world that contains value" (115). On the other hand, the Natural Law view assumes that the self is always surrounded by a reality outside itself to which the self ascribes value. Although Antonaccio thinks that Murdoch prefers the Natural Law view, she quotes "Metaphysics and Ethics" to reveal Murdoch repudiating that view's assertion that "the individual *only* has importance, or even reality, in so far as he belongs to the framework" (quoted, 115). Whereas many would claim Murdoch as a Natural Law moralist, Antonaccio underscores the philosopher's selective preservation of one liberal insight in particular: "the individual must not be absorbed without remainder by any framework" (116).

Mediating Tension between Metaphysics and Empiricism

This proposition leads Antonaccio to the corollary that Murdoch finds a middle course between two risky alternatives, a "view in which the self wholly transcends its relation to nature, history, and community by virtue of its freedom and a view which dissolves or assimilates the self into these relations" (116). Antonaccio's careful development of Murdoch's moral theory reveals the latter's reasons for wishing to "mediate the tension between metaphysics and empiricism in her theory of morals by articulating a complex notion of metaphysical unity which allows room for the idea of the contingent individual and the individual's ordinary moral struggle" (124). To perceive reality in any area of life, Murdoch says, demands a "double revelation of both random detail and intuited unity" (quoted, 125). Explicating Murdoch's determination to mediate, Antonaccio cites the assertion in that pivotal 1957 essay that ethics cannot be scientifically neutral: always valuing one thing over another, human beings find value in the world. Murdoch's philosophy has to struggle against the "'one-making' endeavors that attempt to bring a consoling formal (aesthetic and conceptual) unity to a contingent, formless world" (126). Furthermore, Murdoch explains that metaphysics makes "models and pictures of what different kinds of men are like" and that the human being "makes pictures of himself and then comes to resemble the picture" (quoted, 125).

Few other philosophers or novelists can "picture" what Murdoch calls "'the real impenetrable human person' . . . among other such persons against the background of a rich and receding reality" (119); Murdoch does so in her novels. Antonaccio reads *Metaphysics as a Guide to Morals* as an argument in defense of "a conception of the idiosyncratic individual as valuable *per se* in the context of a metaphysical position which remains, somehow, non-systematic and non-totalizing" (127). This individual has a consciousness that is a bearer of value. Murdoch's emphasis on consciousness challenges two contemporary views: "those positions which tend to reduce moral subjectivity to a unitary faculty such as reason or the will, the operations of which become the exclusive focus of ethics; and second, it challenges those positions which tend to reduce the being of the self to a mere cipher in a larger network or totality (whether linguistic or social) which is considered the authoritative source of reality and value" (128). Antonaccio says that according to Murdoch, "consciousness is naturally one-making" and "truth-seeking"; moral life is similar to Plato's Cave pilgrimage from appearance to reality, "guided by an idea of perfection" (129).

Antonaccio dissects the arguments on which Murdoch bases her conception of the Good: Murdoch begins by insisting that "a notion of value or the Good" is the foundation of the consciousness. For her, the Good is "the ground or source of all being and value," not any specific value. She compares "this transcendental argument for the Good to the one-making aspect of human consciousness. . . . Murdoch's transcendental aspect of the Good thus unifies the whole of human life and perception under the sovereign concept of goodness." The other part of the theory "is an empirical argument about how the concept of Good operates in our cognitive truth-seeking activities." Murdoch insists that what humans apprehend not only is "carried out against a transcendental background of value, but also is progressive in its attempt to make discriminations of value in relation to an implicit ideal of perfection" (133). While this concise explanation is a persuasive case for Murdoch's Good, skeptics might ask: if the one-making drive of human beings came to the conclusion of the Good as encompassing what is outside human beings, why is the Good any less open to illusion than the gods human beings have seen as outside themselves?

Antonaccio shows that Murdoch celebrates the same "open-endedness and incompleteness of art" in *Metaphysics as a Guide to Morals*, especially in the final section, "Void," as in her novels (137). In other words, Murdoch's philosophical strategies, like her novelistic strategies, are not always orthodox. Ceaselessly juxtaposing theory and experience, Murdoch makes even her metaphysical journeys pilgrimages without end. Such journeys help individuals to see that even though humans are a unity-making species, pilgrimages with no end can, as Antonaccio insists, force "us from our false resting places" toward truth and reality (137). In addition to interpreting *Metaphysics as a Guide to Morals*, Antonaccio demonstrates that the rest of Murdoch's philosophy, as well as her fiction, is polyvocal, with many voices competing to be heard.

On this point she and Conradi agree. In addition to opening up a third possible answer to the simplistic, yes-or-no question of whether Murdoch writes philosophical novels, Conradi supports Murdoch's contention that she was not a philosophical novelist but a speculative novelist who used moral psychology. He demonstrates much earlier than Antonaccio that the 1970 essay "Existentialists and Mystics" "argues for both empiricism and mysticism, which are not seen as in conflict" (19). By doing so, the essay pictures for the reader a clear approximation of the Good human being and argues that the hero of the mystical novel is the "new version of the man of faith, believing in goodness without religious guarantees, guilty, muddled, yet not without hope. This image consoles us by showing us man as frail, godless, and yet possessed of genuine intuitions of an authoritative good" (quoted, 19).

Conradi also observes that Murdoch carries over into her philosophy the idea of a "provisional relation" to conceptualizing or theorizing: in "A House of Theory" she "blamed modern philosophy for having discouraged theorising," in "Against Dryness" she "called for a modern liberal theory of personality," and in *The Sovereignty of Good* she recommends "a dialectic between theory and fact" (43). She continues these arguments in *The Fire and the Sun* and in "Salvation by Words." He makes clear why Murdoch's critics must be careful about putting her in a box: rather than simply placing "absolute trust in theory," she calls for theory that is "local and provisional, not general and imperial" (43). For Murdoch, "Classification by itself produces a world of dead facts, love a world mysteriously alive and inexhaustible" (43). The critic, in crawling "under the net" of theory, must explore not only the structure but also "those particulars which break away from and blur the structure, and give us the artful illusion that the work is overflowing back into life" (44).

Conradi's dynamic book, with its attention to clarity of argument and its rigorous exploration of the texts, has fostered a broad and multidisciplinary analysis of Murdoch's work. In turn, Antonaccio's interest has recently focused attention on Murdoch's unorthodox philosophical strategies. The collection Antonaccio coedited, *Iris Murdoch and the*

Search for Human Goodness, grew out of a multidisciplinary conference in 1994 at the Divinity School at the University of Chicago, sponsored through the D. R. Sharpe Lectureship on Social Ethics, which had the goal of exploring "whether there are ethical principles sensitive to the religious and cultural heritages and enlightened by contemporary knowledge adequate for the evolving needs of society in its search for purposeful life on this planet" (ix). While addressing a particular agenda, scholars from various disciplines came to the Chicago conference to examine issues that still underlie the critical reception of this woman of genius.

Antonaccio and the other contributors demonstrate that readers of Murdoch's novels cannot afford to ignore the philosophical aspect of her oeuvre. Literary critics stress that readers must beware of her irony; for example, Conradi says, "Like Plato, Murdoch always veils with irony the highest truth she wishes to show us" (107). Perhaps Backus missed some of her irony, but it is more likely that he has ignored the spiritual aspect of her work; he seems to lack a spiritual calm and would probably not want to submit to the Buddhist-like meditation that Antonaccio finds in *Metaphysics as a Guide to Morals.*

Artist and Philosopher Employ the Same Strategies

Is Murdoch, then, a philosophical novelist? Antonaccio demonstrates that Murdoch the philosopher and Murdoch the artist both use the strategies of meditation and mediation, but in each case she is dealing with different tensions: form and contingency in the novel, metaphysics and empiricism in philosophy. Conradi escapes the bind of binary thinking in another way, by opting for a new definition of what Murdoch does. Respect for Murdoch's dislike of totalizing theories and categories welcomes such an approach, an approach that respects reality — or mystery.

Wishing to practice "open-endedness," I have chosen in this study to highlight the polyvocal quality of Murdoch's criticism and to encourage the reader to decide. Ultimately, Murdoch's philosophy has contributed to the postmodern view that language produces a surplus of meaning, making it difficult to distinguish philosophy from art in that, as Clifford Geertz points out, "all disciplines and all genres have become 'blurred'" (767). Murdoch's writing characteristically struggles with making sense of the modern cultural process that creates a gigantic distance between the various phenomena of life and such blurred representations of them. Her readers, like Murdoch herself, must consider the potential distortions to which both philosophy and art are prone.

Notes

[1] For example, Freud parallels Plato in believing that "artists are neurotic children and incorrigible liars" (PA 88), and both writers theorize a concept of energy (an Eros) that supplies human beings with the ability to change.

Works Cited

Antonaccio, Maria. "Form and Contingency in Iris Murdoch's Ethics." *Iris Murdoch and the Search for Human Goodness*. Ed. Antonaccio and William Schweiker. Chicago and London: U of Chicago P, 1996. 110–37.

Backus, Guy. *Iris Murdoch: The Novelist as Philosopher, The Philosopher as Novelist, "The Unicorn" as a Philosophical Novel*. Bern and New York: Peter Lang, 1986.

Burke, John J. "Canonizing Iris Murdoch," *Studies in the Novel* 19.4 (Winter 1987): 486–94.

Conradi, Peter. *Iris Murdoch: The Saint and the Artist*. New York: St. Martin's, 1986; rpt. 1989.

Forster, E. M. *A Passage to India*. New York and London: Harcourt Brace Jovanovich, 1952.

Geertz, Clifford. "Blurred Genres." *Critical Theory since 1965*. Tallahassee: UP of Florida, 1986. 766–67.

Gerstenberger, Donna. *Iris Murdoch*. Lewisburg PA and London: Bucknell UP, 1975.

Monk, Samuel Holt. *The Sublime: A Study of Critical Theories in XVIII-Century England*. New York: MLA, 1935.

Murdoch, Iris. *Bruno's Dream*. New York: Viking, 1969.

———. *A Fairly Honourable Defeat*, New York: Viking, 1970.

———. *The Fire and the Sun: Why Plato Banished the Artists*. Oxford: Oxford UP, 1977.

———. *Message to the Planet*. London: Chatto and Windus, 1989.

———. *Metaphysics as a Guide to Morals*. New York: Viking, 1993.

———. *The Sovereignty of Good*. New York: Schocken Books, 1970.

———. *Under the Net*. New York: Viking, 1954.

5: The Realist Dilemma

ROM THE BEGINNING OF MURDOCH'S CAREER critics have asked
how well her novels fit into the realistic tradition and what she
means when she argues that realism is the style that best captures the
individuality of human beings. Publicly she embraced traditional realism, insisting that art must recover the nineteenth century's interest in
character if the novel were to be revitalized at end of the twentieth
century following its flirtation with modernist style from 1914 to 1965,
or what she considered the novel's twentieth-century escape into solipsism. In her 1959 essay, "The Sublime and the Beautiful Revisited,"
she argues that nineteenth-century novels, unlike twentieth-century
ones, "are victims neither of conventions nor of neurosis. . . . And the
individuals in the novels are free, independent of their author, and not
merely puppets in the exteriorization of some closely locked psychological conflict of his own" (quoted in Gerstenberger, 19). This statement is central to Murdoch's critical reception, because by contending
that the good artist gives characters freedom it precisely captures the
relationship between her moral and aesthetic principles. Furthermore,
she says that the twentieth-century novel is inhibited by clichéd conventions and stereotyped settings, whereas "the social scene" in the
eighteenth- and nineteenth-century novels gave life to the development
of the characters.

The Larger World beyond Solipsism

In "The Sublime and the Beautiful Revisited" Murdoch criticizes science, especially behaviorism, and philosophy for assenting to a theory
of personality incapable of capturing real human beings in solid, fleshy
characters. Literature requires realist artists, she says, who can show
readers the larger world beyond the subjective one that solipsistic
ideological conditioning imprinted on twentieth-century minds. Elizabeth Dipple explains that the responsibility of such a presentation of
human character would challenge any artist's capacity to give attention
to all the formal aspects of "narration, moral intrusion, point of view,
closure — all the terms comprising our vocabulary of form" (39). In
other words, such an artist must be immersed totally in what formalist
critics label form and content. But since Murdoch's seeming goal of

"the absolute emptying of the author's personality and power from the work of art" is as impossible as the realism it implies, Dipple concludes that the realistic novelist has always had to be ironic to get close to the truth. She distinguishes Murdoch's approach, which she calls "autonomous realism," from the realism of assessment, which is more tied to form. Because realism is a metaphorical convention, Dipple reiterates that "no writer can be totally realist (there is no human mirror in the roadway [as Stendhal suggested]) and still impose form" (39). Dipple's language suggests that Murdoch's job is especially complex, since the realist must accomplish the impossible. As evidence that Murdoch accepts this challenge, Dipple points to the essay's insistence that Murdoch's reader "don the hair-shirt of reality" (348).

Murdoch Questions Aesthetics

Murdoch's preference for the mode of the nineteenth century reflects her rational and moral attitudes toward the sublime. Immanuel Kant served as a whetstone to the development of Murdoch's aesthetic. "The Sublime and the Beautiful Revisited" is one of three essays that his concept of the sublime provoked her to produce; the others are "The Sublime and the Good" (1959) and "Against Dryness: A Polemical Sketch" (1961). These examinations of art ask: What is the nature of art? What constitutes great literature? And how does an artist make moral judgments? Peter Conradi explains that Murdoch wanted to revise Kant's notion of the sublime, since it can "become an excuse for an exalted and solipsistic self-regard." She agrees with Kant's comparison of "the sublime and *Achtung*, or respect for the moral law. . . . She would, however, supplement Kant's natural sublime . . . by a humanist sublime, in which the spectacle of human life itself, and the reality of persons other than ourselves, becomes the most proper trigger. . . . The good man, her ideal candidate for the sublime, in a sense the sublime's true-born citizen, might feel 'delight, terror, but not, if he really sees what is before him, superiority'" (110–11). For example, John Keats might become ecstatic when he contemplates people, as well as when he contemplates birds or funerary urns. Richard Todd says that in her argument with Kant's theory of the sublime Murdoch provides "the notion that the common essence shared by art and morals is love, 'the extremely difficult realization that something other than oneself is real'" (43).

"Against Dryness" is a profound and tightly packed essay that links the development of the novel, as well as its health, to twentieth-century philosophies (linguistic empiricism and existentialism), cultural ideology, and social conditions. Reacting against the scientific and anti-metaphysical disposition of her age, Murdoch posits that "the 18th century was an era of rationalistic allegories and moral tales. The 19th century (roughly) was the great era of the novel; and the novel throve upon a dynamic merging of the idea of person with the idea of class" (12). For her, the dilemma that the earlier centuries had created remains problematic: in the eighteenth and nineteenth centuries philosophy argued that the individual existed "against a background of values, of realities which transcend him," and in the twentieth century the individual is "stripped and solitary" (12). Simplistic existentialist fantasies of total freedom and total rationality led to a lack of attention to reality. A primary concern is that "with the removal of Kant's metaphysical background the individual is seen as alone" (10); such a concern for the condition of human beings without God, in tandem with her preference for moral philosophy over linguistic philosophy, drew her into the existentialist camp, but only momentarily. Even though she diagnoses the novel as in declining health, she remains hopeful that it is one of the few instruments available for measuring and probing these moral questions now that philosophy has become scientific and mathematical: "literature . . . has taken over some of the tasks formerly performed by philosophy" (15). Whereas "the 19th-century novel (. . . of course there were exceptions) was not concerned with 'the human condition,' it was concerned with real various individuals struggling in society" (13). The twentieth-century novel, however, declined when the general malaise of modern Western culture set in. For example, that Sartre's model for his characters is what she calls "Totalitarian Man," a Romantic who complains and surrenders to neurosis. The other extreme, "Ordinary Language Man," is also not representative of real people; he is a puppet who chooses what the conventions of society have dictated ("The Sublime and the Beautiful Revisited," 254). Murdoch's goal is to capture full-bodied human beings, "mess[iness]" and all (*A Fairly Honourable Defeat,* 216).

Distinguishing twentieth-century novels as crystalline or journalistic, she argues that the former, being the most immediately serviceable for the serious writer, usually seem to be the superior novels of the time, apparently because they capture the inner world of unified values. The dryness she opposes is the lack of resourcefulness in just such texts, which do not represent solid, opaque, contingent persons against a broad view of social reality that allows for the depiction "in a nonmeta-physical, nontotalitarian, and nonreligious sense, [of] the transcendence of reality" (14). She finds it disturbing that early-twentieth-century writers prefer this "ideal of 'dryness' . . . (smallness, clearness, self-containedness)," which Kant "required art to be" and which T. E. Hulme, T. S. Eliot, Paul Valéry, and Ludwig Wittgenstein sought as a gemlike perfection (13). This kind of escape from reality, as she sees it, does not contribute to the health of the novel. Critics might well disagree: do not Joyce's Molly and Leopold Bloom and Virginia Woolf's Mrs. Ramsay represent solid, opaque, contingent persons?

Murdoch labels as "journalistic" the novel that is simply "a large shapeless quasi-documentary object, the degenerate descendant of the 19th-century novel, telling, with pale conventional characters, some straightforward story enlivened with empirical facts" (13). Neither kind, crystalline or journalistic, attempts to struggle with the dilemmas of the moral problem of the world — the possibility of experiencing the Good when there is no God. Moreover, Murdoch points out that lack of spirituality, or what Wittgenstein saw as "diseased human understanding" (Edwards, 224), has made it difficult for artists to create robust characters. Such concerns, along with the journalistic-crystalline dichotomy she constructs to address it, are pervasive topics in the criticism. Frank Baldanza, Dipple, and Conradi all emphasize that this early essay is crucial to any explanation of Murdoch's position.

"Against Dryness" lays out not only Murdoch's aesthetic values but also the reasoning process she follows in arriving at them. She understands that novels often have to solve, or at least address, problems that other disciplines ignore or cannot or will not arbitrate. She recognizes that one of her tasks as a novelist is to bridge the centuries, bringing the nineteenth-century focus on human beings as real "free characters" ("The Sublime and the Beautiful Revisited," 271) into twentieth-century literature so that novelists who have ideas, concepts, or visions of a clearer reality can use the novel to propose them for public consumption and discussion.

Murdoch as a Traditional English Realist

Because Baldanza's criticism of Murdoch did much of the early groundwork so well, and because he had to arrange the material tightly on a small palette, he is an excellent source of basic information. Baldanza's 1974 explanation that Murdoch wanted to be seen as the traditional English realist became the accepted position: "As a novelist, Miss Murdoch clearly belongs in the mainstream of the late eighteenth- and nineteenth-century tradition in the English novel. . . . She has no affinity with the plotless, stream-of-consciousness, mood reverie of James Joyce, Virginia Woolf, or Katherine Mansfield; Miss Murdoch's 'realism' retains many of the nineteenth-century Naturalistic assumptions." In technique, "'point of view narration,' . . . is largely irrelevant to her work" (16). For all his insights, some of Baldanza's statements date his contributions. For example, the reader will see that Dipple and Deborah Johnson, among other contemporary critics, find this statement about Murdoch's use of point of view problematic. Other critics take Baldanza to task for using the term *objectivity* as one would use it in a pre-Einsteinian world, as in: "She shares . . . a spread-out view of a society that maintains 'objectivity' in the handling of a wide variety of recognizable persons. Her view of society is implicitly hierarchical, and her attention is largely focused on the upper reaches of the middle class, even though her politics are likely to be left-wing" (16). Todd and Conradi discuss this idea of social hierarchy in great detail, and Conradi particularly disagrees with Baldanza's assumption.

Like A. S. Byatt, Baldanza elucidates such usages by Murdoch as *open and closed novels* and *transcendental realism.* Zeroing in on the latter term from "Against Dryness," Baldanza applies it to Murdoch's moving beyond "all the accepted realistic conventions of character, setting, and plot": "she then almost insensibly starts to use highly likely [i.e., believable] elements within this context to force to erupt within a set scene something outrageous, quirky, fantastic — so that the reader finds himself embroiled in a particularly unique situation that is wildly far removed from the premises on which work set out" (21). Appreciating the Murdochian characteristic of surprising the reader, Baldanza does not criticize the technique as later critics do. The kind of "eruption of the unexpected" that occurs in her novels is, according to him, "a testimony to the richness of reality, and it is not an anti-real element" (21).

Todd by no means judges Murdoch to be simply a realistic novelist. He opens his *Iris Murdoch* by gallantly wrestling with reasons why she does not want to abandon nineteenth-century realism; its analysis of humanistic values and its ability to realize "character" are crucial, he says, to her project (14). He illustrates by explaining the vibrancy of her absorption in the French intellectual life after the Second World War. For instance, "her early — and at the time unfashionable — championing of the work of Elias Canetti" and her empathy for the "fantasy realism" of Gabriel García Márquez demonstrate her involvement in the values of historical and cultural context, international thought, and experimentation with language that captures a new reality (14).

Instruments for Questioning Reality

Todd's most important contribution may be his emphasis on Murdoch's phrase "work for the spirit" (which Dipple took as the title of her 1982 study). He comes close to saying that Murdoch's novels, not always realistic in the traditional sense, are, instead, instruments for questioning reality (or "work for the spirit"): "manifestations of curiosity about the elements and assumptions which made the novel a serious form of art, in so far as they constitute an extended enquiry which has itself deepened and grown complex as time has gone by" (14). The following sentence illustrates how innovative Todd was in 1984 in summing up Murdoch's potential stature: "She has given serious and extended thought to the difficulties underlying the whole enterprise of writing fiction in an age and culture which evinces highly ambivalent attitudes towards 'greatness' in art and which has become deeply suspicious of the kind of liberal creative impulse which she herself possesses" (98). He pinpoints the seeming contradiction between her books' financial success and their posing of substantive challenges: "She has discerned — as have few other contemporary thinkers — the extent of paradox inherent in a situation in which art-works of whatever kind can become grand, available and iconic, and can at the same time be held, humbly and unassertively, to provide 'work for the spirit.' It is in the context of her distrust for the thinking entailed in this paradox that we should see her attainment of a frankly ritualistic form of fantasy realism" (98). This explanation of her reasons for employing "fantasy realism" is perhaps the most cogent that any critic has offered. Todd also discusses her as a thinker who questions and evaluates others' aesthetic theories. Murdoch reveals "a real alertness to the attractive dangers of artistic form" (99); being a Platonist, Murdoch has the same suspicions that Plato had about the elusiveness of truth and the seductiveness of the artist's imagery. Todd demonstrates that she, a philosopher with "a carefully cultivated, historically aware, and genuinely international literary sensibility (unlike that of other writers who have been associated with the revival of realism in post-war Britain)," has a "deeply examined" position on realism (14).

By contextualizing with historical data "a received view of the post-war British novel," Conradi adds a new dimension to this exploration of the difference between realism and the new realism in Britain in the 1950s and 1960s (15). This new realism came about because proponents such as Kingsley Amis and C. P. Snow were displeased with social realism and wanted to celebrate the geographical regions and to return to the "liberal conscience of Trollope, Wells, or George Eliot" (16).

British writers reacted against both international modernism and Marxist realism: "Social realism came to be seen as a naïve or inauthentic mode, relying on a false view of the unified self, of perception and the innocent eye, and a falsely optimistic estimate of human history. And just as 'realism' came to be seen as a form of whiggish romancing, so 'romance' was to be the new realism" (16). Conradi says that although Murdoch also criticized modernist fiction, her work did not fit into either the new realism or the reaction it evoked. Rather than seeing her as a liberal or a social realist, he emphasizes that her first novel, *Under the Net*, is a devastating critique of liberalism. Declaring any experimenting she does with form to be "peripheral" (16), he says that she does not fit into any modernist camp.

Dipple Contextualizes Realism

Baldanza, Dipple, Todd, and Conradi have all understood that Murdoch's vision includes a much broader range of content and form than strict historical realism would allow. Of the four, Dipple focuses the most on defining and historicizing what contemporary critics mean by *realism*. She contextualizes Murdoch's use of the nineteenth century's definition: "the realist writer was, in Balzac's term, merely a secretary or recorder of society, and . . . the author's production was, as Stendhal expressed it, 'a mirror in the roadway' which accurately reflected the traffic of life. Essential to this kind of thinking is the automatic and necessary retreat of the authorial voice. The desired product was large, 'baggy,' prolix, uncontrolled. At its best, the idea produces the marvellous heterogeneity of description and the open-endedness Murdoch so admires in such writers as Tolstoy and Dickens and sometimes so brilliantly achieves in her novels" (37–38). Dipple's explanation helps Murdoch's readers to recognize the similarity between Balzac's definition and Plato's attitude to art as a craft and the artist as a craftsperson, as opposed to the Romantic and elitist concept of ecstatic inspiration — which itself describes the solipsism Murdoch associates with modernism. She sees herself as a craftsperson who makes novels instead of pots.

Conflation of Literary Realism and Reality

In discussing the narrative point of view, Dipple explains that the traditional way to develop a novel is to have its narrator stand apart, as if telling a story about others, rather than expressing the writer's own ideas or feelings. Here she grapples with a central contradiction: realism shows "how strain occurs between an insuperable universal authorial urge towards ideology and the transmutations of ideas which take place when powerful characters take over the novels. . . . Murdoch's work both participates in the struggles of previous great realists and is made new and particularized by her own decisions and innovations, for certainly her work provides major innovations besides her perception of transcendent reality" (37). In describing Murdoch's unusual conflation of literary realism and reality Dipple makes one of her greatest contributions to Murdoch's critical reception. "In Murdoch's work, the discovery of reality is both historical (generally, contemporary England) and transcendent — a curious and radical intermeshing which defines her idea of the operation of love. The hopeless quest for reality, for knowledge, for the good" is disquieting and leads the characters and the readers to ruminations and, possibly, to misadventures (34). For Murdoch and Dipple the reader's task is to "accept the world we live in and not to settle for the one we continually create by our infinitely capacious illusions" (34). In conveying not only the superficial details of everyday life but also, in a Platonic sense, the larger meaning that lies beneath that surface, "realism involves seeing what is there, and behind and informing what is there is reality itself, a true perception of the world sought humbly. . . . This reality is a development of Platonic thinking, and is an idea alien to the conventional literary realism" (33–34); Dipple says that readers who find Murdoch's novels depressing bring to them "a refusal of [Murdoch's] radical idea of realism" (33). Dipple sees Murdoch's understanding of reality and her ability to capture it in the novel form as her contributions to the ailing novel of the twentieth century.

Dipple cites René Wellek's explanation of nineteenth-century realism to illustrate that the early historical view of realism must be superseded if one is to allow Murdoch to be a realist. Obviously Murdoch has an ironic view of the kind of oversimplification one finds in Wellek's account of historical realism: she does not, like the nineteenth-century realist in his account, reject "the fantastic, the fairy-tale-like, the allegorical and the symbolic, the highly stylized, the purely abstract and decorative"; her realism does not reject "the improbable," "pure chance," "extraordinary events" (quoted, 38). Pointing to the subtle distinctions historical changes have made in the received notions of realism, Dipple, like Baldanza, celebrates Murdoch's innovations, saying that Murdoch modifies such notions by substituting Plato's conceptions of reality for strict journalistic reportage of surfaces. Although her characters experience life's unexpected blows while failing to achieve transcendence, "they do know about virtue or holiness." Murdoch employs Plato's idea of the Good to demonstrate "religious apprehension that lies at the core of . . . [her] work and removes it from simple realism into a more serious realm where an external other presents the reader with an idea against which the fiction can profitably be placed" (8).

Murdoch Too Platonist to Trust Mere Imitation

Comparing Lindsay Tucker's analysis of this abstract Platonic stance with Dipple's is useful. Tucker points out in her introduction to *Critical Essays on Iris Murdoch* (1992) that "while it is true that [Murdoch] has consistently argued the need to recreate realism, it is also true that [her] brand of realism departs in important ways from what we have come to know as literary realism — what Dipple calls historical realism — the kind of realism a writer can evoke when she pays 'creative attention' to her/his civilization (Dipple, 31)" (9). Tucker adds that the "creative realist" is responsible for the reader's immersion in the "idea play" of the novel. The difficult task for the writer is to encourage the reader to forego his or her fantasies — a gigantic feat for any human being. Tucker thinks that this task is more important to Murdoch than imitation is: "mimesis in not involved in Murdoch's definition of realism; she is too much a Platonist to trust mere imitation" (9). The reader of a Murdoch text must view "what lies beyond it, what is ultimately Platonic *reality*" (9). This point suggests that Tucker thinks Murdoch expects her readers to have some knowledge of Plato. Tucker agrees with Dipple that the novelist conflates "literary realism and reality"; moreover, she voices a familiar complaint that Murdoch and her critics often use terms that have "a disturbing tendency toward truism. . . . Yet . . . whatever conceptual banalities reside in Murdoch's Platonic pronouncements, they become anything but banal when played out in the world of her fiction" (9). Tucker is referring to "generalized concepts involving freedom, goodness, beauty, love, and reality" (9) and phrases such as "deep structures of reality" (*The Fire and the Sun*, 83).

Finally, to "place Murdoch in her own age," David Gordon summarizes her position in 1995 in terms of the realist tradition in fiction (3). His *Iris Murdoch's Fables of Unselfing* is, in part, a dialogue with Murdoch's critics. He says that she understands that the "élan" of the nineteenth-century novel is "not yet spent": she is "happy in the tradition" of "Jane Austen, Charles Dickens, Emily Brontë, George Eliot, and of course Henry James" (3); she can write comedies of manners like Austen and James, "reflective passages" like George Eliot, and depictions of erotic impulses like Emily Brontë, Thomas Hardy, and D. H. Lawrence. Seeming to disagree with Dipple, Gordon deems the historical present in the novels to be deliberately vague; the characters "live in myth" or, as Margaret Scanlan observes, the characters lack awareness of "a shared world of public history" (quoted, 5). Gordon agrees with the other critics that Murdoch has a paradoxical nature: "If Plato fed her romantic yearning for a truth beyond appearances, Weil fed her anti-romantic distrust of individualism and the assertions of the will, stirring in her a moral passion for an image of suffering unsentimental and severe enough to be called an 'un-selfing'" (5). Furthermore, he suggests that she is paradoxical when he agrees with Conradi about her realism.

The Paradoxical Nature of the Novels' Realism

Conradi says that Dostoevsky's description of his realism — "what 'the majority call fantastic and exceptional'" (quoted, 4) — makes clear the paradoxical nature of Murdoch's realism. If this description applies to her novels, then several questions remain: To what extent does the purity of a novel's realism determine its excellence? If the major critics agree that Murdoch's realism is like no other realism, then what are their criteria and which novels are the best? What appeared realistic and superior in 1959 may have changed, because literary taste has, as a result of theoretical movements of the late 1960s become more tolerant since Byatt published the first book of criticism on Murdoch. Often, early critics consider the more realistic novels and the superior novels to be the same; often, when critics complain about a novel, they are questioning its lack of realistic consistency in bringing such things as the magic in *The Sandcastle* or the Gothic elements in *The Unicorn* or *The Time of the Angels*. Almost all of her critics agree that Murdoch most often uses some form of realism; their varying definitions of realism account for the controversy that is central to Murdoch studies.

Because Dipple seems to have been the most genuinely interested and to have done the most thorough job of exploring and assessing Murdoch's progress in achieving an artistic or historical realism in her novels, it is useful to retrace her classifications while comparing her analyses (133–35) to those of Todd, Gordon, Tucker, Gerstenberger, Baldanza, and Conradi.

The Success of Murdoch's Early Novels

Dipple judges that *Under the Net* (1954) and *The Bell* (1958) are the most successful novels of Murdoch's early period, ostensibly because they convey a sense of wholeness and harmony that fits easily into the realistic tradition. Furthermore, in capturing the reader they escape the kind of confusion nascent abstract systems cause in such novels as *The Unicorn* (1963) and *The Time of the Angels* (1966). None of the other critics would disagree with Dipple's generalization that there is a great distance between Murdoch's first ten novels and "the subtle images and hard-won modified spiritual optimism of *The Black Prince*" or her pronouncement that "in spite of the success of *Under the Net* and the technical excellences of *The Bell* and *The Unicorn* a general sense of unease progressively settled in among her readers, who grumbled about tricks and prolificacy" (133). Why, some readers were asking, if these are novels of formal realism, are there so many surprises and exaggerations?

Not all of the critics agree with Dipple that these "complaints lost their validity" with the publication of *The Nice and the Good* (1968). But most would agree with Gordon that "the period from 1961 to 1966 . . . is usually thought to be her weakest" (117). More significantly, Gordon argues that each of the novels of the period "makes new moves both conceptually and formally" (116). He says that commentary on this period originated in "Murdoch's own distinction between 'closed' and 'open' forms," between novels that are tightly plotted (*The Flight from the Enchanter* and *A Severed Head*) and those that are relaxed (*The Sandcastle* and *The Bell*). In her interview with Harold Hobson in 1962 Murdoch said that her goal was to write open novels but that she felt more affection for her closed novels because they conveyed more of her feelings (116). Since the open novels allow for greater depths of characterization, one might assume that the author would consider them as more realistic in the nineteenth-century sense. Dipple believes that Murdoch began, with *The Nice and the Good,* to achieve her goal of constructing open novels, books that have more characters and in which more of those characters are well developed: this novel "establish[es] the greatness of her reputation in the twentieth century" and "does mark her liberation from a certain obscurity of meaning and tight formulaic patterning that hindered the reader's grasp of much of what she was doing in the earlier novels" (133). Gordon says that Conradi chooses to date this inception with *A Fairly Honourable Defeat* in 1970, "perhaps because the intermediate novel, *Bruno's Dream,* partly returns to the older mode" (138). For Gordon and these critics the later novels are superior to the early ones.

Dipple blames the first three critical studies of the novels, those of Byatt, Wolfe, and Rabinovitz, for overemphasizing existentialism, for employing "almost exclusively the language of Murdoch's philosophical and literary critical essays," and "for tagging her erroneously and simplistically as a philosophical novelist" (133). She devotes minimal attention to influence studies, because "they reduce the energy and originality of the fresh fictional powers of Murdoch's imagination" (157). Dipple sees 1962 to 1966 as Murdoch's most uncertain period. Extolling the merits of *The Unicorn* and *The Time of the Angels,* she says they must be read in a new way: with unusual foresight. Dipple understands that part of Murdoch's problem during these early years was that she was working out the stages of a new turn in her mature work, a turn that was already alienating some of her established audience.

Admitting that "the first ten novels are puzzlingly dissimilar and ultimately of unequal interest" (134), Dipple categorizes their differences: "(1) the novel of tricks where plotting dominates: *Under the Net, Flight from the Enchanter, A Severed Head, The Italian Girl, The Red and the Green;* (2) the ruminative novel characterized by deepening of character: *The Bell, An Unofficial Rose;* and (3), which is closely connected to (2), the increasingly religious novel which is concerned with definitions and enactments of good and evil: *The Sandcastle, The Bell, The Unicorn, The Time of the Angels"* (136). Todd's analysis of the early novels depends, on the other hand, on aesthetic ideas Murdoch developed at the time she was writing them. In three critical essays, "The Sublime and the Beautiful," "The Sublime and the Beautiful Revisited," and "Against Dryness," he says, Murdoch works out her dispute with Kant about art: "It is therefore precisely the 'unutterable particularity' of nature and not (as we might be compelled to argue from Kant) its formlessness which should excite our *Achtung* (attention)" (43). Calling the first phase — that of the 1950s — Murdoch's struggle with existentialist problems, Todd emphasizes the novels' realistic qualities and traditional conventions.

For him, as for Dipple, *Under the Net* (1954) is, on the whole, a traditionally realistic text built on the quest motif, the picaresque adventure, "a genuinely European novel, with wide literary debts" (26). Murdoch's impersonation of a male writer-narrator in the protagonist, Jake Donaghue, parallels her theme of miming. A hack writer and potential artist with no possibilities, Jake puts most of his energy into survival. His emotional quests for a mentor and a lover lead him to recognize his vanity and solipsistic narcissism. Jake's discovery of "the other," Todd explains, "affects his attitudes towards words and writing, producing a recovery of specificity and a new attitude towards creativity" (28–29). Furthermore, the "detailed accuracy of the descriptions of London and Paris" is more complex than traditional realism requires (30). This novel explores moral realism and celebrates the human being as artist and his or her predicament, but it is also complex in its reminiscence of Hamlet's predicament: "For Murdoch, [*Hamlet*] can be seen as a play concerning a man's heroic inability to submit to the conventional forms of expression which are available to, and demanded by, his predicament" (29).

The Enchanter Figure

Whereas Todd sees Murdoch's second novel, *The Flight from the Enchanter* (1955), as generally busy, the plot being "too complex for the book's length" (32), Dipple notes that a new style emerges, revealing "complexity, inter-relatedness, strength of imagery, even indirect didacticism" (136). Dipple examines many themes, characters, and situations that will continue to evolve in Murdoch's mature novels. Of major importance in Murdoch's movement toward historical realism is the dance of the enchanter figure and the victims of power, often eastern European characters displaced by war. Micha Fox, the dark power figure, pits weak characters against each other. His discussions of categorizing are enlightening, as are his actual godlike categorizing of certain tropes: "the unicorn girl [innocent virgin], the siren, and, most importantly, the wise woman" (144).

Todd emphasizes Murdoch's preoccupation with the power figure, which no doubt grew out of her experiences during the Second World War and its aftermath. In addition to pointing out the number of foreigners involved, he discusses the dilemma Murdoch faced with her desire for both the ideal and the real, a paradox that continues throughout her work: "There are inherent paradoxes here, involving the relation between pattern and contingency, fantasy and the right to freedom of the free, full, rounded character, which have lasted as issues throughout her work" (33). He concludes that the novel "leaves us more with an impression of the universality of power rather than of its complexity" (33). While suggesting Murdoch's potential for changing realism, Todd calls attention to her power, as well: "the gods and demons who make their appearance here need not be inconsistent with realism, for they are 'there' in the novel in so far as they are seen to be created by the characters, not by the perverse imagination of the author — so that the author simply, so to speak, 'observes' them in action" (34). Todd observes that Murdoch allows a new freedom in her psychological realism by emphasizing the driving power of early memories to dominate and control the mind.

Murdoch's perhaps most conventionally realistic novel is *The Sandcastle* (1957); Todd judges that "while in many ways the quiet and everyday world offered in this novel is one which [Murdoch] believes the novelist should not consider unworthy of attention, it is a world to which her own fictional talents are simply not best suited" (38). He points out that the novel "has been criticized for its decided thematic similarity to the conventional literature of women's magazines" (36). What Murdoch conveys especially well is the protagonist's lack of awareness of the traps into which he is falling. Obviously, Murdoch learned a great deal about freeing up the character to have to deal with his own internal drives.

Both Todd and Dipple acknowledge the importance of *The Sandcastle* in its preparing Murdoch for writing *The Bell* (1958), which Todd calls another "adventure within a closed environment" (40). Granting that *The Sandcastle* and *The Italian Girl* are the only novels that can legitimately be called failures, Dipple says that *The Sandcastle* predicts an important Murdochian theme and is a bridge to *The Bell,* a novel with "an increased and pointed emphasis on the past and its ability to poison and pervert the present" (146). Furthermore, Dipple adds that "in spite of its failures and irritations, [*The Sandcastle*] also contains Murdoch's first serious religious examination of the moral life of the good" (144), a major theme in her later texts.

The Bell as Murdoch's Most Important Early Novel

Critics generally recognize *The Bell* as the most important early novel in its presaging of just such a serious moral pattern for Murdoch's subsequent fiction. Todd describes the pattern as "the compulsive repetition of an action which has been damaging in the past" (42). What he discovers to be new in this novel is Murdoch's insistence on bringing the reader up to date on the backgrounds of some of her characters. He says that this practice is so obvious that Frank Kermode mentions not only the "dullness" but also the necessity to the plot of some of the expository prose. Taking a more positive stance, Dipple celebrates *The Bell* as a crucial novel in that "the would-be hero," Michael Meade, represents a man caught in a Murdochian rat-run: he "feels that his failure in making a sexual advance to the innocent Toby constitutes a cyclic *déjà vu*" (146). Such a failure, even though accompanied by prayer and religious striving, is characteristic of dilemmas of Murdoch's subsequent major characters. Dipple emphasizes in this fourth novel a pervasive theme of entrapment that many of Murdoch's later protagonists (e.g., Hilary Burde in *A Word Child*) experience: "Michael's guilt lies constantly in some back chamber of his mind, haunting his dreams even before the frenzied dance of the complex plot really begins" (146).

The book is a measure of Murdoch's artistic process partly in its development of rich imagery that carries the burden of the characters' precognitive material. The concepts of evil and guilt coalesce with the image of the medieval bell, suggesting a "perversion of what had once been a great and positive thing" (147). Dipple devotes the most attention to the novel's "increasingly religious content," finding that such material and "the open inexorable destruction of false idealism and the attack on guilty dependence on the past [in addition to Murdoch's "generous ruminative mode"] give this novel a clarity of intention its predecessors did not quite have" (147). For Dipple, another strength of *The Bell*, beyond its strong characters, is its simpler plotting; she finds the plots of the earlier novels annoyingly "hyperactive" (147). She claims that *The Bell* provides two significant emphases that reflect Murdoch's motivation to move in a new direction: her "two principal inclinations — towards the religiously moral and the highly-plotted secular" fuse here, presaging Murdoch's mature style (145–46). The technical skills, however, that she had to practice in the six novels between *The Bell* in 1958 and *The Time of the Angels* in 1966 seem to have distracted her, Dipple thinks, from the "more subtle talent of transmitting perception" (154). Dipple is especially hard on the closed or highly plotted novels, and the gothic ones. She sees Murdoch's focus on drama at this time as having relieved her of her need to write closed novels.

Murdoch's Problematic Period

Murdoch's most severe critics agree that the period beginning with *A Severed Head* (1961) is problematic. Although that satire was popular for "its worst features," Dipple thinks, its picture of society is dreadfully harsh. Working toward an end product that is funny, even dazzling, the author reveals "a more pessimistic attitude towards her characters than the first four books suggest" (148). It left as its trademark a new type of character: "a long parade of self-satisfied, emotionally greedy and superficial, wealthy, middle-class, middle-aged women" (148). These characters "adorn their activities with the products of their education," and these critiques of psychoanalysis and existentialism "point to a basic artificiality in the use of civilized devices" (149). Dipple admits, however, that *A Severed Head* is a "comic masterpiece . . . redolent of real evil" (150). It became a successful play, and Murdoch's critics suggest that she needed to be wary of her successes, which could have tempted her to move in the direction of a slick, superficial style.

Gordon, looking at form rather than at content, discovers more skill in this novel than Dipple does: it "begins to break new ground in connecting erotic adventure to power by way of the myth of Apollo and Marsyas" (125). Todd, on the other hand, finds that this "cunning comedy in a virtuoso manner" (49) "ushers in" a new period that he calls "the most problematic of her career" (46). With this new emphasis on sexual adventures of the wealthy bourgeoisie, embellished by heavy drinking, fetishistic clothes, and abortion, Murdoch travels far afield from her stated goals (46). According to Todd, some critics saw in its urbanity parallels to E. M. Forster. What is important to Todd, however, is that the protagonist, Martin, has to reenact his past unawareness, as do earlier and later protagonists such as Michael Meade, Hilary Burde, and Charles Arrowby. Perhaps critics sometimes fail to search for Murdoch's goals: perhaps she enjoyed using old genres to critique contemporary behavior.

An Unofficial Rose (1962) broadens this issue by using shifting centers of consciousness to tell a story of obsessional actions that generations repeat, unaware of the pattern. It is also, according to Dipple, "the first clear example of a fairly honorable defeat" of good by evil (150) — a theme destined to become Murdoch's major one. Dipple laments that this novel could have been excellent but is "defeated by its ultimately over-extended formal contrast between the demonic and angelic, evil and good, would-be artist and saint, amorality and morality, form and formlessness" (150). The simplistic binary pairing destroys what will, later in Murdoch's oeuvre, become complex paradox. Dipple finds the plot disappointing, the defeat of good by human error, contingency, and evil "not as interesting as it might be because . . . Ann, the protagonist, is too pallid to carry her central role" (150). Todd, on the other hand, insists that the novel is "a formally very beautiful work with a number of contingent graces which tend to mask the form, so that the reader's overall response is one of subdued, aesthetic pleasure at the blend" (50).

A problem that links this novel to *The Flight from the Enchanter* is that "the chain of unrequited affections, for instance, seems here, as implicitly in *A Severed Head,* almost willfully self-parodic. The 'symbolic' potential of events and objects is now so strong as to make it hard for a reader to accept unreservedly the notion that such potential is bestowed by the characters alone: the novelist is evidently playing a part too" (50). Todd's emphasis on Murdoch's willful self-parody is significant: why would he not want her to be self-parodic? Can a self-parodic stance not contribute to Murdoch's moral investigation? She was a comic writer who was comfortable parodying herself and was humble enough to laugh at such play. The important issue is how much power Murdoch relinquishes to the characters in the novels.

Todd points out that later, in *The Nice and the Good*, the exercise of power is "more closely related to obligations to society" (51), whereas in *A Severed Head* it depends heavily on wealth. He suggests that Murdoch is lucky to escape her Jamesian seduction during this period by substituting a Shakespearian form (53).

According to Todd, the gothic novels, such as *The Unicorn* and *The Italian Girl*, are relentlessly dark and "negatively viewed even by Murdoch's sympathetic critics" (54). Part of the negativity may come from the questionable realism: "It remains hard to see how much of the action in these novels, and in *The Red and the Green* and *The Time of the Angels*, can be credited, even in terms of the fantasy-realistic fiction Murdoch claims to write. All four novels deal with peculiarly self-destructive families, and incest comes to be seen almost as a way of conveying internecine destructiveness and the raw nerve-endings of suffering" (54). Perhaps in the future less traditional critics can mine these novelistic strategies with more empathy. Because many critics think that the gothic novels veer off from Murdoch's realistic path, this study will examine some of them in more detail as marking a trend toward postmodernist fiction.

Murdoch's Gothic Novels

Among the gothic novels, critics analyze *The Unicorn* (1963) most thoroughly. Baldanza says that it plays with all the gothic clichés: "sexual feudalism, castles perilous, Courtly Love, *la belle dame sans merci*, sleeping beauty . . . , Homosexuality, Lesbianism, incest, suicide, and several violent murders" (106). For the themes and atmosphere, Murdoch has written that she is indebted to the Brontë sisters and Sheridan Le Fanu. Dipple finds that Murdoch's masterful blending of "the oppressive echoes from the tradition . . . the claustrophobic atmosphere of the alien landscape [Ireland] . . . [and] Hannah Crean-Smith's imprisonment, cloy and sicken the spirit — as indeed they are meant to do" (151). Although an outstanding achievement among the first novels, this text juxtaposes storytelling and magic in a way that is distressing to Dipple. She describes it as an "elegantly wrought, significantly artificial gothic novel with a tight endgame closure which skims the surfaces of tragedy" (265). For her, the novel explores magic, and, while it is only vaguely cognizant of the morality of its characters, "its real subject is the sources of magic in the human mind and that magic's translation into action once a context has been provided for it" (266). She says that while the novel "is a good book which diagnoses the confusions and desires of the spiritual life, . . . *The Sea, The Sea* [1978] explores the same theme in a more complex way" and has an "apparently hidden centre" (266). The implication that *The Unicorn* demands less work on the reader's part is somewhat humorous, in that *The Unicorn* is the only novel about which two complete books of criticism have been written. (In arguing that Byatt still has the best analysis of *The Unicorn*, Dipple earns the harsh criticism of Guy Backus.) Dipple calls the novel a psychomachia; traditionally, the unicorn is "a Christ hunted by mankind who cannot begin to understand their motives in doing so, and then suffering in captivity as a human soul" (267). Hannah serves as a Christ image, but she is, equally, a realistic character who "functions as an ordinary sinful human being, and one whose self-images, including that of a godly Christ identification, are as much a fiction as are the many ways the other characters try to apprehend her" (267).

The Italian Girl (1964) is like *The Unicorn* in "tone, ideology and direction" (152), but it remains Murdoch's major failure as a novel. Referring to it as an "unintentional parody of its author's usual amusement and expertise in plot turns," Dipple explains that its weakness is that it is "out of place in Murdoch's development"; she suggests that it is a recycled early attempt at novel writing (152). It became a play in 1967, when Murdoch collaborated with James Saunders. Todd comments that there is "almost universal agreement among Murdoch's critics" that the dramatic adaptation is more successful than the novel (57).

Dipple and Todd also agree that the historical novel focusing on the week prior to the Irish Easter Rebellion of 1916, *The Red and the Green* (1965), is carefully researched. Dipple discovers a more expansive world in this novel than in *The Italian Girl*. She says that although the novel has possibilities, "the whole thematic issue stumbles before the automatic romanticizing date of the 1916 uprising, and one is left with simply another version of that famous event, ingeniously fitted to the larger Murdochian mode" (153). The writer who best evaluates this novel is Donna Gerstenberger, who in her seventy-nine-page monograph *Iris Murdoch* (1975) finds Murdoch approaching the subject of Ireland "with a good deal of self-conscious ambivalence" (51). For whatever reason, Murdoch distances herself with various strategies: the "Irish Question" is always a riddle with no expected answer, "the *Epilogue* takes place in England in 1938," and the novel never achieves "the feeling and the involvement Yeats embodies in the poem," i.e., in "Easter 1916" (51). Gerstenberger says that Murdoch, with scrupulous thoroughness, gives an academic analysis of the Easter Rebellion, examining it from every possible angle. In doing so, however, she fails to capture emotion, either her own or the characters'. Gerstenberger suggests that Murdoch's attempt to be objective allows many views to struggle dialogically but that this juggling act does not capture the reader's imagination. Furthermore, she agrees with Rabinovitz, who criticizes the novel for its unrealized setting; for Gerstenberger, the setting fails because the author does not allow herself to reveal any of her own emotions about the Irish issue (32).

Assuming that Murdoch might have used the Yeats poem as a model, Gerstenberger finds the epilogue problematic. She is surprised by Murdoch's presentation of Frances Bellman's overstatement of the Irish cause at the end. The author has not prepared the reader for the Romanticism of the final voice, and, of course, the novel cannot work like Yeats's poem, with a survivor presenting the coda. Gerstenberger would remove the epilogue: "it is not like Murdoch as a novelist to accept romanticized absolutes about historical events or to see value in such judgments" (68). The novel's metaphors alone mitigate against a romanticized conclusion. Tending to oversimplify the thematic *Red* and *Green* of the title, readers underestimate the title's complex connotations. Gerstenberger's reading demonstrates how packed these words are with connotations far beyond the political references to the histories of the English and the Irish: notably, the greenness of the characters in their search for the truth and the bloody redness of the sacrifices they make. Gerstenberger suggests that if one reads *The Red and the Green* in context with Murdoch's other novels, one might find that the author is working out some blend of naturalism and allegory (61).

Another of the claustrophobic, near-gothic novels, *The Time of the Angels,* is, for Dipple, "a novel in the process of breaking away from the aggressively stylized patterns that Murdoch gave full rein to for some time after her fourth novel" (155). Fearsome characters penetrate the psyches of readers, convincing them that evil exists. In this novel Murdoch finds the "flawless ability" to convey the "devouring of Carel Fisher's spirit by darkness" without tricks (154). From this novel onward Murdoch was "no longer controlled by the fecundity and charm of her devices" (155). Conradi emphasizes the significance of the imagery, referring to the rector's first name, Carel, as a "cloistered enclosure," calling to mind other unstable cloisters such as Imber Court in *The Bell* and Gaze Castle in *The Unicorn.* The rector's second name alludes, of course, to the impotent Fisher King, made famous in T. S. Eliot's *The Waste Land.* Conradi celebrates the novel as a black farce, juxtaposing spiritual and secular worlds that compete to survive in the aftermath of the Second World War and the bombing of London (132). One recognizes Murdoch's abiding interest in examining how the inner life of a naturally spiritual creature can survive without a God and how the breaking apart of an old, stable world can loose psychological forces that destroy Christian values. In this novel she focuses on what such changes have wrought on the young: is their inheritance to be amorality? Conradi is awed by Murdoch's genius in making beautiful poetry out of the ugly and ordinary thinginess of London life. He comments on the ways in which all the characters seem to be bachelors who cater for themselves. This point and his discussions of enclosing space must have been an inspiration to Deborah Johnson when she wrote her 1987 book on gender issues in Murdoch's novels. These issues are part of this study's chapter on postmodernist strategies in Murdoch's fiction.

The Critical Success of *The Nice and the Good*

Dipple finds that after a long period of testing and trying Murdoch's talents came together in *The Nice and the Good* (1968). She ranks it as excellent because Murdoch achieves her stated aim of removing herself from her work; Murdoch often talked about striving to achieve negative capability, or allowing the characters freedom from authorial power. But she was never an autobiographical writer; therefore, Dipple is apparently suggesting that Murdoch was dissatisfied with earlier novels because she controlled her patterns more than she had intended. Dipple says that Murdoch's growth "demanded both ideological and technical achievements, and one can claim that Murdoch at her weakest, during her second early period [i.e., 1961 to 1966], was partially writing her excesses out of her system. . . . Murdoch's mature novels exude a greater aura of clarity than the earlier ones, but are harder to perceive adequately" (156). These novels are unapproachable; knowledge of Murdoch, her philosophy, or her other novels does not help one to interpret them: "character and action have found a free technical medium in which simplicity and pattern are generally elusive for most readers" (156). Dipple makes clear that as Murdoch approaches the goal of negative capability, she creates novels that are richer and more difficult to interpret.

   Not only the aim of selflessness but also the submersion of ideas into the particulars of the story are obvious in *The Nice and the Good*. Dipple thinks that Murdoch has achieved a minor miracle here. The mystery of human life is the subject of the realist artist, and no realist can perform the miracle required — the bland realism of description must replace the realism of assessment where the novel is "a forum for airing moral ideas" (156). Murdoch has at least accomplished such an airing: "her strong moral achievements are well submerged in the natural realistic body of her major novels" (156). In this novel Murdoch's influences, such as Plato, Simone Weil, and Freud, do not hold sway: the characters figure out what the Good is "in the real world without bookish help" (157). Dipple quotes Murdoch's own description of this change: the novelist told W. K. Rose in a 1968 interview that in her early novels her characters were "arguing against easy existential definitions of freedom"; by the late 1960s, however, they were concerned about love.

> I think [freedom] might have been [my main subject] in the past. No, I think love is my subject. I have very mixed feelings about the concept of freedom now. This is partly a philosophical development. I once was a kind of existentialist and now I am a kind of platonist. What I am concerned about really is love, but this sounds very grandiose. One is always telling a story, making jokes, and so on. I think the novel is a comic form. (quoted, 158)

Dipple interprets Murdoch as proposing that the job of the novel is to tell stories and make jokes, while conveying details realistically: the genre is "characterized by irony — that immeasurable and puzzling gap between the fictional, with its attendant flimsiness and falseness, and the true, characterized by starkness and almost unendurable spiritual discipline" (158–59). For Dipple, this novel is Murdoch's first that fleshes out the idea of the Good, the first in which Murdoch finds her subject and establishes her style (168).

Creating a Shifting Perspective

Dipple sums up by saying that characters in Murdoch's early novels struggled against "early existential definitions of freedom"; during this phase the characters' struggles are not "mere exercises" but "part of a felt and total sense of the characters as personalities living through cogitations" (158). Moreover, at this point in her career Murdoch's ideas and her sympathy for her characters had become one, and her "overall strength and conviction of authority" emerged (158). Her theme of "the untraversable distance between the nice and the good" (165), although balanced by "a brittle gaiety" (166) at the end of the novel, initiates the author's serious exploration of death. Although realism is Murdoch's major stylistic mode, Dipple finds *The Nice and the Good* working hard and successfully on subtle formal strategies. She notes the movement of the narrative voice from character to character, creating "shifting perspective" (157). Often, Murdoch analyzes the same scene from many different points of view, playing one against the other.

Gordon agrees with Byatt and Dipple that this text is "the first novel of a new period; Conradi prefers to date this inception only a little later, with *A Fairly Honourable Defeat* (1970)" (138). Gordon and others find that the subsequent novels are longer, looser, less controlled, and more various and that they reveal more reflection by, and more profound ordeals for, the characters. *The Nice and the Good* begins what Gordon labels "The Major Phase" because it treats demonization in a less conventional way: "After 1968, the demonic is associated with the protagonist's burden of remorse or obsession carried over from the past and posing a moral danger in the present" (139). His one caveat about the later novels is that they do not explore the cultural phenomena of the twentieth century, even though they use such phenomena as subject matter. Instead, novels about Marxism and the Holocaust, subjects with which Murdoch was personally familiar, examine "the fate of religion in the contemporary world and, specifically, the emergence of a spiritual figure who can provide what the age requires" (172). These novels return to the mysterious enchanter figure instead of learning from "the middle novels[,] whose protagonists struggle with *inner* demons" (172).

One way to dodge Gordon's criticism about the pervasiveness of the enchanter figure is to emphasize Murdoch's more clearly defined demand for imperfection in her novels. In *The Nice and the Good* the Good, "known primarily by its unreachable distance from the all too flawed characters," overpowers those who apprehend it but are unable to control themselves (Dipple, 167). To be able to apprehend good, the quester must have reached extreme circumstances. At this point Dipple analyzes Murdoch's pessimism, insisting that "realism is notoriously connected to pessimism" (168) — a link that also applies to comedy.

Insofar as *The Nice and the Good* represents an advance in depicting goodness, Dipple raises the question whether the next novel, *Bruno's Dream* (1969), demonstrates "any significant moral developments in the characters" (168). The answer is that Murdoch juxtaposes a group of characters around a dying man, Bruno, and an artist figure, Miles, a mediocre man who cannot convey the truth satisfactorily. Bruno's dying is a realistic diagnosis of a human being's perceiving "what life and death are" (168); rather than "see[ing] reality (nature)," other characters in the novel see only their own perceptions of it (172). Murdoch contrasts Miles with more dynamic characters, among whom Dipple appraises Danby and Bruno as "extraordinary productions. Their humility before the substance of the unpredictable real world, present and past, is a quality they share in different degrees, but Murdoch's conception of them goes beyond their moral qualities. Although Miles's awfulness is also extremely well done, in Danby and Bruno Murdoch takes a major stride forward in character projection" (171). Dipple says that this novel achieves a free realism that Murdoch has not totally attained previously. In addition, she says that Murdoch uses Miles's demonic qualities as an ironic teaching device to belittle the artist. Dipple sees *Bruno's Dream* as more significant than do other critics, especially Cheryl Bove, whose *Understanding Iris Murdoch* does not categorize it as a major novel.[1]

A Commitment to Grim Realism?

Like *Bruno's Dream*, Murdoch's next novel, *A Fairly Honourable Defeat* (1970), is, according to Dipple, committed to "grim realism" (181): few characters can be happy in a real world, a theme Murdoch probes throughout her career. Both this novel and *An Accidental Man* (1971) examine human unhappiness by acknowledging a "formal demonism" and by "analyzing the evil of selfish mediocrity" — the assertion in *Bruno's Dream* "that people are too muddled to be demons" (181). In *A Fairly Honourable Defeat* the characters are not particularly bad but are victimized from the outside by a charmer. Dipple describes the allegory as a new kind of battle between a Christ figure, Tallis, and a Satan figure, Julius. The latter interferes in the lives of others: he "is surprised not only at Tallis's unimpressive demeanour, but at his embarrassed courtesy towards him, his humility and his messiness, and the result of this surprise is a new version of the Christ-Satan conflict. . . . Christ declines to fight or judge, so Satan has to go to him with his confession" (184). Tallis the good man is an illustration of negative power: because he is inactive and waits, the Satanic figure Julius fills the vacuum and rules the scene (185).

Dipple is specific about this novel's accomplishments, which have helped her weave Murdoch's growing aesthetic together. Her exegesis focuses on allegory, involving Christ and Satan and adding God the Father (Leonard) and the human soul (Morgan): "these . . . identifications are subservient to the transmitted sense of real personality in the characters. The resulting redefinitions nevertheless carry the points Murdoch wishes to make: evil is not absolute but desires to be stopped and judged by good; good is there but small, messy and impotent; mankind is hopelessly involved in selfishness; God is moribund; the life-giving power of the Holy Spirit is dead; Christianity is finished" (186). At the same time, Dipple insists that this system of ideas is of little importance to the casual reader, who will rightly absorb the novel not as allegory or mythology but as realism — a bourgeois commodity. Dipple, however, always apprehends that there are threads in a Murdoch novel that are not realistic, such as the character Julius, who dabbles in magic. Furthermore, Dipple uncovers, buried in Rupert and Julian's conversation about puppets, the "major cultural document," Plato's *Laws*, that lies behind the text and informs the reader that "the artist-magician-puppeteer," more powerful than a realistic character, exists to take advantage of the vulnerabilities of the other characters (186). The good characters are emptied of personality and are, therefore, examples of negative capability who might easily succumb. Furthermore, Dipple comments that *A Fairly Honourable Defeat* is Murdoch's most significantly titled novel: "a fairly honorouble defeat" names the conclusion in several novels, the first clear example of which is *An Unofficial Rose* of 1962 (150). No matter how much spiritual energy characters can muster, the final reality appears to be the repeated "defeat of good by evil" (150). Such an ending is central to tragedy.

In his realistic reading of Julius's holding court in a "South Kensington world," Conradi concentrates more than Dipple on the particulars of destruction and suffering. Morgan, a poor soul who needs strength, enjoys returning to her sister and brother-in-law because "they make her feel continuous" (166). Conradi explains that dismemberment is "a commonplace Neoplatonic symbol of the fall into multiplicity" (167). Several characters are chastised because in their vanity they do not understand that a lack of "self-preservation" makes them vulnerable to demons. Conradi argues that the extreme afflictions in the lives of Tallis and Julius — such as a maniacal killer raping and murdering Tallis's sister, and Julius's living through the war in the Belsen concentration camp — come from Murdoch's interest in Simone Weil, who experienced "the defeat of good by evil" (161). The belief that Conradi attributes to Weil, that "extreme affliction is passed on by all but the saintly" (169), is at the heart of the novel.

Conradi examines "two lesser but still undismissible works" (210) in which he finds degrees of realism: *The Sacred and Profane Love Machine* (1974) and *Henry and Cato* (1976). Whereas the former plays with magic, the latter carries on the realistic tradition, diverging only in terms of psychological devices that one can consider postmodernist, such as inducing the kind of palpable terror in the reader that a John Hawkes novel can. Conradi says that "*Henry and Cato* takes the chiasmus that marks the end of *Bruno's Dream* — Lisa and Diana exchanging roles of nun and hetaera [or courtesan] — and also marks the last part of *The Sacred and Profane Love Machine*, with Emily [mistress] and Harriet [wife] exchanging roles inside and outside society — and makes it into the central device of the plot" (220). Conradi's proof is that whereas Henry begins as a man who rejects material happiness, he eventually opts for it; and Cato, a Catholic priest, who begins the novel thinking himself unhappy, loses his faith, betrays his sister, and kills his love before he realizes that he had been well off. Henry and Cato "are romantics and puritans who dramatise their predicaments in such a way as to narrow their vision" (223).

A Quasi-magical Context

Henry and Cato, The Sacred and Profane Love Machine, and *A Fairly Honourable Defeat* are generally realistic, but Harriet in the second and Rupert in the third are "hurt beyond help by too much decentring" (108). Because Murdoch writes about characters who plunge into "the world's messiness and the indeterminacy of consciousness," she requires the freedom of psychological strategies (109). Conradi says that "not everyone will become what the Tibetan sage Milarepa termed a 'bride of desolation,' living in direct contact with the world's power and beauty and horror, unmediated by the defences of the ego" (108), but that is what happens to Harriet and Rupert. Being denuded by beauty or horror is too much for a human being to live with. Harriet certainly experiences too much pain when everyone deserts her: her husband, her friend Monty, Edgar, the children, and even a fictional fantasy character. Conradi refers again to Weil, who argues that there are "forms of suffering so intense that they . . . repel the sympathy of the onlooker" (214). Many readers experience that repulsion in this novel. Conradi's response to those who find Harriet's death arbitrary is that her husband wishes her dead and that Emily, the mistress, prays for her to die. That "thoughts are both dangerous and consequential is one of the messages shared by all the books" (216). Conradi's point is that Murdoch carefully creates an environment that eventually assents to "a quasi-magical context in which bad thoughts cause accidents" (216).

For Dipple it is significant that what appears to be the main structure of *The Sacred and Profane Love Machine* is only appearance. The world of the novel seems to rotate about the psychiatrist Blaise Gavender and the two families he creates, one with his wife and one with his mistress. The reader is, however, according to Dipple, more drawn to and empathetic with Montague Small. The outward structure hides an internal rhythm that Monty dominates. One of Murdoch's strategies in the novel is the doubling of the characters; another involves dreams, hauntings, and eerie phenomena. Dipple explains that Murdoch is "expanding perception and depicting the more awesome and terrifying reaches of the mind" (229).

Murdoch as Experimentalist

Admittedly, novelists have applied psychological strategies to their texts from the beginning of the development of the novel without being categorized as experimentalists, let alone as postmodernists. But Murdoch's fourteenth novel, *An Accidental Man* (1971), cannot escape the label. Some critics prefer to think of it as a fluke; few critics besides Dipple and Heusel appreciate its excellence. In it Murdoch continues to diagnose the problems of selfishness and fantasy by releasing the accidental man Austin Gibson Grey from authorial control, to "trick the reader into believing in the absolute and free realism of his being" (Dipple, 199). Accident prone, out of control, and unconscious of making avoidable mistakes, Austin is convincing as an embodiment of accidentalness. Dipple says that the ironic strategy for Murdoch was to focus her attention to the peripheries of the novel and to "boldly over-us[e] formal devices" (199). Here is a novel in which Murdoch says she chose to withdraw as a presence, convincing Heusel that such a strategy was actually more pervasive in other novels, as well, than has heretofore been examined. Two strategies that Murdoch employs more often in her later and her better novels are magic realism and decentering.

Murdoch's Time of Great Flowering

Perhaps Murdoch conquered the realist dilemma to her satisfaction in the late 1960s. Whether her major creative phase began in 1968, as Byatt, Dipple, and Gordon would have it, or whether her time of "great flowering"[2] occurred in the 1970s, as Conradi proposes, undoubtedly her texts bloomed. Critics may never be able to account for this qualitative flowering, but the quantitative changes become obvious when the length runs sometimes to five hundred-plus pages. The new dimension that Murdoch's looser, more open novels took on pleased literary critics, but journalistic critics most often found her bizarre antics vexing. For them, the books became stranger and stranger as she began to include more magic and other such postmodernist strategies. Some critics concluded that she was simply engaging with a postmodernist world. At this time the realistic qualities of the mature novels begin to blend with new postmodernist qualities, the seeds of which had always been present in her fiction.

This study does not propose that all the novels preceding *An Accidental Man* are realistic and that all novels following it are postmodernist; instead, it suggests that Murdoch's experimentation does not follow a straight path but surfaces when her novels work to solve problems she has set herself. The division here is neither chronological nor arbitrary but practical. The half dozen novels most discussed in terms of their experimentation and most often classified as postmodernist, which flesh out the last chapter of this study, sound the depths of Murdoch's creativity and test the creativity of her critics.

Notes

[1] Cheryl Bove divides Murdoch's novels into four periods: "Early Major Works (1954–1962)," "Major Works of the Middle Period (1968–1973)," "Later Major Works (1978–1980)," and "Latest Works (1983–1989)." She discusses what she considers lesser works in the chapter "Other Novels and Plays," in which she includes *The Sandcastle, A Severed Head, The Red and the Green, An Accidental Man, The Sacred and Profane love Machine, A Word Child,* and *Henry and Cato,* and in the chapter "The Gothic," in which she includes *The Flight from the Enchanter, The Unicorn, The Italian Girl, The Time of the Angels,* and *Bruno's Dream* (133–89).

[2] Often, one critic's choice of Murdoch's best novel is a text that another critic ignores. John J. Burke says that *The Sacred and Profane Love Machine* (1974) and *The Philosopher's Pupil* (1983) are "among the best of her work, and I agree with almost everyone about the merits of *The Black Prince* (1973)." Not agreeing that the 1960s were "the doldrums" for Murdoch's writing, he praises *The Unicorn* as "an exceptional piece of work." He thinks that "the real turning point in Murdoch's career" is *The Bell* (494). For Harold Bloom in *Iris Murdoch,* on the other hand, her best are *The Good Apprentice* (1985), *The Black Prince* (1973), *Bruno's Dream* (1969), and *A Word Child* (1975). Bove lists the last two among "Other Novels and Plays."

Works Cited

Baldanza, Frank. *Iris Murdoch.* New York: Twayne, 1974.

Bloom, Harold. Introduction to *Iris Murdoch: Modern Critical Views.* Ed. Bloom. New York: Chelsea House, 1986. 1–7.

Bove, Cheryl. *Understanding Iris Murdoch.* Columbia: U of South Carolina P, 1993.

Burke, John J. "Canonizing Iris Murdoch." *Studies in the Novel* 19.4 (Winter 1987): 486–94.

Conradi, Peter. *Iris Murdoch: The Saint and the Artist.* New York: St. Martin's, 1986; rpt. 1989.

Dipple, Elizabeth. *Iris Murdoch: Work for the Spirit*. Chicago: U of Chicago P, 1982.

Edwards, James C. *Ethics without Philosophy: Wittgenstein and the Moral Life*. Gainesville: UP of Florida, 1982.

Gerstenberger, Donna. *Iris Murdoch*. Lewisburg PA and London: Bucknell UP, 1975.

Gordon, David J. *Iris Murdoch's Fables of Unselfing*. Columbia and London: U of Missouri P, 1995.

Heusel, Barbara. *Patterned Aimlessness: Iris Murdoch's Novels of the 1970s and 1980s*. Athens: U of Georgia P, 1995.

Murdoch, Iris. "Against Dryness: A Polemical Sketch." *Encounter* 16 (1961): 16–20. Rpt. in *Iris Murdoch*. Ed. Bloom. 9–16.

———. *A Fairly Honourable Defeat*. New York: Viking, 1970.

———. *The Fire and the Sun: Why Plato Banished the Artists*. Oxford: Oxford UP, 1977.

———. "The Sublime and the Beautiful Revisited," *Yale Review* 49 (December 1960): 247–71.

Todd, Richard. *Iris Murdoch*. London and New York: Methuen. 1984.

Tucker, Lindsey. Introduction to *Critical Essays on Iris Murdoch*. Ed. Tucker. New York: G. K. Hall, 1992. 1–16.

6: Postmodernist Experimentation

CRITICS WHO USE MURDOCH'S REALISM, or traditionalism, as an easy way to dismiss her lasting artistic contribution to twentieth-century literature fail to recognize that each novel is for her an experiment, a way to test shifting views of reality. Her statements about her desire to write like some nineteenth-century writers did not hinder her from experimenting throughout her career to see how the seventeenth-, eighteenth-, or nineteenth-century worlds of the novel would look and work in the twentieth century and what the implications of such an experiment would be. As Peter Conradi explains her experimenting: she "combines . . . inner and outer visions [of human inner wildness] in a way that looks traditional, yet properly disturbs us too" (*Iris Murdoch: The Saint and the Artist*, 291). Perpetually inventing strategies and scrupulously weighing them, Murdoch worked to achieve dynamic narratives that will continue to prod her readers into thought.

The Strategy of Defamiliarization

One method Murdoch's novels use to coax readers further away from personal fantasy and to provide a clearer picture of reality is defamiliarization. Perhaps more than any other critic, Elizabeth Dipple illustrates that Murdoch's novels participate in what Viktor Shklovsky described as "baring the device," thereby revealing that art "is not transparent but opaque . . . a willed simulacrum" (Harmon and Holman, 51). Such estrangement, called *ostranenie* by Shklovsky and his fellow Russian formalists, is a strategy for demonstrating that "art does not strive . . . for verisimilitude" but continues "to remind us that it *is* art" (Harmon and Holman, 144). Because for this formalist "as perception becomes habitual, it becomes automatic" (Shklovsky, 58), the "function of literary language" is "to break up predictable patterns — of sound, grammar, plot — by means of conspicuous defamiliarization . . . that restores freshness and vitality to language" (Harmon and Holman, 222). Indeed, Murdoch theorizes in *Sartre, Romantic Rationalist* that "we can no longer take language for granted as a medium of communication. Its transparency has gone. We are like people who for a long time looked out of a window without noticing the glass — and then one day began to notice this too" (26). She goes so far as to empathize with the modernists' dilemma, "the need to work within a desiccated language" (Heusel, *Patterned Aimlessness*, 86). Drawn to Sartre because he wanted "to find a middle way (a third force) between the ossification of language and its descent into the senseless" (*Sartre: Romantic Rationalist*, 36), Murdoch criticizes his inability to understand that confronting the strangeness of the other, or alterity, might be progress toward that end and is certainly a necessary ingredient in the novel.

Murdoch has the protagonist of *The Black Prince* label as "switching gestalt" one of her techniques for making what is familiar suddenly seem new (e.g., Bradley Pearson misinterprets Julian Baffin to be a Hindu priest and pieces of a love letter to be flower petals). Perhaps mistakenly, Dipple thinks that Murdoch distrusts "her own forms," that she employs strategies to turn aside "audience expectation" and plunge "the reader into an alien atmosphere which inclines to frustrate and disappoint"; she says that by doing so, Murdoch expands "the accepted frame of the traditional novel," creating strategies that "run counter to the tale-spinning talents which constitute fiction's magic" (*Iris Murdoch: Work for the Spirit*, 265). Murdoch undoubtedly has many other reasons for turning aside audience expectation, such as breaking boundaries of form and content, creating allusiveness, and multilayering.

Dipple is unique as a critic, however, in being able to demonstrate that Murdoch works "to convince the reader that what is most contrived in her work, most authorially controlled and most magical, contributes to a larger function" (265). To illustrate, Dipple discusses *The Unicorn* and *The Sea, The Sea* in a chapter of *Iris Murdoch: Work for the Spirit* titled "The Dangerous Road," echoing Murdoch's statement on a BBC radio program in 1978 that "the road to goodness is a dangerous road" (quoted, 274). She argues that each novel encourages the reader to walk that road — to become a detective and to search and unearth the rich center. For her such an occupation is *active* reading. Each reader is learning how to live in a new world; while some want to know the world to its very roots, or radically, others do not.

A Surplus of Sense, Action, and Meaning

It might surprise some that Murdoch has, in discussing the dangerous road, preempted an end-of-the-century jeremiad for the kind of art that dares defy the status quo, "works that stretch into subtler vistas when you thought they'd settled . . . works with enough intertwining, self-referential, neural complexity to make you feel both lost and found"

(Fulton, 47). A passage in Alice Fulton's essay in *The Nation*, "A Poetry of Inconvenient Knowledge," refers to Gary Lee Stonum's analysis of the poetry of Emily Dickinson, but this description of a reading experience could as easily have referred to Murdoch's novels: "to read all of Dickinson's poems is 'to risk the vertigo characterizing the reader's sublime, a bewilderment in the face of some vast surfeit of meaning'"; Stonum describes the sublime as "an affective and effective power that draws attention but also eludes or even disrupts pleasing harmonies and intelligible schemes" (quoted in Fulton, 47). Fulton explains that "The sublime arises from a poetics of inclusivity and synthesis, of gorging, stuffing to capacity. Of muchness as a means to euphoria. Excess that transcends the natural. Extremes" (47). Murdoch's tale-spinning techniques include defying the status quo, disorienting the reader, focusing on extremes, and including just such a "muchness," which itself reflects the surplus of meaning that postmodern theorists say that all language produces. And as this study has repeatedly demonstrated, Murdoch's ubiquitous moral viewpoint spills over into everything she writes. Readers misunderstand her radical point of view and her radical literary agenda, as Dipple has explained it, precisely because, like Elias Canetti — one of the intellectual giants with whom Murdoch jousts and one whom Fulton cites — Murdoch stands against her time, creating a rich, imaginative realm, a place many artists lack the courage and freedom to enter. Critics have often criticized her for being old-fashioned, because they do not understand why she refused to write as other contemporary writers, who reject character and plot or, at the least, see them differently from the ways the nineteenth-century novelists did. Dipple's answer to these critics is that Murdoch's oeuvre is an active confrontation of the traditional with the experimental, "an unruffled demonstration of what fiction can actually do now as opposed to how it functioned in the past, how it can be said to operate, and what its limitations and necessary ironies are" (*The Unresolvable Plot*, 189).

In regard to including a "muchness," David J. Gordon quotes Peter Conradi as observing about Murdoch's novels: "There is always more event, story, incident than the idea-play can use up" (2). Conradi explains that "this surplus of sense and action over meaning" creates the baffling aura of the novels (*Iris Murdoch: The Saint and the Artist*, 31). Moreover, Murdoch captures in a passage in *Nuns and Soldiers* her penchant for muchness: referring to novels she is reading, Anne Cavidge declares that they are "marvelous, but too much" (quoted in *Iris Murdoch: The Saint and the Artist*, 105). Conradi argues that Murdoch is disagreeing with Sartre's "horror of the contingent": the contingent is for her the "'too much' which characterises novels and makes

them . . . exemplary art-forms" (105). In other words, novels are vehi-
cles for muchness. Conradi goes on to analyze this muchness in relationship to Kant's sublime. Gordon agrees with Dipple that Murdoch's
project is radical, saying that Murdoch uses her novels to test, experiment, and create effects. In his discussion of unselfing as it relates to
masochism and Simone Weil he says, "Murdoch is primarily testing the
idea's fictional possibilities rather than asserting it as doctrine"; she is
arguing that "the danger of egoism . . . [is] highest [in] religion, love,
and art" (9). To emphasize muchness in the novels, he quotes Howard
Moss: "Part of the effect of these books is their wild extensiveness, their
overexpansion, as if a mind too inventive to stop, and imagination too
replete with images to let go, an intelligence that still has something
further to say on the subject could not quite hear the end of the score,
that resounding final chord that would let the whole tray of wonders
slide off her lap" (9).

Since the reviews of her first novel, critics have disagreed about
Murdoch's theoretical leanings and the way they impinge on her stories. Her existentialist interest in authors such as Samuel Beckett and
Raymond Queneau, "both heirs of the Existentialist school of the Absurd" (Baldanza, 31), led critics to question her interest in the absurd.
Like Byatt, Baldanza refers to these authors as sources for *Under the
Net*. An awareness of the absurdist view of reality is present there and in
all of Murdoch's subsequent novels. As early as 1966 Wolfe suggested
the difficult task for the author and the reader: "Iris Murdoch sees no
reason for subscribing to a human-centered interpretation of reality
[which she analyzes in *Sartre, Romantic Rationalist*]; her novels bristle
with events that defy both rational explanation and human volition"
(210). Because Murdoch exposes her readers to the contingent, she se-
cures the link between the inside self and the outside world, not ignoring one or the other, and sensitizes readers to the responsibility of
allying one's "fragmentary, inchoate sensibilities with the intractable,
discontinuous world he inhabits. The superimposition of one kind of
eccentricity or disorder upon another must be enacted without any
items or aids except the individual's understanding of himself as a social
being" (210).

The Charge of Un-realism

Even Conradi, who is less than enthusiastic about postmodernist theoretical investigations into literature, allows that Murdoch has been influenced heavily by Fyodor Dostoevsky, in whose texts "All is
permitted" (*Iris Murdoch: The Saint and the Artist*, 91). Here Conradi

is referring to morality in *A Severed Head*, but elsewhere he says that both Murdoch and Dostoevsky go far beyond what is traditionally considered realism. In his list of similarities between Murdoch's writing and Dostoevsky's, Conradi finds some characteristics that one would associate with postmodernism, although he does not identify them as such. He does argue, however, that "both writers defend their work against the charge of 'un-realism' and do so in the name of a higher or deeper realism, arguing that real life is much odder and more fantastic than we pretend, more kin to the Gothic conventions they set to work in their books" (291). In Murdoch and Dostoevsky readers relish "extremes of arbitrary coincidence, melodramatic manipulation of the plot, sensational temporal compression. . . . Both utilise man-god superheroes, or villains, who herald a new age of terrors and argue that 'All is permitted,' and both give their devils the best tunes, testing out their own best pieties to [the] breaking-point, and leaving the reader to experience the book in a welcome yet disturbing freedom" (291–92). Conradi makes the point that Murdoch's writing is beyond realism, but he does not name her strategy.

Because Murdoch's world of the novel is so various and because many of her devoted critics see her project as radical or revolutionary, a reader is wise to discover all means possible to explore that world. Dipple insists that Murdoch's "impulse is dialogic" (*The Unresolvable Plot*, 187). Her application of many and various theories to Murdoch's novels demonstrates her desire to open up Murdoch's texts to new kinds of scrutiny. In a paper delivered in 1994 Dipple is optimistic about the future of literary study, because so much "beneficial criticism" exists ("The Green Knight and Other Vagaries of the Spirit," 139). In celebrating Murdoch's infinite variety, Dipple applies to Murdoch's novels not only the criteria Bakhtin uses for Dostoevsky but also such disparate techniques as those of Shakespeare, Venetian Ovidian painters, and *mise-en-abyme*. In a discussion of Bakhtin and Murdoch, Dipple mentions Caryl Emerson's concern with "the one problem Bakhtin's work on Dostoevsky fails to confront" and says that authors such as Murdoch need to work on issues inherent in the dialogic or polyphonic novel that Bakhtin never tackled: "by the very demands of its ambition, [the polyphonic novel] defies unification, and is therefore always formally troubled" (*The Unresolvable Plot*, 187). For Dipple, critics are professionally bound to consider all theoretical perspectives. The health of Murdoch criticism is best served by critics who are willing to search out and find new optics through which to examine her storytelling brilliance. Murdoch's novels deserve the attention of all critical lenses.

Granted, as Conradi proposes, Murdoch's many authorial strategies have precedents throughout literary history. Many that Murdoch uses overlap with others that one can call traditional — except, that is, the gender-based experiments. Many of her techniques that might seem radical enough to be postmodernist coincide precisely with devices she had been using all along as a realist, devices that, indeed, had worked for Laurence Sterne two centuries earlier; in the second half of the twentieth century Murdoch used them in her own way, in her own combinations, with her own flair, and for whatever purposes, to create her radical vision. The critic's role is to continue to speculate about them.

This chapter focuses on critics who explore and celebrate the innovation of Murdoch's experimentation and demonstrate its significance at the end of the millennium, unearthing vital ideas that other critics have ignored. These professional readers trace an increasing emphasis on experimentation in the novels of the 1980s. Murdoch's strategies have commonalities with those characteristics first attributed to postmodern writing: indeterminacy, contingency, irony, deferral of meaning, and subversion of positivism (Heusel, *Patterned Aimlessness*, 271 n. 5). Postmodernism eschews what it considers the elitist pomposity of high culture, just as the Bakhtinian model of literature celebrates the low form: the novel, the form that the partially educated traditionally read and that women, knowing no Greek and Latin, wrote. Murdoch is a postmodernist writer in her rejection of at least "three elements of High Modernism: its sophisticated formal experimentation, its elitism . . . , and its tragic sense of alienation, which she calls romantic solipsism" (271 n. 5). Unlike the high modernists, she finds no reason to jettison the palpable, fleshy characters readers of novels so love: "The death of the character need not follow the death of God" (89). It is the solipsism of the modernist that Murdoch cannot stomach; in her desire to shun elitism in both form and content, she is a postmodernist.

Murdoch's Polyphony

Murdoch clearly revels in experimentation as a part of novel writing: for her, literature must reflect changes in the culture. She distances herself from traditional conventions, such as the unified character and the narrator, which she uses as tropes; an example is N in *The Philosopher's Pupil*, a narrator who does not know everything that is going on. To capture contingency, she uses polyphony, many voices superimposed, and the carnivalesque, a spectacle without a stage; in *Nuns and Soldiers*, for example, she uses playful and indeterminate language games. The early pages of the novel, beginning with the word — and, perhaps, the mantra — *Wittgenstein,* are a "network of reverberating fragments of language that allows the novel to structure itself through accretion around the puzzlement of the . . . characters, suggesting a socially constructed self located within networks of discourse" (Heusel, *Patterned Aimlessness,* 58). Here she ignores the realistic criteria of authenticity, autonomy, and unity. Moreover, the first-person narrators of *A Word Child, The Black Prince,* and *The Sea, The Sea* — her word-children or wordsmiths — experience indeterminate outcomes, the reader having to organize and judge the ambivalent evidence.

Three of Dipple's texts lay out her groundbreaking insights into the artistic reasons for Murdoch's experimentation. In *Iris Murdoch: Work for the Spirit* (1982) she demonstrates that Murdoch, to critique and possibly dispel the reader's own fantasies, allows psychological stereotypes and magic realism — the supernatural, myth, dream, or fantasy — to invade a realistic story to make a serious comment on reality (e.g., a vision of Christ in *Nuns and Soldiers*). Readers might consider this goal didactic, but such a goal is not unusual for contemporary novelists. Moreover, as a Renaissance scholar Dipple is able to place the novels in a broader context than that which is imagined by most critics; she can, therefore, more easily recognize the implications of Murdoch's manipulation of older genres. In more recent texts, such as *The Unresolvable Plot* (1988) and articles (1995 and 1996, respectively) on *Jackson's Dilemma* and *The Green Knight,* Dipple proposes that Murdoch often uses novels to test out ways of looking at age-old literary and cultural problems in the twentieth century: that is, they are chronotopic (time-space) experiments. For example, in reworking Shakespearean comedy as another popular genre, the novel, Murdoch "parodies the technical demands of the genre: young lovers, star-crossed contingency leading to a deep peripeteia, comedic closure with lots of marriages . . . the brittle, imposed magic of it all" ("Fragments of Iris Murdoch's Vision," 6). By clothing her contemporary ideas in a variety of older forms, Murdoch achieves a complex intertextuality, various strands of which appeal to various kinds of readers. She has often named her models — Shakespeare, Tolstoy, Dostoevsky, George Eliot, and Marcel Proust — but no one before Dipple describes so specifically the way Murdoch tests out her ideas about humanity, psychology, and literature by clothing them in those earlier writers' forms. Murdoch uses all of these strategies to get the attention of, and thereby defamiliarize, the reader.

Taking a different tack — a feminist perspective — Deborah Johnson shows that Murdoch's reasons for such defamiliarizing are more clearly cultural than Dipple suggests. Johnson proposes in *Iris Murdoch*

(1987) that Murdoch presents in her novels deeper critiques of Western culture than critics had previously recognized. Using the "novel [as] her means of testing reality" (Metcalf, quoted in Johnson, 113), Murdoch interrogates the foundations on which Western culture has rested, including gender-based specular and goal-oriented assumptions (e.g., the stereotypes of males as subjects and females as objects and the Western search for perfection or progress). Furthermore, Murdoch uses "archaic worlds" in texts "simultaneously dramatizing and distancing [certain] feelings" (Johnson, 65) about which she seems both cautious and ambivalent; an example is masculinist assumptions in a patriarchal world, assumptions with which the reader — and, apparently, Dipple — might also be uncomfortable. For Johnson such authorial ambivalence is a split that reveals unvoiced possibilities in Murdoch's novels.

Taking a cue from these two critics, Barbara Stevens Heusel's *Patterned Aimlessness* (1995) explores the philosophical and psychological patterns underlying the world of these novels. Focusing on the narrative strategies encourages readers to search for ambiguity and indeterminacy. Moreover, Heusel argues that Murdoch "redefines . . . the boundaries of the novel of formal realism in order to address moral issues that are still unresolved" (x). Heusel also investigates Murdoch's position as author in relation to her characters, her expectations about the role of the reader as participant, her role as historian and intracultural and intertextual guide, and her postmodernist narrative effects. Discussions of these issues are invaluable to a readership ready to move beyond the surface of Murdoch's novels.

All of these critics have searched avidly for answers to the questions: To what extent does Murdoch experiment? What form do her experiments take? As late as 1982 Dipple dismissed Murdoch's tendency toward contradiction as "game playing," even as she acknowledged that such melodramatic devices demonstrate the "connection between the external other of Platonic reality and the traditional literary realism, and in spite of her tricks and confusing surfaces, this is where the life and the essentially experimental aspect of her fiction reside" (*Iris Murdoch: Work for the Spirit,* 5). If Dipple is right about this thrust of Murdoch's work, then these often melodramatic contradictions are necessary to her novels. Anyone who has read *The Fire and the Sun: Why Plato Banished the Poets* recognizes Dipple's point: Murdoch agrees with Plato that art, artifice, and artists are suspect, an unusual belief at the beginning of the twenty-first century, and this study of Plato associates the magic of storytelling with the misuse of "theories, ideology, and religious materials" (5). Dipple says that Murdoch incorporates such suspiciousness in *The Black Prince,* where she argues that paradox teases "all art into ironic and comedic frames" (5). Dipple shows how central such paradox is to Murdoch's craft: "on the one hand [her] oeuvre illustrates her commitment to reality and her practice of a firm defensible realism; on the other hand her games, tricks and ironies indicate her reluctant acquiescence to the artifice and unreality of the form" (5).

Dipple concludes *Iris Murdoch: Work for the Spirit* by focusing on this problem, using as an example the relationship of form and the concept of the Good in *Nuns and Soldiers.* Murdoch explores the various contradictory and comical ways the artist figure Tim Reede bumbles while searching for the right form. Murdoch puts the muddled artist, to say nothing of the reader, through his comic paces by using intricate imagery — "tight nets and meshes of form as opposed to rich, organic life which parallels but subtly alters her long-standing contrast between form and formlessness, or between lies and truth" (347). But Dipple's purpose here is to pinpoint Murdoch's generosity in giving her characters and readers a story "more productive of amelioration than . . . some of the heart-sickening novels of the recent past" (348). This novel closes with a demonstration of Murdoch's ability to give attention "to the entire panoply of people who clothe her novels"; this attentiveness is, for Dipple, "the compelling force which shapes the fictions" (348). She says that "the perpetual idea of a moral imperative as shown by the touchstone characters of the good serves as a reminder of what we half wish to be" (348).

Magical Literary Devices

The artist, however, has no choice about using what Plato called "magical devices" to enchant the reader and produce form. Murdoch has to practice this magic as all artists do, but "this is all a subservience to the patina and not reflective of the deep uses of fiction" (5). Analyzing where Murdoch fits into the tradition, Dipple places her closest to American experimentalists: "her nearest relatives are Saul Bellow, Isaac Bashevis Singer and, in a small way, British writers fundamentally interested in magic — John Fowles and Muriel Spark. The difference lies in the fact that for Murdoch, as for Singer, magic is a tool which must be used ironically and not believed in; the real area of significant fiction . . . is for Murdoch unmagical realism as it was practiced by Shakespeare and the great nineteenth-century novelists, and towards them she aims" (5–6). In contrast to Conradi, who sees magical devices as gothic, Dipple labels magic experimental.

Various levels of magic help Murdoch clothe realistic material in mystery to show the incomprehensibleness of life and the tendency of individuals to be deceived by their own illusions. In *The Unresolvable Plot: Reading Contemporary Fiction* (1988) Dipple catalogues her study of the magic devices that impinge on daily life. For example, in *The Philosopher's Pupil* (1983), she says, the inhabitants of the town accept that there are "'funny times' when people act strangely and nature erupts" (201). The atmosphere is similar to the kind Shakespeare creates in *King Lear* or *The Tempest:* characters refer to the signs of the zodiac and accept their predictions routinely. The magic signs multiply: mysterious incidents of flying saucers, an eight-year-old animist who sees some people as "doubles," and men "plagued by the language of the birds, a phenomenon of seventeenth-century language theory that contended that in a shamanist universe the original tongue of the original Adam is still heard as birds converse" (201). Dipple examines a long list of magic occurrences in the novel to demonstrate that "Murdoch strives to keep human experience in a vexed, undetermined area where certitude is alien" (201). The magical hubbub reminds the reader of the difficulty of distinguishing reality from illusion in much of Murdoch's fiction or, for that matter, in life.

The Good Apprentice

Dipple also uses *The Good Apprentice* (1985) to show that objective perception is not easy — often, it is not possible. She says that the novel juxtaposes a new combination of the "illusionist magic and redemptive theology" as they impinge on the Good (201). Here "religious fantasies and magic redemptive devices" and religious rationalization, such as *We must accept the will of God,* distort the perception of the characters; the good eschew magic, others do not. The title suggests that Murdoch asks the reader to judge one character as the good apprentice; but actually, according to Dipple, there are two: the young stepbrothers Stuart Cuno and Edward Baltram. Edward, the prodigal son, participates wholly and guiltily in the dynamic flux of life; Stuart's apprenticeship takes the strait and narrow path. Both learn that compromises are the key to the discovery of the Good. Focusing the conversations of the other characters on Stuart, Murdoch leads the reader to assume that Stuart is "a man in error and a death-bringer"; actually, he is a good individual who has quit school to "study virtue" (202). In assuming up to this point in the story that his profession will be computer science, Stuart speaks for Murdoch when he dwells on the "crucial ethical differences between human and artificial intelligence": "A machine can't even simulate the human mind . . . because we are always involved in distinguishing between good and evil" (202). Stuart remains good throughout the novel, "where he describes his decision to train as a schoolmaster of the very young as the only means of effecting change in society from its roots" (203). As a teacher he can help children learn to think, to meditate, and to love, possibilities that call attention to the soft spot Murdoch seems always to have had in her heart for teachers.

Magic in this novel manifests itself when other characters, who are not good, proceed as if psychology and religion had supernatural power. Dipple sees this theme as emanating from Murdoch's fear that "a cultural and spiritual Logos might be removed from the world. . . . And for her, ethical thought is entirely dependent on the survival of subtle and complex language" (202). When certain professions utilize their skills as if they can wield charms and spells, dangerous psychological debris can work loose and damage the vulnerable. Magic enters the plot through Edward's uncle, the psychotherapist and puppeteer Thomas McCaskerville. Dipple says that the reader sees McCaskerville as a quasi-philosophical practitioner who believes in the negative psychological theory of R. D. Laing "that suffering aids in spiritual development" (204). McCaskerville is treating Edward for his guilt after he has accidentally given a friend a fatal drug overdose.

Another kind of magic, however, helps Edward more than psychotherapy does. It emanates from "an enchanted Gothic" place similar to the eerie houses in *The Unicorn* and *The Sea, The Sea*. Dipple compares the bizarre architectural monstrosity, the home of Edward's father, to the form of Murdoch's novel because each "lacks an easy formal coherence," and "the perceiver has to learn its logic and beauty" bit by bit (205). Edward's quest for his real father, Jesse Baltram, who lives in the magic house, uses not only religious parable but also oedipal myths. Magic supplies Edward with consoling fantasies that keep him alive. In his fantasies he creates parallels between his behavior and that of the prodigal son, and he thinks of himself as being marked like Cain and wandering the earth. Murdoch often chooses stories from the Old Testament as rationalizing strategies to help characters grapple with their psychological chaos. Such rituals keep them sane but do not help them reach the Good. For example, Murdoch shows that Edward's sudden irrational attachment to Jesse — "ultimately a product of his inventive and self-protective imagination" — works as an obstacle on the way to the Good. His vision of Jesse "has the nebulous origins in a séance, and the combination of determinacy and chance that lead to its confirmation is questioned but unanswered in the plot process" (205). Each young man finds "systematic symbolic centers" that "supply false readings of the circumstances" (205). Jesse "walks Christ-like on water toward his son" (207). Just as at the end of James Joyce's "The Dead" snow is general all over Ireland, for Murdoch religious fantasies and magic redemptive devices cloud the perception of her characters, as well as the perception of their counterparts — a majority of people at the end of the twentieth century.

The Sea, The Sea

An even more frustrating kind of magic for critics and general readers alike is that in *The Sea, The Sea*. While many of Murdoch's novels have examined the broad outlines of spirituality — for example, *The Bell* suggests the possibility of a religious and moral life, and *The Unicorn* "diagnoses the confusions and desires of the spiritual life" — *The Sea, The Sea* goes to the very roots of the matter, interrogating the need for spirituality (*Iris Murdoch: Work for the Spirit*, 266). Dipple says that "by understanding Murdoch's extensive fictional devices we can apprehend with increasing clarity its apparently hidden centre" (275). She emphasizes the difficulty of the reader's quest, which Murdoch frustrates with false hopes, mistaken assumptions, and deceptive truths. Murdoch uses a realistic style to focus on the details of Charles Arrowby's life and his memories, even as she weaves them together in a multilayering effect. The realism "is counterbalanced by an undertone at once demonic and connected to the spiritual reaches of the good, and it behooves the reader to sort out, distinguish and connect context with undertone" (275). The reader is enthralled by Charles's stated purpose in the book: telling the story of his life. But "as in the case of the medieval idea of the *alieniloquium* (a speaking of things other than those it purports to do, which is fiction's strength and perhaps its bane) there is a sustained questioning of the spiritual life, a study of the devastation of magic in all its forms and a profound psychic landscape whose symbolic quality very slowly, in small, subtle steps unfolds" (275).

Readers have discovered the deep-seated seriousness of the two tragicomedies, *The Sea, The Sea* and *The Black Prince*, when they understand that Murdoch has constructed these novelistic worlds to be violated by the real world, much as the godhead in the guise of a swan breaks into Leda's Greek world or into the Virgin Mary's Christian one. Indeed, Dipple says that a major idea in each text is "the breaking in of the real world on the crafted form" (277). She shows that in the middle of a richly realistic novel Murdoch finds it necessary to widen her net and present the reader with "the eerie" and "the uncanny" (277). In *The Sea, The Sea* poltergeists confront the narrator, Charles, a Prospero figure: in his new seaside home the green vase falls, the mirror crashes, faces peek in at him, and later other characters die mysteriously. Murdoch makes it clear that Charles, who has recently retired as a theater director, cannot handle this new life; his neurotic inability to live as an adult even in retirement grows out of obsessive attachments he fabricated in the past (281).

In her much-quoted 1977 BBC interview with Bryan Magee, Murdoch explained a few symbolic identifications that she had in mind when she wrote this novel: "the theatre is the world, Charles is a naïve, the sea is empty" (Dipple, 281), and Hartley, Charles's childhood sweetheart, is a "phantom Helen" (quoted in Dipple, 291). His cousin James Arrowby, who has experienced first hand the spirituality of Buddhism, is not like the "largely unconscious Charles[;] he is acutely aware of its nature and dangers as well as of its task in seeking goodness and evoking the whole of the spiritual life" (Dipple, 289). James is a spiritual man who almost achieves goodness through his special powers. Dipple explains that both Charles and James are on what she calls in a chapter title a dangerous road. The spiritual path James takes is much more powerful and, therefore, more alive with magic than the egotistical one Charles chooses, even though Charles has produced a degree of magic on the stage.

For the initial encounter of these two characters Murdoch uses realistic details to paint an unsettling psychological scene of sibling rivalry. Suffering a hangover, Charles views the paintings in the Wallace Collection through a dreamlike, sepia scrim, as if they were scenes fading from his own past life. Murdoch embellishes this eerie visual effect with the hammering of the workmen, which reminds Charles of a theatrical device he had borrowed from the Japanese theater to create suspense (Dipple, 290). Dipple finds this scene emblematic of the kinds of psychic reality Murdoch renders throughout the novel: "The sense of eeriness and doom, the hammering which connects to both heartbeat and *hyoshigi* [wooden clappers that announce doom], and the dramatic entrance of James combine to take this scene into a psychic area where one questions external reality" (290). Murdoch's brilliant combination of realism and the uncanny sets up a matchless atmosphere of dizziness, disorientation, and doom.

The Philosopher's Pupil

Disorientation and doom are also pervasive in *The Philosopher's Pupil* (1983), which Dipple says is a "strong mixture of [the] traditional and experimental" (*The Unresolvable Plot*, 189). Two of Dipple's crucial remarks about this novel are appropriate here. This carnivalesque novel about scandal, gossip, and journalism argues, according to Dipple, that textual misreading is characteristic of contemporary readers, because even careful readers trained to recognize indeterminate meaning can assume such meaning to be the same as a lack of meaning. Furthermore, characters, like people, are "endlessly unknowable" (192). She explores these two issues as she interprets Murdoch to be developing them in the novel. First, misreading of texts is a recurring theme in *The Philosopher's Pupil*. For example, Murdoch asks both readers and a character, Father Bernard, to rethink their interpretation of Stéphane Mallarmé's "Quelconque une solitude" in *Petit Airs*. Hattie Meynell, a serious girl who reads French, comes up with several new possibilities that impress the priest. But Dipple says that Murdoch does not have the priest study any of the possibilities, because although he recognizes that his reading is self-indulgent, he lazily settles for his "fantasy interpretation" (190). After giving other proofs, Dipple concludes that Murdoch indicts "both the closed system illustrated by the reader who has made up his mind what the text means and . . . the hazy idleness of another sort of reader who dismisses a poem as just a poem, with which the mind cannot be actually or fruitfully engaged" (190).

The second theme illustrates "the Bakhtinian overlapping of roles" and poses the question: "Where does one person end and another person begin?" (191). Characters are objects of study for Murdoch; human consciousness is a moral value she has worked to record. In "Nostalgia for the Particular" (1952) she called for philosophical research on "inner mental happenings" (243), and forty years later, in *Metaphysics as a Guide to Morals* (1992), she continued to make the same plea. Conradi quotes Murdoch's character Plato in her dialogue "Art and Eros" to demonstrate that "the characters'delusion that they are autonomous is held up as a mirror to us" (*Iris Murdoch: The Saint and the Artist*, 79). Although she perpetually interrogates her various narrators, she is especially playful in *The Philosopher's Pupil*. Dipple says that this Jewish narrator, named N, inhabits a kind of Shakespearean neverland, which he calls Ennistone (N's Town), and she demonstrates that Murdoch uses this character to explore the role of the narrator in fiction: "the narrator whose sense of his job gives us a pointed definition of how Murdoch views the problems of narration and the task of the story-teller" (188). In Bakhtinian fashion, Murdoch makes N "so interested in his characters that he irritates them with the symbiotic relationships he sets up; fictional himself. . . . He intrudes not only as a narrative voice but as a character who interacts with his so-called creations at a personal, quasi-realistic level. . . . The reader is carefully led to realize that because N is dealing with the vast complexity of human character and motivation, there are of necessity areas too perplexing for his mastery" (193). Moreover, Dipple shows that Murdoch appears to agree with Umberto Eco's semiotic theories, which suggest that some authors write open texts for "the model reader whose freedom to move with considerable interest and accuracy within the narrative has been foreseen by the author" (192).

In her article "The Green Knight and Other Vagaries of the Spirit; or, Tricks and Images for the Human Soul; or, The Uses of Imaginative Literature" Dipple makes a superb advance in Murdoch criticism by demonstrating the ways in which Murdoch's recent novels *The Good Apprentice* (1986), *The Book and the Brotherhood* (1987), *The Message to the Planet* (1989), and *The Green Knight* (1993), like certain contemporaneous poems and novels, "infuse reading with an apprehension of the path through experience, to a knowledge of the radical insufficiency of material existence, and hence to the divine" (139). For example, a theme Murdoch discusses in *The Green Knight* is the tendency of all human beings "to want a world energized by spirit" but to have to relinquish this desire and survive in the mundane (167). Dipple makes several new claims about these novels. Because Murdoch's strategies detach the reader from determinate meaning, the novels force the reader to imagine multiple interpretations; furthermore, Murdoch requires the reader to follow a kind of mirrored regression, or *mise-en-abyme* path. Moreover, Murdoch's brand of realism, which captures a tawdry world of "infinite interpretational regress[,] is hermeneutically analogous" to her understanding of the quester searching for the Good (144).

Mise-en-abyme Structure

Dipple cites C. S. Peirce's discussion of representation in his *Collected Papers* to argue that Murdoch's "novels can be seen as participating in a version of realism the reading of which demands a *mise-en-abyme* structure. . . . In an increasingly secular world, one central use of literature as practiced by Iris Murdoch is to detach us from the illusion of determinate meaning, in both fiction and the spiritual life" (144–45). When Dipple proposes that this slow and careful regress will help the reader absorb Murdoch's infinite intertextuality, she is referring not only to the usual root stories and strategies from Shakespeare but also to Renaissance painters' treatments of stories from Ovid: "Murdoch's art lives in a milieu of oblique commentary on Shakespeare's techniques as well as on those she has learned from her enormous interest in the Venetian Ovidian painters of the cinquecento, particularly Titian" (145). Having taken the reader on an intertextual mini-tour, Dipple says that one of her purposes is to show how "imagery, metaphors, and allusions work, as one senses that within every one of her fictions books endlessly talk to books within the minds of the narrator, the characters, and the readers, who share the process of constructing a world in which the images and stories of the past beget story after story in the present" (146). Murdoch's work on methodology unites readers as they visit and revisit in her novels some of the defining artifacts of western culture: art "from Judeo-Christian texts, Buddhism, Hinduism" (146).

Because these works move beyond the binary focus of the saint-artist plot to one in which a single character bears "an enormous weight of metaphoric power beyond the boundaries of the possible" (168), Dipple says that they are Murdoch's most ambitious novels from both a literary and spiritual perspective and judges them "tough, experimental, tenuous, unabsorbable" (168). The last sentence of her article indicates the kind of mystery to which Murdoch continues to return: "Murdoch, who has never read the work of Mikhail Bakhtin, operates fully within his definition of the 'unfinalizability' of the literary work — that sense that the last word about our lives cannot be written nor the final analysis achieved" (168). Like Johnson and Heusel, Dipple argues that postmodernist lack of closure is characteristic of Murdoch's later novels.

The Green Knight

In one of this group, *The Green Knight,* Dipple's emphasis is on the apocalyptic figure Peter Mir. He goes further than other characters to make concrete what Dipple means when she claims that Murdoch wants her realism to interact with "real life" (166) — obviously, an impossible goal. Murdoch creates in this analogue to the Green Knight, who "goes from death to resurrection and life in the world and back to death," a character who lives in "two worlds — the metaphoric and the real. His stumbling presence ties the novel more firmly to the 'real' than anything else in the book" (167). Dipple suggests that, like Christ before him, he begins a new era and then leaves the characters on their own. One might more accurately say that he exists metaphorically in both the temporal and the eternal worlds. The character with whom he interacts most significantly is a spritelike adolescent girl named Moy, who lives in the present and absorbs with love the suffering in the world.

In addition to suggesting Murdoch's successful uniting of the real world and the fictional, Dipple examines the richness of this group of novels that defy easy interpretation: "Because the novels are so crowded with myriad details, all significant from one point of view or another, any reading feels small and eccentric in the face of the crowded, resonant text. The multiple interpretations called out by Murdoch's work defy the single reading, or the smug sureness of the theoretician" (144).

Feminist and Masculinist Perspectives

Observing that Murdoch tests reality from a gendered perspective, Johnson explores several strategies that help the author mimic male narration, play off feminist and masculinist perspectives, and create doubled-voiced discourse in her texts by transgressing gender boundaries and using irony and erotic symbolism. Her goal is to interrogate Murdoch's engagement "with some of the most problematic, puzzling and irritating aspects of the fiction, its often explicit assumption of 'masculinist' perspectives and values, and its curious reluctance, for the most part, to deal directly or non-ironically with woman's experience" (xi-xii). She explains that Murdoch couches her political pronouncements, including her feminist statements, in a "cautious way" (xiii). Anxious to avoid what she calls a "narrowly feminist" reading, Johnson responds to Dipple's discussion of male narrators (xi). Johnson says that Dipple's text betrays her significant interest in the subject of the "presence of a male first-person narrator, and the absence of a corresponding female voice" (2). She criticizes Dipple for saying that a biographical-psychological reading would be necessary to investigate this imbalance; Johnson says that the male narrator is "a rhetorical strategy" and needs to be explained by no text outside itself (3).

Drawing on feminist and psychoanalytic theory, Johnson grounds her discussion in Mary Jacobus's essay "The Question of Language: Men of Maxims and *The Mill on the Floss*," which asks, "What *does* constitute the 'feminine' in writing[?]" (9). Johnson also cites Luce Irigaray's argument that the logic of discourse itself subordinates the feminine and that "the systems of representation at work in discourse are 'masculinist' in that they are self-reflexive and specular" (10). A question Johnson raises in regard to Murdoch is one that Elaine Showalter has asked about other women writers: whether the novelist's strategy of using first-person male narrators is a form of evasion or whether the role-playing is a strategy of subversion that liberates patriarchal structures. She finds more in the texts than the "ironic distance and implied didactic attitudes" that Dipple does (13). At the core of Western narratives, Johnson says, quoting Roland Barthes, is "the drive toward origins and ends," the trajectory found in Plato's Myth of the Cave and Sophocles' *Oedipus Rex*. Barthes theorizes, according to Johnson, that "(every unveiling of the truth) is a staging of the (absent, hidden, or hypostatized) father — which would explain the solidity of narrative forms, of family structures, and of prohibitions of nudity" (13). Johnson judges Murdoch to be critiquing centuries of history and culture.

The novels, according to Johnson, are radical statements that provide a vision for the twenty-first century. The patina of the novels may be traditional, seemingly masculinist, but their inner core promotes radical ideas that are feminist. For example, Murdoch's search for the Good is about unselfing (becoming unselfish) and bonding with others, not a search for a father or for some ultimate truth that will bring about progress. Johnson claims that Murdoch creates worlds in the novel that are socially as well as aesthetically significant in their disruption of such traditional patterns and that she unyieldingly investigates over and over characteristics of the psyche most readers would prefer to ignore. The following passage proposes the depth of the patterns Murdoch wants to disrupt in the late twentieth century's decentered world of displaced persons: "the various ways in which we lay waste our creative energies, and . . . the power struggles which make up life in an aggressive society." To address these problems "Murdoch offers a surprisingly fresh and radical vision of the human (and, as I have argued, in many ways, specifically female) struggle both for self-definition and for connection with others." Throughout her writing Murdoch displays "an in-touchness with some vital feminist issues, and can speak to the feminist need for re-readings of the world, even though she cannot ultimately be claimed as a feminist writer" (112). Furthermore, since Murdoch is investigating the moral responsibilities incumbent on individuals who reject a personal God and is writing a certain kind of novel because she has a particular kind of worldview, her narratives depict cultural situations in which agnostics and atheists must intellectualize their ethical behavior.

The Bell

During the kind of cultural upheaval Murdoch suggests, it is not unusual for a novelist to depict characters as disoriented; by the time Murdoch began publishing novels, modernism had perfected the art of capturing such an existential plight. *The Bell* (1965) is Johnson's choice for illustrating not only the general bewilderment of humanity but also the special bafflement of a group of religious laypeople, and, more important for Johnson, the perplexities Murdoch assigns to her female characters. A group of laypeople form a religious community, Imber Court, in order to live better lives. The Abbess, leader of a nearby cloistered community of Anglican nuns, describes to Michael Meade, the leader of the lay community, the predicament that potentially good people have in the twentieth century: she says there needs to be a "buffer state" between the abbey and the world, "a reflection, or benevolent and useful parasite, an intermediary form of life." She says that there are people who cannot live in the world or out of it: "They are a kind of sick people, whose desire for God makes them unsatisfactory citizens of an ordinary life, but whose strength or temperament fails them to surrender the world completely, and present day society, with its hurried pace and its mechanical and technical structure, offers no home to these unhappy souls" (82). Murdoch's personal experience with displaced persons after the Second World War made her especially empathetic to people's fear and disorientation in the face of rapid change, drawing her to investigate such individuals living inside and outside the technological culture — especially women.

Johnson scrutinizes the novel's feminist subtext by exploring two of its sustained and subtle symbols, the bell and the fruit garden. Crucial to Murdoch's exploration is Catherine Fawley, who is preparing to become an Anglican nun. It seems to be no accident that readers first encounter this postulant much as they do Eve in John Milton's *Paradise Lost:* laboriously attempting to control the wildly flowering plants and keep the garden in check, chores traditionally supposed to please the god of order. Johnson emphasizes Murdoch's representation of an infinite number of women who are enclosed in such walled gardens and other, more confining, structures and who, as the female lay leader says, "stick to the traditional tasks" (quoted in Johnson, 81). To document the female tension, unease, and fecundity in the novel, Johnson cites the head mother's "inane pieties," "the heat," the younger women's unreleased creative exuberance, and their fear. Johnson says that the feeling of fear exudes from a "thwarted female potential" that "hangs over the scene" (81) — much as, perhaps, the narrative about Eve is about lost creative potential. In her need for sympathy Catherine has much in common with Dora Greenfield, an art student who is visiting the community to make up with her estranged husband: "the female subtext, with its stress on sympathy and practical help, offers some obliquely illuminating contrasts to the main story-line," which involves "different kinds of isolation within community" (81–82). The first is the emphasis on the sexuality manifested by these women and its history in the courtly love tradition as evoked in the novel by a myth in which a fourteenth-century postulate commits suicide because she has an illicit lover. Murdoch suggests that the young women are potentially available to help each other and are likely to communicate more easily and thoroughly than the men, who have similar problems of disorientation. Michael Meade, for example, will never communicate with Catherine's twin brother, Nick Fawley (91), with whom he has had a homosexual affair and from whom he is now estranged. An alcoholic, Nick is recuperating at Imber Court.

Murdoch is able to turn the divided self of Dora to creative account, but Catherine ends the novel suffering from schizophrenia. The reader assumes that Dora's bewildered emotional state, and Catherine's, are similar; each must, as Dora thinks, try "somehow to break into the idle motionless scene" (quoted, 83), the scene at the lay community from which they are psychically separated. Each has a problem with identity; each is alienated from herself and from the outside world. Johnson helps the reader see that female entanglement, alienation, bewilderment, and then "extinction of will" (*The Time of the Angels*, 204) are states that Murdoch analyzes in novel after novel. Here Murdoch shows that these two young women, who seem to have nothing in common, are like the new bell that is dressed carefully for its rite of passage: naïve but not innocent. Murdoch also shows how they are comparable to Mother Clare, the nun who saves them from drowning when Catherine attempts to commit suicide and Dora tries to rescue her. Both are comparable also to the nun in the fourteenth-century myth who commits suicide because she has no control over her relationship with her lover.

The Bell is typical in that the male viewpoint dominates; Murdoch's concealing the self of women while presenting the male viewpoint is crucial to Johnson's analysis of the novel's irony. Women are confined not only by enclosures in the setting, such as gardens and rooms, but also by more symbolic constructs, such as plots that lack closure and Plato's cave structure, which for women represents both the mind and the womb. The medieval bell has a different symbolic meaning for each character. Whereas for Toby Gashe, an adolescent visiting the community, it represents a rite of passage from "(sexual) ignorance to (sexual) knowledge" (84), it is most frighteningly significant for Dora, the novel's most fleshed-out female character. When Toby discovers and, with Dora's help, recovers the bell, it overwhelms her as both a work of art and a sexual symbol: "It was black inside and alarmingly like an inhabited cave. Very lightly she touched the great clapper, hanging profoundly still in the interior. The feeling of fear had not left her and she withdrew hastily and switched the torch on. The squat figures [represented on the bell] faced her from the sloping surface of the bronze solid, simple, beautiful, absurd, full to the brim with something which was to the artist not an object of speculation or imagination" (quoted in Johnson, 84–85). Clearly a representation of Eros, the bell embodies in its past, in its function in the narrative, and in its shape "inescapable connections between erotic and spiritual love" (85), evoking the courtly love tradition. Therefore, when Murdoch uses a "'Dora-centred' perspective," the symbolism presents a "'double-voiced discourse'" (85–86), a masculinist viewpoint as filtered through a woman.

Johnson supports her claims that the walled gardens, the cloistered community, and the restrictive female occupations represent the degrees of confinement that help define female history by demonstrating the way early feminist criticism construed the cave imagery of Plato and Freud. Sandra Gilbert and Susan Gubar questioned, for example, how a woman could make the cave's "negative metaphoric potential" positive (quoted, 87). But most of Johnson's emphasis is on Irigaray's exploration of the cave as a masculine image of the womb. She cites many of Murdoch's references in other novels to Plato's cave to demonstrate that there is "a dialogue between the public 'male' philosophical voice and the private 'female' poetic voice" (95). The latter voice undermines the assumptions of the former. For example, Murdoch expresses her poetic voice when she has Dora release the butterfly from the dusty train. Dora, in turn, releases herself from her chains at the end of the novel.

Artistic Masks

Using *The Black Prince* as an illustration of Murdoch's exploration of her own artistic process, Johnson points to Murdoch's "need for partial concealment of the self" behind the masks of other artist characters (45). She says that a comment by Bradley Pearson is a playful removal of the author's mask for an instant: "What can one do but try to lodge one's vision somehow inside this layered stuff of ironic sensibility, which, if I were a fictitious character, would be that much deeper and denser?" (quoted, 45). Johnson demonstrates that Murdoch enjoys "the creation of separate, self-contained fictional worlds" while simultaneously projecting "her more personal sense of connection between artistic, erotic and religious experience through the meditative narration of her *persona*, Bradley Pearson" (45). In her novels Murdoch emphasizes "the de-centring effect" that male first-person narratives give to "the unequal power relationships which exist between men and women" (8–9). Men such as Bradley, Charles Arrowby in *The Sea, The Sea,* and Hilary Burde in *A Word Child* are "almost Jacobean in their intense misogyny"; they fail to see the obvious, Johnson says, because they talk too much (8). She proposes that Murdoch manipulates her articulate and powerful male heroes, and the "quest" motif, to create an ironic picture of reality. Zeroing in on this tendency, Johnson questions whether the novelist uses "male mimicry" to evade or critique masculinist culture. Johnson finds Irigaray's work on "male mimicry" the most useful tool for tackling a woman writer's potential method of "undoing the repressive (patriarchal) structures encoded in language itself" (9). Such "exposing through imitation" is advantageous, according to some feminist theorists, in recovering "the operation of the 'feminine' in language" (9). Johnson says that the first novel, *Under the Net*, critiques the solipsistic, Cartesian male "questing hero of so much modernist (and post-modernist) fiction" (25) instead of celebrating him as an existentialist hero, as is often the case in criticism.

Johnson does not go so far as to label Murdoch "an exponent of *écriture féminine*," but she does employ Freudian psychology to examine a major question in Murdoch criticism: Is Murdoch ignoring and evading Western institutional sexism by using male narrators, or is she manipulating "role-playing and male narration in her novels . . . as liberating devices, subversive of male-dominated structures and modes of perception" (12)? She says that Edmund in *The Italian Girl* and Martin in *A Severed Head* "trace the journey of a male hero into a comic version of Thebes, where he . . . remains caught for good in the toils of erotic (self) deception" (14). For Bradley Pearson, on the other hand, "'the world [is] transfigured' . . . into a state not bound by his normal, narrow ego-consciousness. His vision is enlarged through the destruction of some of his most cherished illusions" (14–15). Referring to Conradi's arguments on the psychotherapeutic value of the novels as "expression[s]" of 'the movement towards the saving of Eros, the clarification of passion or education of desire,'" Johnson writes that Conradi is interested in conveying "the provisionality of life-myths which lead us to repeat roles in emotional systems whose patterns are laid down early" (15–16). Against this statement Johnson juxtaposes her innovative question: What particular forms of identification are available here for *female* readers, when the myths define them only as objects?

Quest-Narratives

Johnson says that "the playfulness of Iris Murdoch's quest-narratives works precisely to expose or foreground . . . a splitting of the female subject" or a female getting caught in what Teresa de Lauretis calls "the two mythical positions of hero (mythical subject) and boundary (spatially fixed object, personified obstacle)" (quoted, 16). Murdoch achieves this exposure of such cultural assumptions through the text's revelation that the quest *topos* is "inadequate or illusory as a model" for life (16). But more complex and more important to Johnson is the subtext of the .*"female* Oedipus conflict (never a direct or sustained object of authorial focus)." In *The Black Prince* Julian's questionable love for her father, Arnold Baffin, "throws a questioning light on Bradley's exalted reading of his own love-story." In *The Sandcastle* Rain's struggle with "separation both as woman and as artist from her dead father is a shadowy and enigmatic area for Mor [who is considerably older] in his bittersweet romance with her" (16). Many other women, such as Franca in *The Message to the Planet,* have this same problem, never growing up to be adults.

Johnson demonstrates Murdoch's reliance, beginning with her first novel, on the conventions of the theater, especially Shakespeare, showing that life is made up of people playing roles, and on illusionistic storytelling strategies harkening back to Plato's cave allegory. Murdoch also continually relies on the conventions of the 1950s Hollywood cinema, often comparing the darkened movie theater to Plato's cave. Johnson uses illustrations from this first novel, *Under the Net,* to clarify Murdoch's double-voicedness and to examine the male protagonist's specular viewpoint. Jake views these women as a series of body parts reflected in a series of mirrors in a beauty salon. In Murdoch's evocation of a *mise-en-abyme* structure, Johnson points out that he sees them as synecdoches: "'elegant heads . . . in various stages of assembly,' 'a row of well-dressed backs,' 'a large number of fascinated female eyes'"; the novel employs images of women "wearing masks of make-up, elaborate coiffures, high-heeled shoes" (23). She thinks that Jake's specular viewpoint might well carry the burden of Murdoch's own detachment and critique of such "fashions and conventions which codified femininity in the early fifties" (23). This male quester understands that women are "always a little more unbalanced by the part they have to act" in life (24).

Jake, like Murdoch, is an artist who is "in the process of continually revising and questioning his assumptions about maleness, femaleness, sexual glamour, personal and political power" (25). Johnson argues that Murdoch's doubleness is evident in "the space which she carefully maintains between herself and her first male narrator, a space which is beautifully conveyed through the persistent theatrical imagery of masks, roles, decors, stage properties, all of which influence the ways the characters behave towards one another" (25). Johnson's implication that Murdoch might have had some of the same feelings as Jake is fascinating and demands further study. Later, Heusel will demonstrate that theatrical strategies help give Murdoch's novels a Bakhtinian flavor.

Johnson claims that Murdoch clothes herself in traditional male power and privilege not only in creating a controlled, detached narrative voice but also in her multiple, elaborately Shakespearean plot structures. Murdoch's experimentation with the Gothic has allowed her to delve into bizarre subjects such as incest, with its various Freudian manifestations. Like the Gothic plays Murdoch has written, such as *The Three Arrows* and *The Servants and the Snow,* Johnson thinks that *The Unicorn* and *The Time of the Angels* reveal an authorial detachment that is unique. Johnson suggests that Murdoch could be trying to "exorcise uncomfortable feelings about female imprisonment/oppression" by basing the story "upon acts of male choice" (65). Other texts she mentions that render a sharp division between the male and female spheres are *The Red and the Green, The Italian Girl, A Severed Head,* and *An Unofficial Rose,* most of which explore "terrible family relationships [that] are played out in terms of diabolical triangles, all doomed repetitions of the original Oedipal drama" (65). Johnson says that Murdoch's emphasis on strict detachment is significant and deserves further study.

In addition, Johnson cites Judith Wilt's description of the "doubly-fathered father" to argue that Muriel Fisher's father, the rector Carel in *The Time of the Angels,* is both father and priest to quite a few women in the novel, but especially to his two daughters. Although Murdoch dares to analyze the kind of female misery that Tennyson evokes in "The Lady of Shalott," including "images of bowers, mirrors and tapestries" (67), she manages to remain detached and simply suggest "veiled references to Tennyson's text [as] . . . the male tendency to 'textualise' the woman, to reduce her to text or to myth"; she has carefully worked out a strategy for utilizing "the vocabulary of courtly love, the woman as *princesse lointaine,* enchantress and Lilith" by setting up such anachronisms ironically or jokingly (67). Johnson also remarks that Charlotte Ledman's depression in *An Accidental Man* evokes images "reminiscent of Tennyson's 'Mariana in the Moated Grange'" (68). Although Johnson criticizes Murdoch for colluding in "'textualising' the woman," her critique of the courtly love tradition explores the physical and psychological destruction that male "textualising" manifests. At the climactic moment of *The Time of the Angels* Muriel, "gazing into the depths of the mirror in which the act of incest is reflected, . . . achieves simultaneously a process of painful self-realisation; she becomes herself a Lady of Shalott and succumbs to Elizabeth's own living death" (68–69). Even in the early novels, the Gothic strategies and settings help Murdoch frame explorations of moral issues.

Other critics might say that Johnson is referring to what Murdoch calls objectivity, a concept much maligned at the end of the twentieth century. Johnson is the first critic to ask whether Murdoch manages to evoke the inevitable outcome of traditional scientific objectivity without colluding with its patriarchal stance. Earlier critics had simply assumed that Murdoch's philosophical training gave her an unusual capacity to place herself, as writer, outside or beyond her cultural surroundings. Johnson implies that scientific objectivity is another potential framework for Murdoch to play with. For example, Johnson says that Murdoch's concern is "to treat certain kinds of socially and culturally induced female misery . . . within carefully established limits" (66). Being traditionally "objective" protects the author and reader from the pain of the actual reality. But one must add that Murdoch's statements about feeling that, being Irish, she had grown up as an outsider might imply that her capacity not only for empathy but also for distance come from this source. Therefore, her ability to go beyond Tennyson and contemplate why these women in literature, and life, are imprisoned in rooms, literary conventions, and language reflects her philosophical and moral acumen. Murdoch no doubt wants to communicate what Johnson describes as "the world which closes in on Muriel" when she discovers what she should have recognized all along as being "a nightmare of the abuse of patriarchal authority" (69): her sick stepsister being sexually abused by her father. Johnson argues that Murdoch's texts require unexpected change followed by a complicated unraveling of the plot to critique the absurdity of such patriarchal assumptions of privilege. The phrase Conradi uses for Dostoevsky seems to fit here: a freedom that is interpreted as "all is permitted" (*Iris Murdoch: The Saint and the Artist*, 91). Johnson does not mention Virginia Woolf in this context, but one is nevertheless reminded of the allusion in *To the Lighthouse* to the monster in the children's room covered by Mrs. Ramsey's shawl but never removed, as a veiled symbol of the prevalence of hidden Victorian incest. Earlier, however, Johnson does make this comparison when discussing a Murdoch reference to Sartre: Murdoch "shares something of Woolf's striving after an aesthetically rendered *plurality* of vision and her stress on human sympathy and interconnection. She also shares Woolf's playfulness, her subverting of set assumptions about gender roles and gender identity through a dramatically presented series of roles and disguises" (24–25). Here she conjures up *Orlando* and Woolf's understanding that all aspects of life, especially language, are clothed in the Cartesian paradigm, with its stereotypes of subject and object.

Any reader who watches the metamorphosis of Julian Baffin in *The Black Prince* — a young woman, mistaken for a boy, twice dresses the part of Hamlet and eventually denies her attachment to the protagonist — knows that Johnson is on target about Murdoch's employing masks and male mimicry to distance herself as she simulates the split consciousness of female characters. Any reader who has attended to the images in mirrors in *Under the Net, The Bell,* and *The Time of the Angels* understands that such play presupposes not only the split but also the isolation, the lack of identity, and the paralysis of will of a majority of female characters. Moreover, anyone who reads *The Sea, The Sea,* in which Charles Arrowby as Prospero works his magic, knows that Johnson is right about the nightmare of patriarchal abuse that Hartley, Murdoch's "phantom Helen" (quoted in Dipple, *Iris Murdoch: Work for the Spirit,* 291), endures. As Johnson demonstrates, Murdoch goes to great lengths to separate her female characters from society, to show their consequent disorientation, to reveal misogynist male characters, and to detach herself from the fray.

Murdoch's Bakhtinian Lens

Murdoch's copying of Shakespearean mimicry of all kinds, especially the gendered variety, and her modeling of set pieces on Dostoevsky's could not long escape comparisons to those of her models: Todd and Conradi have written entire books on these subjects. Similarly, her weaving of strands of Shakespeare's and Dostoevsky's texts into her novels has led a few critics to recognize the importance of the theories the Russian critic Mikhail Bakhtin used to analyze the texts of these writers. This kind of intertextuality, in which Murdoch revels, is at the crux of Bakhtin's innovative ideas about the function of the novel. While discussion of the texts of these other writers is beyond the scope of this study, readers of Murdoch can enhance their understanding of her novels through knowledge of them.

Dipple, Conradi, and Heusel all mention Bakhtin in relation to Murdoch's novels, and Murdoch's husband, Bayley, brought up the subject at a speaking engagement the two had at Cambridge. Given the publication of Caryl Emerson's English translation of Bakhtin's *Problems of Dostoevsky's Poetics* in 1984 and Murdoch's dozens of public statements regarding her influence by Dostoevsky and Shakespeare, it is no surprise that English-speaking critics began in the 1980s to recognize the parallels between Murdoch's texts and Dostoevsky's and Shakespeare's. When Heusel asked her in an interview in 1987 about her reactions to Bakhtin's theories, Murdoch replied that she did not know his work; in a personal conversation in 1999 Bayley said that this response was typical of her. She was not often interested in such literary theories; however, her independently creating strategies to which the terms *dialogical* and *carnivalesque* are applicable gave Heusel good reason to analyze her fiction through a Bakhtinian lens. In her playful overturning of Western cultural assumptions and weaving of dialogical language games in which two voices from different social strata create a bond, Murdoch comes quite close to the daring of literary masters she most admires.

Although Dipple recognizes Murdoch's and Bakhtin's narrative insights and novelistic goals to be similar, she never develops the likenesses. She does discuss, however, Bakhtin's interest in the semantic function of literature and in the relationship of the narrator to the characters, and she mentions Murdoch's chronotopic experiments and her Dostoevskian interest in otherness. Bakhtin compares this power relationship to that of the relationship between God and man or Christ and man; Dipple says that Bakhtin, Dostoevsky, and Murdoch are alike in insisting that "an anti-solipsistic communication . . . [,] Martin Buber's 'I-thou' recognition of the other[,] is essential" (*The Unresolvable Plot*, 186). All three writers explore the relations between Christ and man and man and man. In *Problems of Dostoevsky's Poetics* Bakhtin explains dialogic style as "an idea that encompasses the capacity of the author to envisage the fully individuated being of the characters as well as the ability of the characters to perceive and respond to each other's precise nature and spirituality"; "The very idea of the dialogic . . . withholds the power of clear statement from the fiction" (Dipple, *The Unresolvable Plot*, 187) — therefore, monologism is discouraged. Dipple is reiterating what Murdoch believed: that people and stories are endlessly unknowable. Using N, the narrator of *The Philosopher's Pupil*, as an example, Dipple bewails the tendency to read characters as alter egos of the author; she finds this tendency not only distressing but a way of denying integrity to the character and the author (192). Just as Murdoch focuses most directly on character, so do Dipple and Heusel.

Heusel's *Patterned Aimlessness* is the first book to focus on applying Bakhtin's ideas to Murdoch's fiction. She prepares for such a comparison by analyzing the influence on the novelist of Ludwig Wittgenstein's ideas about language, morality, and aesthetics. In Murdoch's play with strategies from all traditions — spectacle, the contingent swirl of discourse, narrative point of view, parody, and stylization — she creates her own unique fictional world, which unintentionally displays many of the characteristics of Bakhtin's polyphonic novel and parallels his celebration of dialogic discourse. This expanding of the boundaries of the novel form by using traditional conventions as tropes allows Murdoch to capture the contingent. Without doubt the novels demonstrate that she is fascinated aesthetically with what Bakhtin calls the carnivalesque: "'a spectacle, but without a stage; a game' . . . mirroring the folk game; erotic orgies, mirroring ancient sacred worship" (Kristeva, 78, 82; quoted in Heusel, *Patterned Aimlessness,* 277 n. 1). Each of her novels fits Bakhtin's criterion in being a social phenomenon celebrating language as it is being used. Since Bakhtin's understanding of language and its social function is similar to those of Murdoch and Ludwig Wittgenstein, Heusel appropriates Bakhtin's "concepts, terms, and definitions" to demonstrate Murdoch's wide-ranging play with genres and novelistic strategies (100).

Celebrating Language

Looking at the way Murdoch's strategies evoke the language theory Bakhtin applies to Dostoevsky helps alleviate some of the seemingly insoluble problems about whether or not Murdoch is a philosophical novelist. It also makes clear that she has valid literary reasons to disorient her readers and to use sensational devices. In fact, Heusel argues that "most of the faults that readers find with Murdoch's fiction can be categorized under the rubric of the novels' strong carnivalesque flavor" (119). Murdoch's novels, Heusel proposes, tend to be polyphonic discourses emanating from an imaginative world of the novel that is grounded in historical confrontations between the concepts and languages of ancient Greek culture, Judeo-Christian culture, and the neo-Platonic adjustments to Christian culture. These historical struggles between authority and freedom are the background to Murdoch's explorations of the empowerment of the reader (the reader's participation in the texts) and of the characters to whom she sometimes gives free rein.

But more important, Heusel grounds Murdoch's interest in the discourse of "the other" in her first published analysis, *Sartre, Romantic Rationalist* (1953), a vast storehouse of the author's comments on the language crisis of the twentieth century, the novel in crisis, and the significance of realism. Murdoch criticizes Sartre's novels for failing to dramatize solid characters defining themselves in relationship to "the other," characters who are different from them. Murdoch's philosophical analyses indicate that the prerequisite for empathy is learning to pay attention to the beings outside one's ego — that is, truly to love others. Heusel argues that dialogical discourse, what Bakhtin describes in *The Problems of Dostoevsky's Poetics* as "dynamic utterance in which at least two voices are superimposed and create a 'bond'" (quoted in Heusel, *Patterned Aimlessness,* 86), is a major ingredient of Murdoch's moral outlook. Superimposing philosophical discourse and literary criticism dialogically in *Sartre, Romantic Rationalist,* Murdoch illustrates in her well-crafted philosophical argument the necessity of the discourse of "the other," a point she reiterates in *The Fire and the Sun: Why Plato Banished the Artists.* For her, both the discourse of the novel and that of philosophy superimpose multiple voices.

Heusel insists that the discourses Murdoch includes in her novels of the 1970s and 1980s and "the utterances of her most memorable characters demand readings that take into account the social context of discourses and the ways they intersect" (100). Because language is basic to all human interaction, and because any utterance can have contested interpretations, Murdoch "creates narrative strategies to explore not only verbal content but also the contingent flux and the nonverbal part of utterance, the gestures and the anticipation" (100). Bakhtin's theoretical concepts are appealing and accessible sources of such social language theory. Heusel demonstrates the compatibility of Murdoch's practices with Bakhtin's ideas about the narrative voice that stands among the other characters, not above them. Morality is always of consequence, language being "inherently a social, historical, and ideological creation: words resonate with centuries of meanings and uses"; Murdoch's fiction is decidedly a "critique of monologism" (100).

To help the reader visualize the novels, Heusel assumes their background to be the aimless universe Murdoch discusses in her philosophy and assumes that Murdoch peoples the foreground with a few unselfish characters whom she intersperses among a huge crowd of psychologically distraught characters. The results Heusel describes as a cacophony of voices and madcap escapades: Murdoch views life as "an aimless universe whirling around 'anxiety-ridden' human beings who impose patterns on the formlessness in order to stave off physical and psychological chaos." Constructing a novel and populating it with such characters allows Murdoch to illustrate what she calls in *The Sovereignty of Good* "the 'falsifying veil[s] which partially [conceal] the world'" (quoted, 156). Following Murdoch's large patterns — "her interconnecting schemes of caves, networks, labyrinths, and cycles" of space and time (156) — teaches the reader to search for concealed reality not only in literature but also in life in general.

The function of the carnivalesque is to reveal and change society's natural stratifying impulses, and Murdoch's novels play out such struggles between the powerful and the less powerful forces in society — the most noticeable of these less powerful forces being women. Heusel demonstrates that Murdoch's world of the novel combines Plato's cave allegory with this carnivalesque questioning of social hierarchy, illustrating Bakhtin's argument that "authors release stratifying impulses with which they attempt to subvert socioeconomic hierarchies of power within their novels" (*Patterned Aimlessness*, 100). Even more basic, however, is that Murdoch takes an unusual stance among late-twentieth-century novelists, "humbling herself" and "becoming incarnate in the world of her characters, a habit characteristic of Dostoevsky, whom Bakhtin praised for that ability. Murdoch, like Dostoevsky, . . . acts as the . . . architect-choreographer who provides imaginative strata," leading "her characters occasionally in soothing, beautiful language, but most often in wild, staccato clashes" (100–101). She employs a concept that is similar to Bakhtin's metaphorical strata, in which characters can act out and define their rituals. He explains that "represented characters in a novel exist in order to find, reject, redefine a stratum of their own; formal authors exist to coordinate these stratifying impulses" (*The Dialogic Imagination*, 433). To guard against being controlled by her private fantasies, Murdoch establishes a spacious playing ground, a big plot with exaggerated diachronic and synchronic spaces. She voiced her goal in regard to characters in an interview with Malcolm Bradbury in 1977: "one starts off — at least I start off — hoping every time that this [creating characters] is going to happen and that a lot of people who are not me are going to come into existence in some wonderful way" (quoted in Bradbury, 114). Drawing on Murdoch's description of her composing process in which she refers to the creative "cauldron" of her imagination (Heusel, "A Dialogue with Iris Murdoch," 9), *Patterned Aimlessness* suggests that Murdoch metaphorically chooses "characters from a storehouse in her mind" during the composing process, from metaphorical spaces that resemble Bakhtinian strata (269 n. 12). She "supplies her characters with personal as well as physical space so that the author is just one among many" (216).

An Accidental Man

Two of the many novels that illustrate Bakhtin's theories and use the Dostoevsky's subversive strategies and irreverent carnivalesque discourse are *An Accidental Man* and *The Philosopher's Pupil*. They demonstrate in their polyphony Murdoch's attempts to equalize her authorial desire to create form and the struggle of realistic characters to be independent in her aimless universe. In each novel she is testing her own views of morality, and reviewers have harshly criticized her for this testing. *An Accidental Man* (1971) begins a major phase of novelistic experimentation. With the Vietnam War and its arguments about private and public responsibility as background, this novel explores what Bakhtin labels "the social veracity of discourses, such as professional discourses, and the social history of those who speak the discourse" (quoted in Heusel, *Patterned Aimlessness*, 105).

In examining *An Accidental Man* Heusel argues that what Todd criticizes in the novel in his *Iris Murdoch: The Shakespearian Interest* — its lack of organic unity — is the very basis of Murdoch's Bakhtinian flavor. Todd is much more conservative about her experimenting in *The Shakespearian Interest* than he is in his later book, *Iris Murdoch*. In the earlier study he is ambivalent about Murdoch's failure to invite the reader "to sense the organic unity of plot and subject which is so characteristic a feature of Shakespeare's maturer drama" (48). He goes on to say that although this novel may, for Murdoch, have an acceptable degree of contingency for a peripheral novel, she thinks "Shakespeare succeeds [when he includes contingencies] in drawing attention away from this relationship between the parts and towards the desired otherness of character, so that what is actually apprehended appears more contingent than it in fact is" (48). His implication seems to be not only that she fails by not "drawing attention away" but also that, since she wants to write like Shakespeare, she would necessarily think that she had failed if she had not achieved organic unity.

Heusel argues, on the contrary, that the organic unity so highly praised during and after the Romantic and high modernist periods is not necessarily relevant in the 1970s. She points out that this novel "is about the contingency of the 1970s, when morality is no longer at the center of philosophy" and a war is destroying nations and families and crushing any illusion of unity (106). From a position closer to the end of the twentieth century, Murdoch is strikingly presenting a point that W. B. Yeats and T. S. Eliot illustrated earlier: that the center cannot hold. She had experienced disintegration in her culture after the Second World War and was in 1970 under no modernist obligation to write an organic work, a perfect jewel of a novel. Instead, she uses her vivid imagination and her novelistic instincts to raise and explore questions that she need never answer.

Heusel counters Todd by illustrating the similarity between Murdoch's statement about *An Accidental Man* and Bakhtin's pronouncements about centrifugal and centripetal forces. Murdoch says that the novel is "a deliberate attempt to exclude the central nucleus and to have a lot of different attachments pulling the plot and the interest away into further corners" and that the characters "have lives of their own and . . . are pursuing dramas of their own which are quite alien to the central story" (quoted in Todd, 48). Michael Holquist and Caryl Emerson explain Bakhtin's view of the novel as a genre that is a "denormatizing and therefore centrifugal force." They write that Bakhtin, in his comparison of centripetal and centrifugal forces in language and culture, finds that "the rulers and the high poetic genres of any era exercise a centripetal — a homogenizing and hierarchizing — influence; the centrifugal (decrowning, dispersing) forces of the clown, mimic and rogue create alternative 'degraded' genres down below" (*The Dialogic Imagination,* 425). Observing a similarity in the imagery in *An Accidental Man,* Heusel argues that Murdoch, understanding the "denormatizing" capability of the novel, demonstrates the "dispersing" forces of the rogues' choosing their own random avenues of behavior, ignoring such traditional, stabilizing issues as marriage and the responsibility of defending one's country in war.

A later statement by Todd helps Heusel explain Murdoch's strategy for working in her moral theme: "the 'peripheral' kind of fiction . . . offers an attractive solution to the problem of how to get the apprehension by one character of the suffering of another across in such a way as to show the part accident plays" (48). After all, Murdoch's major purpose is to create a "moral labyrinth, which dramatizes the horror of endless accidental occurrences causing characters to suffer — the loving characters letting it stop with themselves, but most characters allowing it to reverberate to the next person" (*Patterned Aimlessness,* 107). Moreover, Murdoch's own statement about her goals seems to echo Bakhtin's concepts. Murdoch explained to A. S. Byatt in a BBC interview on October 27, 1971, what she was striving to accomplish: "The counterpoint . . . to the idea that one's life is a series of accidents is, of course, the notion that it is not a series of accidents because one is busy contriving often at . . . even an unconscious level that a certain kind of drama shall be enacted and re-enacted" (quoted in Todd, 45). The issue of refusing to pass on the evil one has experienced is crucial in Murdoch's novels.

In all of them Murdoch is striving for "accidentalness" or the overturning of the status quo, the expected (Rose, 11). In her early as well as her late novels she catches the reader unawares, and astonishment abounds. In *The Severed Head* (1961), for example, "a sophisticated wine merchant has the responsibility of chauffeuring from the airport a woman whose ugly, fat legs distract him from her other attributes, but later, when he falls down the steps into the lap of this seemingly unattractive woman, he instantly falls in love with her," and in *The Sea, The Sea* (1978) "a powerful theater director lures a youth from his mother but does not pay attention to his safety and allows him to drown" (*Pat-*

terned Aimlessness, 260). These examples show that Murdoch gives the characters free rein to act their parts without the help of logic; surprise is central to her strategy, as it is to the carnivalesque in general.

In *An Accidental Man,* however, Murdoch set up circumstances in which characters can defy the orderliness envisioned by the author — or by conventional logic — and create their own way. In this blatantly anti-Aristotelian fairy tale contingency rather than cause rules most often. For example, "the kind and beautiful Dorina Grey escapes the harassment of her irresponsible husband to relax alone in a bathtub and dies when the hairdryer electrocutes her; the same husband, driving drunk, kills an innocent child; at the close of the novel, he marries Dorina's beautiful sister and lives ever after" (*Patterned Aimlessness,* 260). Here Heusel introduces into the criticism of Murdoch's writing the freedom the author enjoys as she juxtaposes multiple genres and strategies, cultural and literary allusions, dialogic play, and the carnivalesque. In attempting to visualize the workings of this plot structure with concrete spatial imagery, Heusel explains that the traditional content is the tragicomic struggling against genres, such as philosophy, theology, history, and journalism, or even styles such as realism, and their traditional strategies. Such play inevitably pulls the comedy off its conventional tracks. The characters, most often the intelligentsia, "create the centripetal force: the majority of the characters enjoy socioeconomic stability, and a number of them either have been knighted or hope to be. . . . The traditional plot is also [a stabilizing force]; boy wins girl, parents hinder match, manly honor intervenes, a marriage ends the story" (107).

Competing against these conventions, the author marshals destabilizing forces that interfere. Murdoch is able to create a radical departure from the effects of previous novels by the "highlighting of prolonged choruses of disembodied voices in entire chapters of letters and of untagged stichomythic dialogues" (*Patterned Aimlessness,* 107). Her strategy demonstrates heteroglossia at work (all utterances "are functions of a matrix of forces practically impossible to recoup" [*The Dialogic Imagination,* 428]): "each chorus, be it dialogue or letters, gives form to the concepts of simultaneity of outside perspectives and of a group of decentered personalities. Like a Greek chorus, these speakers are naïve, blind, and mistaken" (*Patterned Aimlessness,* 107). These letters further the plot at the same time that the stichomythic dialogues interrupt it and throw it out of balance. Such a strategy also necessitates employing literary allusion in a new, creative way. Allusions to *The Waste Land* and *The Tempest* make the reader disregard the subtle and gradual "semantic drift . . . away from a discussion of heterosexual love to homosexual, a shift that is also an issue in *The Waste Land*" (112). Her novel resists categories, challenges Aristotelianism, and employs analogical thought to defy "the expectation of clear causes, fixed referents, and essence" (260).

Another Murdochian strategy in this novel is to use multiple literary allusions to fortify her diagnosis of the societal symptoms that result from a world without God. Murdoch "achieves labyrinthine parallels by situating her character types, both side by side in strata with others like them . . . and vertically, along the deep structure of [Plato's] cave analogy in her world of the novel. The character types, each of whose personalities determine their potential moral choices, have the potential of moving toward the sun" (262). By adding character types from other texts, she can compare and contrast groupings of characters, such as Ludwig with Ferdinand and Hamlet or Gracie with Miranda and Ophelia. The reader can examine these analogies, using this Bakhtinian comparison; Heusel wants to be certain that the reader sees the unusual way in which Murdoch stands among her characters, giving them opportunities to upset the status quo or overturn the logical movement of the novel, rather than hovering above them paring her fingernails, as James Joyce's Stephen Dedalus proposes.

Sometimes readers may misunderstand and assume that the author is as lost as the characters or is losing control. Heusel insists that Murdoch has orchestrated the novel to highlight the alienation and disorientation of both characters and readers. If an author wanted to find a literary model for perplexed and lost characters, where could she find a happier source than *The Tempest*? Murdoch chooses this analogue that requires disembodied voices, whose plotting bubbles over on a fanciful island (108). The comedy, in which Prospero sets the supernatural creature Ariel the task of finding combinations of lost characters, both aristocratic and plebeian, is invaluable to the construction of *An Accidental Man*. Heusel shows that by "putting into play the stylized masque format or opera form, [Murdoch] is able to tune in not only to Shakespeare's comic voices but also to the historical voices that reverberate further back to Shakespeare's analogues" (108). Murdoch invites the reader to compare the bafflement of Shakespeare's "colonists bound for the New World shipwrecked in the *Sea-Adventure* off the coast of Bermuda in 1609" with young men inducted into the Vietnam War and bound for an equally unknown reality (108). Her orchestration of voices inside and outside the text creates eerie music and unexpected magic, which unsettles the group of characters as much as it does any reader.

The author emphasizes self-reflexive linguistic play, or getting out-side the mind to see what it is thinking. Radically unlike other novels, such as *The Bell,* which moves between expository and meditative prose, *An Accidental Man* celebrates conversation: "Murdoch has created nine entire chapters of letters and three chapters composed almost en-tirely of untagged stichomythic dialogues, in addition to one combina-tion of the two. . . . The six-page chapter, a sequence of ten letters and one telegram, not only moves the plot of the novel forward but con-tains the climax of the love plot — Ludwig's decision not to marry Gracie Tisbourne" (109). The contents of Murdoch's notebooks at the University of Iowa Libraries show that the stichomythic dialogues and letters are important statements and that they are the basis for a delib-erate patterning with a void at the center. All the characters are at the periphery, and no one — not even the author — is attending to the center.

This novel's multiple allusions to *The Tempest, Hamlet,* and *The Waste Land* help to develop the theme that the unified self is an illu-sion. The characters are "full of other people's words," confirming Bakhtin's argument that self and language are social. By referring to Prospero's line about "revels" being ended, with which he concludes his daughter's wedding festivities, Murdoch draws on the rebounding voices of "Ferdinand and Miranda, Ariel and Caliban, Ophelia and Hamlet, Gertrude and Claudius, the pub women and the water nymphs, the typist and the young man carbuncular" (112–13). Like Eliot, Murdoch is a masterful choreographer of disparate and divergent voices. Such a tapestry of voices as she has stitched together from many walks of life demonstrates in practice Bakhtin's theory that language is always a patchwork of phrases others have already uttered. According to Bakhtin, stylizing "another's style in the direction of that style's own particular tasks . . . merely renders those tasks conventional" (*Problems of Dostoevsky's Poetics,* 193). That is what Murdoch has done here: she has used allusions from Shakespeare and Eliot or has spoken "in some-one else's discourse" to develop her decentered plot. But she has not created a modernist symbolic configuration that simply radiates many meanings; she has chosen also to "clash" with her sources, achieving what Bakhtin calls parody, "semantic intention that is directly opposed to the original one" (193).

Stylization does not allow Murdoch the opportunity to wield her stiletto wit. To show that her world is out of synchronization, she must clash with her sources. The major events in *The Tempest,* rather than being random, are carefully manipulated by the godlike Prospero, who has the learning of a magician. The aristocratic young Ferdinand who supposedly shipwrecks will make a model husband for Miranda; the voices, the songs, and the movements are also perfection. Murdoch must make clear that in the cynical world of 1970, where a Vietnam War is possible, perfection is neither expected nor even fantasized. Murdoch's text clashes with its sources to create contingency and the slippage of language; Eliot's text creates multifaceted symbolism, the grail hero reflecting Hamlet, John the Baptist, or Ludwig of Bavaria. Whereas Eliot is working to perfect a high modernist form in which content fits form and voices from the past echo voices from the present to simulate organic unity, Murdoch is simulating contingency by creating a form in order to break it: "In *An Accidental Man,* the strategies and the untagged stichomythic dialogue are purposefully inadequate to the needs of the utterances; the inadequacy demonstrates that the middle-class intelligentsia can gossip about pretty pillows and cars and drinks but cannot fill the void of their existence" (Heusel, *Patterned Aimlessness,* 114). They parrot the vacuousness that Murdoch multiplies by alluding to *The Waste Land.* Whereas Eliot's purpose is to radiate many meanings, Murdoch's is to allow for the possibility of no meaning beyond what the vapid voices utter. Murdoch chooses to defamiliarize her readers, complicating their role; lost, they can only guess which voices in the text "belong to whom, which to men and which to women. Whereas the form is vital, the content is mundane" (114).

The Philosopher's Pupil

An even more extreme example of the polyphonic novel is *The Philosopher's Pupil.* In its revitalizing of discourses that Bakhtin calls carnivalesque it critiques journalism, philosophy, and theology. Many details in the novel parallel carnivalesque ritual, and Murdoch focuses on "low Eros (incest, homosexuality, lesbianism, adultery) and on murder and death" (Heusel, *Patterned Aimlessness,* 120). Knowing that comedy began in the communal square, she creates rites in the communal bath that encourage promiscuity and create scandal. The Bath Institute seems to imitate the carnivalesque, which breaks down the "impenetrable hierarchical barriers" between people and allows them to "enter into free familiar contact on the carnival square" (Bakhtin, *Problems of Dostoevsky's Poetics,* 123) The narrator compares the role of the square to that of "the agora in Athens. It is the main rendezvous of the citizenry" (*The Philosopher's Pupil,* 23). Of course, the square's metamorphosis to spa helps Murdoch to combine the ideas of rebirth and communion.

Furthermore, she builds the novel on contrasts and abrupt transitions, achieving a polyphony of competing voices by means of "styles and techniques from the epic, tragic, gothic, picaresque, mythical, and romantic" (Heusel, *Patterned Aimlessness,* 121). Murdoch introduces "all avenues of gossipmongering: characters, narrator, letters, and newspapers"; the narrator, listening to the stories, "plots the course of the river of erratic gossip or scandal" (122). Murdoch even includes carnival curses: the philosopher John Robert Rozanov writes to his pupil George McCaffrey, "I would like to kill you," and calls him "fake fantasy villain, mean weak impotent rat, incapable of evil but spewing out the sickening black bile of your petty spite" (*The Philosopher's Pupil,* 433). These curses stir up in George's unconscious mind psychic energy that pours forth, reverberating evil. George eventually tries to murder his mentor, but the philosopher is already dead.

The potential for layers of discourse is evident in the strategy Murdoch selects for narration: her narrator, N, refers to the setting as N's town — Ennistone — a place "where people idle, gossip, relax, show off, hunt for partners, make assignations, make business deals, make plots" (*The Philosopher's Pupil,* 23). What he knows, he learns from gossip; it is his job to track this energetic river of gossip as it winds throughout the small bedroom community. He relays most of what he encounters to the reader, but he does not know the whole story: he has "had the assistance of a certain lady" (576) who, perhaps, knows more.

The layers of discourse begin to reach a peak of absurdity when a comic exploration of the carnivalesque challenges the reader to analyze two journalistic accounts of a slapstick-comedy scene that evokes a carnival masquerade. Heusel cites Julia Kristeva's discussion of the carnivalesque to name and illustrate Murdoch's strategy: "traditionally, carnival first stages a realistic representation and then, using language to repudiate it, provokes laughter (WDN ["Word, Dialogue, and Novel"] 79)" (*Patterned Aimlessness,* 120). Murdoch's disclaimer about the carnivalesque aside, the scenes follow this pattern exactly. Near the end of the novel Murdoch interposes an occasion of wild Dionysian hilarity foreshadowed by the narrator, who has revealed that a traditional "unholy restlessness . . . attacks the town at intervals like an epidemic" (*The Philosopher's Pupil,* 19). This staged spectacle, representing a convention of the carnivalesque, is a spontaneous, unrehearsed performance of a Saturnalian celebration in which Rozanov is decrowned and Tom McCaffrey, a young local the philosopher chooses to marry his granddaughter Hattie, in effect becomes king momentarily.

The Carnivalesque Flavor

One of Murdoch's funniest examples of the carnivalesque is the wild, cavorting revelry prior to Tom's overturning of the status quo. No one can deny the effort Murdoch expends to make this set piece uproariously festive. In the metaphorical position of carnival king, Tom eventually marries the metaphorical carnival princess Hattie. (But at a low point he is worried that she is "not quite real" and says, "Rozanov is a magician who took me to his palace and showed me a maiden" [490].) Late on a warm summer evening, as the fair on the common ends, people stop dancing at the Ring (an ancient Druid stone ring), and the Green Man pub is about to close, the cast of the play *The Triumph of Aphrodite* noisily marches to the pub, gathering more and more young revelers as they progress. Awash in carnivalesque atmosphere, the groups pursue their merrymaking, "some in mediaeval costume, some dressed as animals, some carrying lighted lanterns," some dancing the minuet, others dancing alone or "sloshing beer and wine into glasses" (383). Someone in a stag's head serves drinks as the procession wends its way on toward the Slipper House, the residence of Rozanov and his granddaughter. The completion of the party at Hattie's home is pure accident. One of the camp followers, Tom, who momentarily tries on a bear head, inadvertently tells the group he is leaving to visit the Slipper House. In the noise a reveler misconstrues the statement and shouts that there is a party at Hattie's. Tom tries in vain to "end the awful carnival" (390). He discovers his close friend, Emmanuel (Emma), with whom he has had an experimental sexual encounter, frolicking in women's clothes on his way to seduce a young woman who is disguised as a man. Her urging Emma to get rid of his wig prompts him to throw it into a ginkgo tree, where others will later read it as a magic sign.

Journalistic Discourse

Murdoch not only constructs narrative effects that are carnivalesque but also works hard to make sure that another low genre like the novel — newspaper journalism — has its comic comeuppance and renewal. Having focused on low Eros (including adultery, homosexuality, lesbianism, and incest) to manipulate such change and renewal, she focuses on this staged spectacle, showing how problematic journalistic discourse is. For example, the *Ennistone Gazette* refers to this incident as the "Slipper House riot" (382). Of course, it was no such thing; but even when Murdoch "reduces the carnivalesque to monotonous duplicity, it resists and retains its energy" (Heusel, *Patterned Aimlessness*,

123). The account begins with the sensational headline "MCCAFFREY PRACTICAL JOKE GOES TOO FAR":

> Extraordinary scenes took place on Saturday night at the *so-called* "Slipper House" . . . home [of] Miss Harriet Meynell and her maidservant. "Rehearsals" of *The Mask of Aphrodite* in the Ennistone Hall broke up in confusion when George and Tom McCaffrey led a drunken rabble to lay siege to the two damsels in their flossy seclusion. Drinking shouting, the revellers, who included [the] parish priest . . . attempted to gain access to the house. . . . Also present were a number of young men in outrageous "drag" and their sponsor, our own Madame Diane. (409; emphasis added)

This energetic version reflects destabilization of the hierarchy and, therefore, still has the potential for change. But Murdoch reveals that with each subsequent report the carnivalesque discourse loses its energy as diatribe, soon becoming moralistic and incapable of forcing radical change and rebirth. Even though the first version amplifies innuendoes and makes a lame joke about maidservants, Tom, howling with laughter, still "evokes the carnivalesque tradition of cleansing the community through laughter" (Heusel, *Patterned Aimlessness,* 124).

The second faux journalistic account focuses on the "hint of lesbianism suggested by deflation of the 'so-called maid'" (124) in the first account. In the other local newspaper the event deteriorates into an "orgy" planned by Hattie. Heusel demonstrates the moralistic attitude of this more fictionalized news item, which strikes "a note of its own, reporting that 'Our Sapphic Sisterhood of Women's Libbers were also there in force, and the *so-called* 'maid' was to be seen hugging and kissing, clasped to the bosom of another long-haired Amazon'" (quoted, 124; emphasis added). Murdoch parodically names this second paper *The Swimmer,* the title connoting water and river, "a collector of garbage and gossip as well as a vehicle for rebirth" (124). The two passages demonstrate the deterioration as the journalese in exposé becomes monological and loses its "double-voiced" ability to renew.

Murdoch has continually revitalized the novel form by incorporating traditional genres and techniques; such mixing allows her, through stylizing and parodying spatial and temporal features, to make old forms convey new concepts. For example, she often parodies technical strategies that earlier authors had employed in road novels such as *Joseph Andrews, Tom Jones, Sentimental Journey,* and *Humphry Clinker.* In such experiments she plays with the familiar, age-old space-time dilemmas, what Bakhtin calls the road chronotope:[1] "A meeting [on the road] is one of the most ancient devices for structuring a plot" (*The Dialogic Imagination,* 98), usually in "*familiar territory*" (245). Bakhtin historicizes this pattern, emphasizing "the immediacy" with which time and space "are felt in actual experience" at the moment of an encounter. He explains that time "fuses together with space and flows in it (forming the road) . . . the course of a life" (244). Borrowing Einstein's concept to study the time and space markers of texts, Bakhtin gave the name *chronotope*, "literally, 'time space' to the intrinsic connectedness of temporal and spatial relationships that are artistically expressed in literature" (84). The chronotope is "essential for the showing forth [in narrative], the representability of events" (250) in the historical world. In light of Murdoch's interest in mapping out quest structures against Plato's cave metaphor, her working with such a basic pattern is not surprising. She most often chooses London as her space and frequently represents the living of life as the moving image of the road (sometimes a Roman road) unrolling, much like a narrative. She chooses distinctive temporal and spatial features from traditional genres and reapplies them to explore new conflicts and to test new power balances at the end of the twentieth century. Dipple makes a similar point in her review of *Jackson's Dilemma* in the *Iris Murdoch News Letter:* "Here we have the romantic Shakespearean source material brought wholesale and transported into the last few years of the twentieth century — just to see how we can look at it . . . whether it can be dealt with within a new chronotopic experiment" (6).

Many of Murdoch's novels dramatize the physical needs of characters struggling between the world of fact and the world of fantasy by calling attention to the moments or intersections of space and time at which their crises, often crises of love, occur. One of her ways of representing historical time in novelistic space is to foreground the automobile and its effects on culture. For her the automobile motif is especially useful for incorporating the sexual, or the unconscious, and the mechanical, or the modernist. That automobiles are instruments that cause accidents on roads in almost half of her twenty-six novels demonstrates her deliberate imaginative manipulation of characters who believe that it is easier and quicker to escape their narrow lives when they can use such a mode of travel. In addition, the automobile allows her to combine violence and contingency with adventure and escape. More specifically, *An Accidental Man, The Bell, A Word Child, The Black Prince, The Philosopher's Pupil,* and *The Good Apprentice* all highlight the automobile as a metaphor for the animalistic drives that exert control unconsciously, an instrument in which people often act out unconscious sexual motivations that lead to destruction.

Murdoch took up realism where she found it in 1954, and she expanded it in numerous directions: the picaresque, gothic, comedy of manners, fantasy, allegory, cautionary tale, fable, parable, mystery, detective story, diary, epistolary novel, and postmodern experimentation including touches of magic realism. Dipple has traced Murdoch's revitalization of Shakespearean themes, Heusel has demonstrated her carnivalesque leanings, and Johnson has prepared young scholars for new studies on gender and sexuality. Murdoch's habit of writing novels to solve problems has left critics a rich heritage that cries out for continued critical analysis.

Notes

[1] Bakhtin approaches genre through a discussion of the chronotopes, "unit[s] of analysis for studying texts" (Clark and Holquist 424). He views genre as "an X-ray of a specific world view, a crystallization of the concepts particular to a given time and to a given social stratum in a specific society" (275).

Works Cited

Antonaccio, Maria. "Form and Contingency in Iris Murdoch's Ethics." *Iris Murdoch and the Search for Human Goodness.* Ed. Antonaccio and William Schweiker. Chicago and London: U of Chicago P, 1996, 110–37.

Bakhtin, Mikhail. *The Dialogic Imagination: Four Essays.* Ed. Michael Holquist, trans. Holquist and Caryl Emerson. Austin: U of Texas P, 1981.

———. *Problems of Dostoevsky's Poetics.* Ed. and trans. Caryl Emerson, Theory and History of Literature 8. Minneapolis: U of Minnesota P, 1984.

Baldanza, Frank. *Iris Murdoch.* New York: Twayne, 1974.

Bradbury, Malcolm. *The Novel Today: Contemporary Writers on Modern Fiction.* Manchester: Manchester UP, 1977.

Clark, Katerina, and Michael Holquist. *Mikhail Bakhtin.* Cambridge MA: Harvard UP, 1984.

Conradi, Peter. *Fyodor Dostoevsky.* Macmillan Modern Novelists. London: Macmillan, 1988.

———. *Iris Murdoch: The Saint and the Artist.* New York: St. Martin's, 1986; rpt. 1989.

Dipple, Elizabeth. "Fragments of Iris Murdoch's Vision: *Jackson's Dilemma* as Interlude." *Iris Murdoch News Letter* 9 (August 1995): 4–8.

POSTMODERNIST EXPERIMENTATION

———. "The Green Knight and Other Vagaries of the Spirit; or, Tricks and Images for the Human Soul; or, The Uses of Imaginative Literature." *Iris Murdoch and the Search for Human Goodness*. Ed. Antonaccio and Schweiker, 138–68.

———. *Iris Murdoch: Work for the Spirit*. Chicago: U of Chicago P, 1982.

———. *The Unresolvable Plot: Reading Contemporary Fiction*. New York: Routledge, 1988.

Fulton, Alice. "A Poetry of Inconvenient Knowledge." *The Nation* (June 14, 1999): 40–48.

Gordon, David J. *Iris Murdoch's Fables of Unselfing*. Columbia and London: U of Missouri P, 1995.

Harmon, William, and C. Hugh Holman, eds. *A Handbook to Literature*, 7th ed. New York: Macmillan, 1996.

Heusel, Barbara Stevens. "A Dialogue with Iris Murdoch." *University of Windsor Review* 21:1 (1988): 1–13.

———. *Patterned Aimlessness: Iris Murdoch's Novels of the 1970s and 1980s*. Athens: U of Georgia P, 1995.

Johnson, Deborah. *Iris Murdoch*. London: Harvester P, 1987.

Kristeva, Julia. "Word, Dialogue, and Novel." *Desire in Language: A Semiotic Approach to Literature and Art*. Ed. Leon S. Roudiez, trans. Roudiez, Thomas Gora, and Alice Jardine. New York: Columbia UP, 1980. 64–91.

Murdoch, Iris. *The Bell*. New York: Viking, 1958.

———. *The Philosopher's Pupil*. New York: Viking, 1983.

———. *Sartre, Romantic Rationalist*. London: Bowes and Bowes, 1953; rpt. New Haven: Yale UP, 1967.

———. *The Time of the Angels*. London: Chatto and Windus, 1966.

Rose, W. K. "An Interview with Iris Murdoch," *Shenandoah* 19 (Winter 1968): 3–22.

Shklovsky, Viktor. "Art as Technique." *Contemporary Literary Criticism: Literary and Cultural Studies*. 2nd ed. Ed. Robert Con Davis and Ronald Schleifer. New York and London: Longman, 1989. 55–66.

Todd, Richard. *Iris Murdoch: The Shakespearian Interest*. London: Vision P, 1979.

Wolfe, Peter. *The Disciplined Heart: Iris Murdoch and Her Novels*. Columbia: U of Missouri P, 1966.

Conclusion

THIS STUDY OF IRIS MURDOCH'S critical reception has set up the major critics' conflicting arguments, analyzed their disagreements, and presented their various conclusions. Except when particular occasions necessitated comment, the study attempted to stay out of the fray. Revealing many perspectives and raising many questions gives readers the opportunity to listen to dialogues among critics and to reach informed conclusions about Murdoch's direction in — and her influence on — the development of the contemporary novel.

Furthermore, this examination organized chronologically the three phases through which book-length Murdoch studies have explored and evaluated her novels: 1965 to 1976, 1977 to 1986, and 1987 to the present. The critics' analyses represent the stages of their understanding, which have relied to some extent on Murdoch's progress in visualizing and determining her own direction. Whatever the arguments and conclusions of these critics may be, each of them struggles with three major questions about Murdoch as a creator of fiction. These questions — To what extent is Murdoch a philosophical novelist? Is she a realistic novelist? Is she a postmodern novelist? — form the three sections of this study. While decrying the act of categorization, as did Murdoch, the study admits that categorization remains an activity, albeit a dangerous one, which is common to all human beings.

Disagreements over answers to these questions separate the critics. From the first newspaper reviews in 1954 to 1976, the early critics, who were exploring the texts of an unknown novelist and needed assurance from Murdoch that their interpretations were plausible, tended to apply her critical statements about literature — and even her philosophical statements — directly to her novels. With a few variations, they generally saw her novels as extensions of her professional life as a philosopher. Even though the major critics were sympathetic to her insistence that she was not a philosophical novelist, they also, after defining the term philosophical novelist to suit their purposes, found it necessary to refer her readers to philosophical texts that might aid in comprehending the novels. Most of these critics, nevertheless, revealed an uneasiness about their own necessary oversimplification of her goals. Arguing that she was a traditional realist, they applied adjectives such as "outrageous, quirky, fantastic" (Baldanza, 21) to her texts.

Writing between 1977 and 1986, the second, less orthodox group began to celebrate Murdoch's uniqueness. As a whole, they were more willing to challenge her statements in interviews and to compare her narrative techniques to those of earlier literary masters. Since Murdoch had become a well-known novelist by this time, the critics focused on contextualizing her work to demonstrate the direction and significance of her contributions to the novel. An influential transitional critic, Lorna Sage, signaled a major change in Murdoch studies in 1977 when she published an essay that convinced many critics that Murdoch not only had no desire to console the reader but that she created intentionally unfinished, imperfect texts to disturb the reader's complacency. Richard Todd and Peter Conradi gave Sage credit for these seminal ideas. The criticism of Todd and Elizabeth Dipple made clear Murdoch's revitalization of Shakespearean themes. Conradi's focus on her spirituality and his study of Dostoevsky as an influence demonstrated that Murdoch's paradoxical position was less puzzling in light of Dostoevsky's description of his own realism: "What the majority call fantastic and exceptional" (quoted in Gordon, 4).

Critics writing after 1986 applied much broader lenses to view Murdoch's novels historically in relationship to the Western tradition of the novel and in relationship to theoretical issues. Dipple and Barbara Stevens Heusel demonstrated her carnivalesque leanings. Deborah Johnson, who is among the first feminist critics to have addressed Murdoch's oeuvre, laid the groundwork for new studies on gender and sexuality. These critics explore the postmodernist characteristics of the novels. It seems certain that discussion of her writing will remain an active part of contemporary literary discourse and will continue to be an important source of information about the development of the novel, the strategies that become literary history.

The body of criticism has arrived at and recorded some major conclusions about Murdoch's stated goals and her descriptions of her own thinking processes. The consensus is that she was an unorthodox quester after the truth, a novelist who devoted her life to recording a broad picture of the human condition. Concluding that the twentieth century had been a period of narcissism, Murdoch dramatized in her fiction individual human idiosyncrasies against an age-old background of Western cultural history. Few novelists have been able to draw on such a thorough education in the academy and in life.

Because she was a professional philosopher, many early critics and at least one later one assumed that demonstrating another philosopher's influence on Murdoch's thinking proved that she was a philosophical novelist. Later critics do not accept such a foregone conclusion. Her wide experiences in the world of philosophy created an eclectic thinker, whose views many more-conservative philosophers have considered unorthodox. She was obviously moved by the work of great philosophers, as she was by artistic geniuses, but she managed to separate her two professions and to use her knowledge of each to complement and enhance the other. Living in two worlds, she could never totally rid her mind of what she knew about the peripheries of her other life — but she could and did control her goals. As a result of her rich life, her oeuvre reveals an extraordinarily enlightened view of reality. Readers must weigh for themselves what percentage of professional philosophical discourse — if any — they find in each novel and then decide whether what they discover interferes with the story. Furthermore, her biographical experiences no doubt affected the scope of her interests and helped determine the choice of subject matter for her novels, although she wrote adamantly that she did not base incidents or characters in novels on real events and people. The critic's categorization of novels into styles was of no interest to her. She wanted the freedom to create her own unique style in each novel. Other than arguing against the solipsism of the modernist stance and for eighteenth-century and particularly nineteenth-century realism, she preferred to ignore such classification.

What is crucial for literary critics is that Murdoch, a natural and consummate storyteller, never gave up on the novel during the 1950s and 1960s, when certain critics were declaring it dead. Her oeuvre continually revitalized the novel form by incorporating traditional genres and techniques; such mixing allowed her, through stylizing and parodying spatial and temporal features, to make old forms convey new concepts. She chose a realistic canvas and a popular genre for her first novel, and in the remaining twenty-five she wove her own unorthodox patterns, mixing comedy of manners and parable, picaresque and gothic, detective story and fantasy, epistolary novel and magic realism.

At the beginning of this study I promised to grant Murdoch's critics the same kind of freedom she no doubt wanted: the freedom to argue about the stages and value of her novelistic output and the effectiveness of her narrative process in fashioning the material world without attempting perfection. Demonstrating the journey these critics made from 1954 to 1995 reveals the complexity of Murdoch's project and the danger of categorizing her as a philosophical novelist, a realist, a postmodernist, or some combination thereof. Her most devoted critics seem to agree that Iris Murdoch embodies the qualities of the good artist.

The critics to whom this study gives voice make clear that criticism has just begun to grasp the potential of a writer who considered herself the outsider, the other. It has been traditional to categorize her as part of the new generation that was throwing off modernism. What effects have her life and work had on Western culture? What does it mean that this humble and shy woman set the reading public afire in the mid-1950s and then continued for forty years to produce provocative stories? From the publication of her first novel in 1954, when *Under the Net* was immediately celebrated as a work in the nascent tradition of Britain's angry young men, to her professorial days at Oxford, when the BBC chose her as the token woman to interview on the series *Men of Ideas,* she defied barriers of all kinds, including gender.[1] Murdoch's twenty-six novels, not to mention the rest of her oeuvre, give scholars ample room to continue delving into her creative cauldron, analyzing her play with gender, genre, and the force that Western culture calls creativity.

Notes

[1] In 1954 critics categorized her first novel, *Under the Net,* with novels such as Kingsley Amis's *Lucky Jim.* Subsequently, when Bryan Magee prepared the book *Men of Ideas,* based on his BBC *Men of Ideas* series, he included a Murdoch interview (No. 14, October 28, 1977), calling it "Bryan Magee Talked to Iris Murdoch."

Works Cited

Baldanza, Frank. *Iris Murdoch.* New York: Twayne, 1974.

Gordon, David J. *Iris Murdoch's Fables of Unselfing.* Columbia and London: U Missouri P, 1995.

Magee, Bryan. "Philosophy and Literature: Dialogue with Iris Murdoch." *Men of Ideas: Some Creators of Contemporary Philosophy.* New York: Viking, 1978. 262–84

Bibliography

Primary Bibliography: Major Works by Iris Murdoch

Novels

[Each novel was published first in London by Chatto and Windus; several months later Viking published the U.S. edition.]

Under the Net. 1954.

The Flight from the Enchanter. 1956.

The Sandcastle. 1957.

The Bell. 1958.

A Severed Head. 1961.

An Unofficial Rose. 1962.

The Unicorn. 1963.

The Italian Girl. 1964.

The Red and the Green. 1965.

The Time of the Angels. 1966.

The Nice and the Good. 1968.

Bruno's Dream. 1969.

A Fairly Honourable Defeat. 1970.

An Accidental Man. 1971.

The Black Prince. 1973.

The Sacred and the Profane Love Machine. 1974.

A Word Child. 1975.

Henry and Cato. 1976.

The Sea, The Sea. 1978.

Nuns and Soldiers. 1980.

The Philosopher's Pupil. 1983.

The Good Apprentice. 1985.

The Book and the Brotherhood. 1987.

The Message to the Planet. 1989.

The Green Knight. 1993.

Jackson's Dilemma. 1995.

Plays

A Severed Head, with J. B. Priestley. London: Chatto and Windus, 1964.

The Italian Girl, with James Saunders. London and New York: Samuel French, 1968.

Three Plays: The Three Arrows, The Servants & The Snow and The Black Prince. London: Chatto and Windus, 1989.

Philosophy

Sartre: Romantic Rationalist. 1953. New Haven: Yale UP, 1967.

The Sovereignty of Good. New York: Schocken Books, 1970.

The Fire and the Sun: Why Plato Banished the Artists. New York: Oxford University Press, 1977.

Acastos: Two Platonic Dialogues. New York: Viking, 1986.

Metaphysics as a Guide to Morals. London: Chatto and Windus, 1992.

Selected Essays, Reviews, and Correspondence

For a comprehensive, fully annotated bibliography, see Fletcher and Bove.

"Art is the Imitation of Nature." *Cahiers du Centre de Recherches sur les Pays du Nord et du Nord-Ouest.* L'Université de Caen, 1978.

"The Existentialist Hero." *Listener* (March 23, 1950): 523–24.

"Existentialists and Mystics: A Note on the Novel in the New Utilitarian Age." *Essays and Poems Presented to Lord David Cecil.* Ed. W. W. Robson. London: Constable, 1970. 169–83.

"A House of Theory." *Partisan Review* 26 (1959): 17–31.

"Knowing the Void" (review of *The Notebooks of Simone Weil*). *Spectator* 197 (November 2, 1956): 613–14.

Letter to the author, 12 January 1983.

"Mass, Might and Myth" (review of Elias Canetti, *Crowds and Power*). *Spectator* 209 (September 7, 1962): 337–38.

"Metaphysics and Ethics." *The Nature of Metaphysics*. Ed. D. F. Pears. London: Macmillan, 1957. 99–123.

"Salvation by Words." *New York Review of Books* (June 15, 1972): 3–5.

"The Sublime and the Good." *Chicago Review* 13 (Autumn 1959): 42–55.

"Vision and Choice in Morality." *Aristotelian Society: Dreams and Self-Knowledge*, supplement 30 (1956): 32–58.

Secondary Works Cited

[Arranged chronologically by year, alphabetically by author's last name within years.]

Monk, Samuel Holt. *The Sublime: A Study of Critical Theories in XVIII-Century England*. New York: MLA, 1935.

Thompson, T. J. T. and E. P. T. *There Is a Spirit in Europe: A Memoir of Frank Thompson*. London: Gollancz, 1947.

Mehta, Ved. *Fly and the Fly-Bottle: Encounters with British Intellectuals*. Boston: Little, Brown, 1961.

Byatt, A. S. *Degrees of Freedom: The Novels of Iris Murdoch*. New York: Barnes and Noble, 1965.

Wolfe, Peter. *The Disciplined Heart: Iris Murdoch and Her Novels*. Columbia: U of Missouri P, 1966.

Civin, Laraine. *Iris Murdoch: A Bibliography*. Johannesburg: University of the Witwatersrand, Department of Bibliography, Librarianship and Typography, 1968.

Rabinovitz, Rubin. *Iris Murdoch*. New York: Columbia UP, 1968. Rpt. in *Six Contemporary British Novelists*. Ed. George Stade. New York: Columbia UP, 1976. 271–332.

Murdoch, Iris. "Existentialists and Mystics: A Note on the Novel in the New Utilitarian Age." *Essays and Poems Presented to Lord David Cecil*. Ed. W. W. Robson. London: Constable, 1970. 169–83.

Baldanza, Frank. *Iris Murdoch*. New York: Twayne, 1974.

Barthes, Roland. *The Pleasure of the Text*, trans. Richard Miller. New York: Hill and Wang, 1975.

Gerstenberger, Donna. *Iris Murdoch*. Lewisburg PA and London: Bucknell UP, 1975.

Byatt, A. S. *Iris Murdoch*. Burnt Hill: Longman Group, 1976.

Tominaga, Thomas T., and Wilma Schneidemeyer. *Iris Murdoch and Muriel Spark: A Bibliography*. Metuchen, NJ: Scarecrow P, 1976.

Magee, Bryan. "Bryan Magee Talked to Iris Murdoch." Modern Philosophy: Philosophy and Literature, BBC *Men of Ideas* series no. 14: Iris Murdoch, October 28, 1977. National Sound Archives, London.

Sage, Lorna. "The Pursuit of Imperfection." *Critical Quarterly* 19 (1977): 60–68. Rpt. as "The Pursuit of Imperfection: *Henry and Cato.*" *Iris Murdoch.* Ed. Harold Bloom. New York: Chelsea House, 1986. 111–19.

Weil, Simone. *The Simone Weil Reader.* Ed. George A. Panichas. New York: David McKay, 1977.

Chevalier, Jean-Louis, ed. *Rencontres avec Iris Murdoch.* Caen: Centre des Recherches de Littérature et Linguistique des Pays de Langue Anglaise, 1978.

Magee, Bryan. *Men of Ideas: Some Creators of Contemporary Philosophy.* New York: Viking, 1978, 262–84.

Todd, Richard. *Iris Murdoch: The Shakespearian Interest.* London: Vision P, 1979.

Kristeva, Julia. "Word, Dialogue, and Novel." *Desire in Language: A Semiotic Approach to Literature and Art.* Ed. Leon S. Roudiez, trans. Roudiez, Thomas Gora, and Alice Jardine. New York: Columbia UP, 1980. 64–91.

Bakhtin, Mikhail. *The Dialogic Imagination: Four Essays.* Ed. Michael Holquist, trans. Holquist and Caryl Emerson. Austin: U of Texas P, 1981.

Dipple, Elizabeth. *Iris Murdoch: Work for the Spirit.* Chicago: U of Chicago P, 1982.

Edwards, James C. *Ethics without Philosophy: Wittgenstein and the Moral Life.* Gainesville: UP of Florida, 1982.

Fletcher, John. "Iris Murdoch." *Dictionary of Literary Biography 14: British Novelists Since 1960.* Ed. Jay L. Halio. Detroit: Gale, 1983. 546–61.

Haffenden, John. "In Conversation with Iris Murdoch." *Literary Review* 58 (April 1983): 31–35. Rpt. in *Novelists in Interview.* London and New York: Methuen, 1985. 191–209.

Bakhtin, Mikhail. *Problems of Dostoevsky's Poetics.* Ed. and trans. Caryl Emerson. Theory and History of Literature, 8. Minneapolis: U of Minnesota P, 1984.

Clark, Katerina, and Michael Holquist. *Mikhail Bakhtin.* Cambridge MA: Harvard UP, 1984.

Todd, Richard. *Iris Murdoch.* London and New York: Methuen, 1984.

Backus, Guy. *Iris Murdoch: The Novelist as Philosopher, The Philosopher as Novelist, "The Unicorn" as a Philosophical Novel.* Bern and New York: Peter Lang, 1986.

Bloom, Harold. Introduction to *Iris Murdoch: Modern Critical Views.* Ed. Bloom. New York: Chelsea House, 1986. 1–7.

Bove, Cheryl Browning. *A Character Index and Guide to the Fiction of Iris Murdoch*. New York: Garland, 1986.

Martz, Louis L. "Iris Murdoch and the London Novels." *Twentieth-Century Literature in Retrospect*. Cambridge: Harvard UP, 1971. Rpt. as "The London Novels." *Iris Murdoch*. Ed. Bloom, 1986. 39–57.

Windsor, Dorothy A. "Solipsistic Sexuality in Murdoch's Gothic Novels." *Renascence* 34:1 (Autumn 1981). Rpt. in *Iris Murdoch*. Ed. Bloom, 1986. 121–30.

Hauptfuhrer, Fred. "The Lost Loves of Iris Murdoch." *People Weekly* 14 (March 1988): 17–18.

Conradi, Peter. *Iris Murdoch: The Saint and the Artist*. New York: St. Martin's, 1986; rpt. 1989.

Geertz, Clifford. "Blurred Genres." *Critical Theory since 1965*. Tallahassee: U P of Florida, 1986. 766–67.

Begnal, Kate, ed. *Iris Murdoch: A Reference Guide*. Boston: G. K. Hall, 1987.

Burke, John J. "Canonizing Iris Murdoch." *Studies in the Novel* 19.4 (Winter 1987): 486–94.

Fletcher, John. "The Birth of a Writer: Iris Murdoch before 1950." *The Iris Murdoch News Letter* 1 (July 1987): 1–3.

Hassan, Ihab. *The Postmodern Turn: Essays in Postmodern Theory and Culture*. Columbus: Ohio State UP, 1987.

Johnson, Deborah. *Iris Murdoch*. London: Harvester P, 1987.

Conradi, Peter. *Fyodor Dostoevsky,* Macmillan Modern Novelists. London: Macmillan, 1988.

Dipple, Elizabeth. *The Unresolvable Plot: Reading Contemporary Fiction*. New York: Routledge, 1988.

Heusel, Barbara Stevens. "A Dialogue with Iris Murdoch." *University of Windsor Review* 21:1 (1988): 1–13.

Shklovsky, Viktor. "Art as Technique." *Contemporary Literary Criticism: Literary and Cultural Studies*. 2nd ed. Ed. Robert Con Davis and Ronald Schleifer. New York and London: Longman, 1989. 55–66.

Blackburn, Simon. "The Good and the Great" (review of *Metaphysics as a Guide to Morals*). *Times Literary Supplement* (October 23, 1992): 3–4.

Tucker, Lindsey. Introduction to *Critical Essays on Iris Murdoch*. Ed. Tucker. New York: G. K. Hall, 1992. 1–16.

———. "New Directions: Iris Murdoch's Latest Women." *Critical Essays on Iris Murdoch*. Ed. Tucker, 1992. 188–98.

Bove, Cheryl Browning. *Understanding Iris Murdoch*. Columbia: U of South Carolina P, 1993.

Fletcher, John, and Cheryl Browning Bove. *Iris Murdoch: A Descriptive Primary and Annotated Secondary Bibliography.* New York and London: Garland, 1994.

Dipple, Elizabeth. "Fragments of Iris Murdoch's Vision: *Jackson's Dilemma* as Interlude." *Iris Murdoch News Letter* 9 (August 1995): 4–8.

Gordon, David J. *Iris Murdoch's Fables of Unselfing.* Columbia and London: U of Missouri P, 1995.

Harmon, William, and C. Hugh Holman, eds. *A Handbook to Literature,* 7th ed. New York: Macmillan, 1995.

Heusel, Barbara Stevens. *Patterned Aimlessness: Iris Murdoch's Novels of the 1970s and 1980s.* Athens: U of Georgia P, 1995.

Antonaccio, Maria. "Form and Contingency in Iris Murdoch's Ethics." *Iris Murdoch and the Search for Human Goodness.* Ed. Antonaccio and William Schweiker, 1996. Chicago and London: U of Chicago P, 1996. 110–37.

Diamond, Cora. "'We Are Perpetually Moralists': Iris Murdoch, Fact, and Value." *Iris Murdoch and the Search for Human Goodness.* Ed. Antonaccio and Schweiker. 79–109.

Dipple, Elizabeth. "The Green Knight and Other Vagaries of the Spirit; or, Tricks and Images for the Human Soul; or, The Uses of Imaginative Literature." *Iris Murdoch and the Search for Human Goodness.* Ed. Antonaccio and Schweiker. 138–68.

Gamwell, Franklin I. "On the Loss of Theism." *Iris Murdoch and the Search for Human Goodness.* Ed. Antonaccio and Schweiker, 1996. 171–89.

O'Connor, Patricia J. *To Love the Good: The Moral Philosophy of Iris Murdoch.* New York: Peter Lang, 1996.

Tracy, David. "Iris Murdoch and the Many Faces of Platonism." *Iris Murdoch and the Search for Human Goodness.* Ed. Antonaccio and Schweiker, 1996. 54–75.

Fowler, Simon, William Spencer, and Stuart Tamblin. *Army Service Records of the First World War.* London: Public Records Office, 1997.

Bayley, John. "Elegy for Iris: Scenes from an Indomitable Marriage." *The New Yorker* (27 July 1998): 45–61.

———. *Iris: A Memoir of Iris Murdoch.* London: Duckworth, 1998.

Bove, Cheryl. "Iris Murdoch." *Dictionary of Literary Biography 194: British Novelists Since 1960, Second Series.* Ed. Merritt Moseley. Detroit: Gale, 1998. 220–43.

Conradi, Peter. "Memoir, Festschrift, Biography." *The Iris Murdoch News Letter* 11 (Winter 1998): 8.

Dunbar, Scott. "Philosophy, Art and Morals: Reflections on *Existentialists and Mystics.*" *The Iris Murdoch News Letter* 11 (Winter 1998): 9–19.

Levy, Paul. "Sunday Lunch with Iris." *The Independent* (London) (25 July 1998).

"Losing Her Mind to Gain the World." *The Sunday Times* (London) (26 July 1998).

Romano, Carlin. "Rortyism for Beginners" (review of Richard Rorty, *Truth and Progress: Philosophical Papers*, volume 3). *The Nation* (July 27/August 3, 1998): 25–33.

Rowe, Anne. "Alzheimer's Appeal." *The Iris Murdoch News Letter* 11 (Winter 1998): 19–21.

Schaefer, Christina K. *The Great War: A Guide to the Service Records of All The World's Fighting Men and Volunteers.* Baltimore: Genealogical Publishing, 1998.

Bayley, John. *Elegy for Iris.* New York: St. Martin's, 1999.

———. *Iris and Her Friends: A Memoir of Memory and Desire.* New York and London: Norton, 2000.

Antonaccio, Maria. *Picturing the Human: The Moral Thought of Iris Murdoch.* New York: Oxford UP, 2000.

Index